Curiosities Series

Arkansas
CURIOSITIES

Quirky characters,
roadside oddities &
other offbeat stuff

Janie and Wyatt Jones

gpp

Guilford, Connecticut

The prices, rates, and hours listed in this guidebook were confirmed at press time. We recommend, however, that you call establishments to obtain current information before traveling.

Photos by Janie and Wyatt Jones unless otherwise noted.
Maps by Sue Murray copyright © Rowman & Littlefield

Distributed by NATIONAL BOOK NETWORK

Library of Congress Cataloging-in-Publication data is available on file.

ISBN 978-0-7627-4894-5
ISSN 2154-2880

Printed in the United States of America

To the memory of Nancy Eugenia Burnett,
cherished friend and inspirational teacher

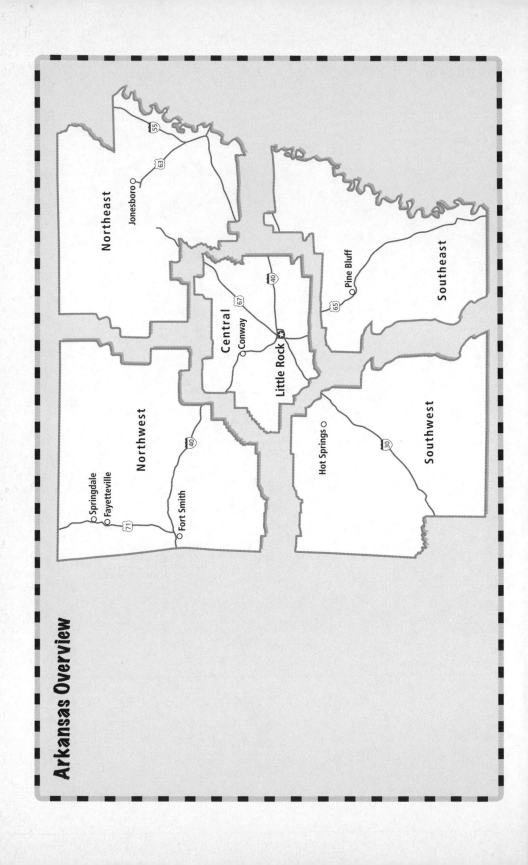

Arkansas Overview

contents

acknowledgments

★ ★

*I*f you play your life backward, you see how even the smallest things have affected you. Most of all you remember the people who have made a difference. Sometimes the biggest influence might be somebody who doesn't remember you or doesn't even know you exist, but without that person you would not be where you are today. We want to take this opportunity to recognize both the people who hopefully already know how much they helped us with this project and those who just saw us in passing.

We want to thank our good friend and research assistant, Barbara K. McDonald, who bolstered our courage during dark days of doubt and helped us become the little engine that could. We owe a debt of gratitude to Wanda McNinch, who knows the state of Arkansas better than anyone else and was glad to keep the road hot when we needed a chauffeur; her hugs worked wonders when we ran out of Valium. To Wanda Necia Jones, thank you for your words of encouragement, your contagious optimism, and your map-reading skills that served so well on the trips you made with us. Thanks also to Susan Hook for all the free shrink sessions, computer lessons, and tolerance of absent-mindedness.

We appreciate the assistance we received from the staff at the Faulkner County Library, with special thanks to Sarah Mattingly, Wade Graham, and Ruth Voss. Thanks also to Lynita Langley-Ware at the Faulkner County Museum.

A big thank-you to the Arkansas Department of Parks and Tourism, an invaluable source of information and photos, with particular kudos to Tim Schultz, Greg Overturf, and Dena Woerner.

Thanks to Kaye Lundgren, Linda R. Pine, and Jennifer L. McCarty at the University of Arkansas at Little Rock Archives and Special Collections for their work in gathering photos for us; to photographers Haley Emerick and Julie Johnson; to all the individuals, newspapers, and agencies who sent photos and leads to us.

Thanks also go to Carol Rolf with the *River Valley & Ozark Edition* and Linda Caillouet with the *Arkansas-Democrat Gazette* for publicizing our search for curiosities.

acknowledgments.

★ ★

Thanks to our archaeological consultants, Marlon Mowdy with Hampson Archeological Museum State Park; Jane Anne Blakney-Bailey with the Arkansas Archeological Survey, Toltec Mounds State Park; and Leslie "Skip" Stewart-Abernathy of Arkansas Tech. And thanks to our geological consultants, John D. McFarland (ret.), Doug Hanson, and Charles Stone with the Arkansas Geological Survey, and to our USDA Forest Service consultants, Jim Jones and Don Bragg.

Again on our home turf, thanks to Alicia Suitt and Addie Bailey at the University of Central Arkansas Torreyson Library; and to Gale Velte, the best mechanic in the state.

Thanks also to the wonderfully informative staff members at various museums, libraries, archives, chambers of commerce, and schools around Arkansas.

And a hearty thank-you to all the people who made this book possible by sharing their stories of the interesting, odd, and downright bizarre.

★ ★

The thrill of sniffing out morsels of trivia for a book about off-beat subjects was like ratnip to us pack rats. We pored over the stacks of old newspapers and magazines that wound through our house like a maze. Our rollover minutes finally rolled over, thanks to all the long-distance interviews we conducted. We discovered, though, that speed is as essential to good reporting as thoroughness. Many of the roadside attractions we looked forward to visiting fell victim to an ailing economy and vanished while we were still doing research. Crystal Caves Motor Court caved in, and Dinosaur Park lumbered to extinction. We especially mourn the demise of our choice pick, Booger Hollow, where tourists vied for the upper throne in a double-decker outhouse. Other curiosities eluded our butterfly net because we couldn't verify their authenticity. If Uncle Charlie said he saw a mermaid in the swimming pool, you'd want to believe him, but would you call the evening news? Probably not—unless he was handy with a camera. Let us now salute some of the curiosities that, for one reason or another, didn't make the cut.

The 1814 Rock of Ages Massacre at Cadron; the skeleton of an alien creature found by a deer hunter near Charleston; giant snakes roaming the bottomlands; Mothman sightings in the Ozark Mountains; a mysterious animal resembling an oversize hyena that was killing sheep in Johnson County; Bigfoot sightings too numerous to mention; the recovery of a flying disc in 1948; the discovery of a metal cup found in a 300 million-year-old coal seam near Sparta; a black panther roaming loose near Conway; and our personal favorite: a Trumann resident who was chased by a creature that leapt from a tree and appeared to be a cross between a dog and an ape. He didn't know whether to toss it a bone or give it a quarter for the organ grinder.

Even when a curiosity is pinned to the public bulletin board, it is soon replaced by another. Change is always just one step ahead of everybody. Arkansas has changed a great deal over the course of our lives—in some ways good; in others, not so much. At times it seems we've been invaded by culture snatchers who want to alter our state into the

★ ★

strip-mall and big-box sameness that threatens to turn every town in America into Anyplace, U.S.A.

Still, before we take our soma pills and don our virtual reality suits, let's take a look at the real reality that speaks to the uniqueness of our state. Where else but in Arkansas would you find an ice-cream flavor called Woo Pig Chewy?

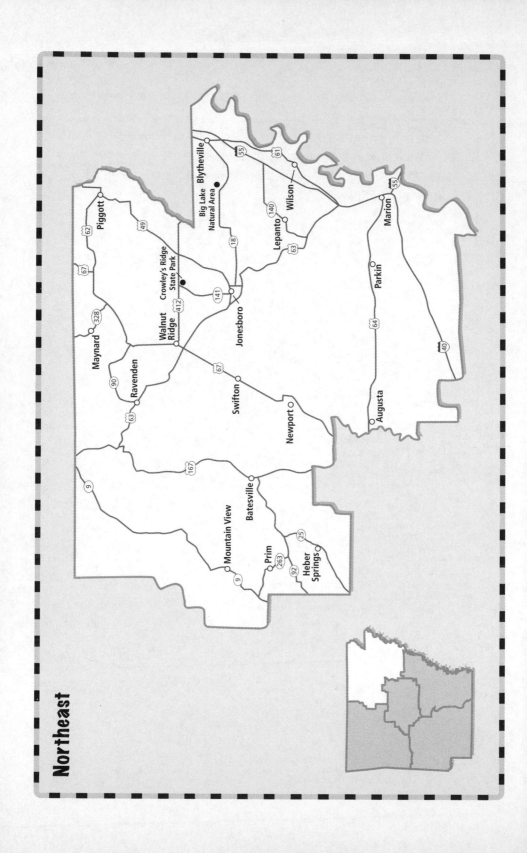

Northeast

1

Northeast

Northeast Arkansas comprises *three distinct and diverse geographical regions: the Ozark Mountains, Crowley's Ridge, and the Delta. Each has something to offer seekers of the curious.*

The port-o-potty has been perfected by the inventive folks in Mountain View, home of the Arkansas Bean Festival and Great Outhouse Race. And if you get a hankering for authentic Ozark Mountain music, Mountain View also bills itself as the Folk Music Capital of the World.

Batesville, one of Arkansas's oldest towns, is home to the Scottish Festival, where men in kilts air out their differences—and their women hope for a good, strong wind.

The history of northeast Arkansas is preserved and protected at places like Parkin Archeological State Park and the Hampson Archeological Museum State Park. There you can see ancient relics left by the first Americans. Such priceless antiquities were too often plowed under by pioneers.

Pioneers of a different sort often stopped at a nondescript building on US 67 near Swifton. Early rock and rollers traveling from Memphis to Little Rock stopped to perform at the King of Clubs, a popular roadhouse. The roster included Jerry Lee Lewis, Roy Orbison, and the King himself, Elvis.

Crowley's Ridge is a curiosity unto itself. Surrounded by Mississippi Delta flatlands, Crowley's Ridge rises 200 feet above sea level. It's kind of like being a basketball player in a room full of jockeys. Some say it used to be part of what is now Tennessee, before the fickle Mississippi River changed course.

★ ★

Grave Secrets
Augusta

Within Augusta Memorial Park Cemetery, an enigma lies under a large marker bearing the name L. J. Crocker. Some believe that the moniker is an alias and that the grave is actually the final resting place of William Clarke Quantrill, the infamous Confederate renegade.

Quantrill burned his name into American Civil War history during the border clashes between the states of Missouri and Kansas. On August 21, 1861, he led a group of 450 men into Lawrence, Kansas, where they executed 183 men and boys and then burned the town. Most historians think Quantrill was wounded and captured in 1865 and that he died in prison in Louisville, Kentucky.

But did he?

In 1867 a wealthy stranger calling himself Captain L. J. Crocker arrived in Gregory, a small town near Augusta, Arkansas. He bought a large farm, helped establish the local bank, and joined the local Freemason lodge.

Rumors circulated about Crocker's true identity. Men familiar with Quantrill noted the stranger's striking resemblance to the guerilla leader. Quantrill was said to have lost a finger. Crocker always wore a glove in public. Crocker's wife, Gabriella, was a relative of Cole Younger. Younger and Frank and Jessie James were former members of Quantrill's Raiders and sometimes visited the Crocker home. In 1910, after obtaining a secrecy oath from his fellow Masons, Crocker confirmed suspicions. He was, he said, William Clarke Quantrill. He asked that his true identity be kept secret until after his death.

Was Crocker the infamous renegade leader? Quite possibly, according to former police investigator David Kennedy of Beebe. He believes that Quantrill escaped and assumed a new identity, aided by members of a secret splinter group of Freemasons known as the Knights of the Golden Circle, composed of former high-ranking Confederate officers. After years of studying the case, Kennedy has

L. J. CROCKER
BORN OCT. 18, 1839 – DIED JUNE 28, 1917
LAURA LEE CROCKER
BORN SEPT 26, 1864 – DIED AUG 1, 1980

CROCKER

Is it Crocker? Or just a crock?

gathered an array of evidence, including photographs, handwriting samples, medical reports, private correspondence, and other documents.

Kennedy, who has written a book on the subject, said, "I thought it would be easy to debunk this myth, but after four or five years I realized I had failed. I kept finding new corroborating information."

Augusta is 75 miles northeast of Little Rock. To visit the cemetery, turn south off US 64 East onto Fifth Street at the armory and go about 1 block. The cemetery will be on your left.

★ ★

Great Scot!
Batesville

For three days each April, everyone at Lyon College in Batesville belongs to the same clan. The McSmiths and McJoneses join the McDougals and McTavishes in a celebration of all things Scottish. The Arkansas Scottish Festival brings thousands of visitors to the campus of Lyon College, which was founded in 1872 by the Presbyterian Church, a Scottish-bred denomination.

We heard bagpipes as we approached the festivities. Some of us love what a good piper can do with reeds and a bag made of sheepskin. Others think the sheep is protesting.

Highland dancers stepped lively in Scottish brogues, cut a rug in the Sword Dance, and had a fling with gravity.

One of us considered entering a sporting event until we realized it was the hammer throw, not hammertoe. The sheaf toss was exciting. Competitors used a pitchfork to hurl wheat-filled burlap sacks over a bar. Other sporting events included the caber toss, more recognizable to us couch potatoes as "Scotty heaves the telephone pole."

All that hurling and heaving put us in the mood for some traditional Scottish food. Haggis is where a sheep eats itself and then the human eats the sheep. We hear it goes down well with tatties and neeps (potatoes and turnips). Pie sounded good for dessert, but it was meat pie. Where did they hide the Scotch whiskey?

Sheep dog demonstrations were fun to watch. They showcased the dog's talent for separating and herding sheep. *Bah, ram, ewe.*

Plaid was the fashion choice for many at the festival. Those who knew their ancestry sported the tartan of their clan. Men who had never tried kilts before found them very liberating. They felt Scot-free. Kilts also presented the opportunity for the lasses to judge the laddies in the Bonniest Knees Contest. Our male half was going to enter until realizing it was not boniest knees. Blindfolded, the young maidens groped and squeezed—short men seemed to get a wee bit more enjoyment out of the experience.

For more information about the Arkansas Scottish Festival, call Lyon College at (870) 307-7000 or (870) 307-PIPE (7473).

A feller could get kilt.
ARKANSAS DEPARTMENT OF PARKS AND TOURISM

★ ★

Shake, Rattle, and Roll
Big Lake

> A lot of people think that the devil has come here. Some
> thinks that this is the beginning of the world coming to
> an end.
>
> —George Crist, a settler,
>   referring to the New Madrid earthquake
>   of 1811–12

It began as a mere sliver of light in the night sky, but it grew into a
comet. Then, in September, a solar eclipse occurred. Domestic animals began acting nervous and erratic. Flocks of birds took flight in
chaotic, panic-stricken patterns. Wild geese and ducks landed near
people or even on people's heads. Snakes awakened from their
hibernation and surfaced in great numbers. Boatmen on the lower
Ohio River saw numerous dead squirrels floating in the river, while
live ones migrated en masse. Rabbits, raccoons, and deer were seen
traveling in groups with bears, panthers, wolves, and foxes. They
approached settlers' cabins, fearing neither man nor one another,
acting as if they were tame.

Lightning struck from out of a clear blue sky, and a traveler near
Memphis saw "two vast electrical columns shooting up from the
horizon at sunrise" like searchlights in the sky.

On December 16, 1811, the first shocks struck. The ground shook
and began rolling in waves as cracks and crevasses opened. The largest were up to 1 mile long by 20 feet deep and many yards wide.
Trees exploded as crevasses opened beneath them and split their
trunks from bottom to top. There was a hissing noise like the sound
of gas escaping, and the odor of sulfur filled the air. Lights flashed
from out of the ground; sand, wood, rock, and fist-size bits of coal
blew out of the earth.

Red mud and clay boiled up from the river bottom, turning the
water the color of blood. Crevasses opened in the riverbed, and
whirlpools pulled boats underwater, never to be seen again.

6

As the one hundred inhabitants of Big Prairie fled their town, the sandy soil it rested on began to liquefy and houses sank into the ground. Today the Mississippi River near Helena occupies the site.

Simultaneously, on what is now the Arkansas-Missouri border, a strip of land 4 miles wide and 10 miles long sank, creating Big Lake. The New Madrid earthquake created a total of ten lakes, but Big Lake is one of only two remaining today.

Big Lake is located in the Big Lake National Wildlife Refuge near Manila in Mississippi County. Big Lake NWR's e-mail address is biglake @fsw.gov. The phone number is (870) 564-2429.

And Then There Was One
Blytheville

Art Deco. The name sounds more like a jazz trumpet player than an international movement, but in the brief period from 1925 to 1939, the style sometimes called Art Moderne had a wide-ranging influence on commercial design as well as the visual arts. One of the best existing examples of Art Deco architecture in Arkansas is the restored Greyhound bus terminal in Blytheville. Built for the heady sum of $30,000 in 1939, the building incorporates many of the features associated with the style.

Trivia

Another one-of-a-kind in Blytheville's history was a physician by the name of Benjamin Bugg. In the late 1800s Bugg held the record for the world's longest beard. It measured 6.6 feet. Sadly the good doctor has long since retired to that great golf course in the sky, but there are still Buggs in Blytheville, though perhaps none as hirsute.

Retro chic, doggy style.
ARKANSAS DEPARTMENT OF PARKS AND TOURISM

★ ★

With its flat roof and round corners, the structure's overall look is clean, smooth, and streamlined. Exotic and expensive materials were used in its construction and decoration. Its brick walls were covered with blue and white Vitrolite, a form of baked enamel. The spacious interior lounge and restaurant featured indirect lighting; handsome couches and chairs were chrome-framed with cushions upholstered in royal-blue leather.

Built at the tail end of the Art Deco period, the depot was one of ten such terminals nationwide, with plans for four more. But the outbreak of World War II spelled the end of the Art Deco movement. Materials like chrome, plastic, and leather were all diverted from the public sector for use in the war movement.

After the war, long-distance bus travel went into decline as commercial airlines became more popular and more Americans bought automobiles. The Blytheville station closed its doors in 2001; but just when it seemed as if the old Greyhound terminal was headed for the dogs, civic pride came to the rescue. With plans to make it Blytheville's visitor center, the Greyhound depot was restored. Today it is the only remaining one of its kind in the country and is listed on the National Register of Historic Places.

The depot is located at 109 North Fifth Street in Blytheville. For more information call (870) 763-2525 or e-mail mainstbly@sbcglobal.net. Get your ticket and take a ride back to the future.

Alien Artworks?

Clay and Greene Counties

In 2003 a farmer near Knobel in Clay County got word from a local ultralight aircraft pilot that someone or something had visited his wheat field and flattened the stalks, creating a design in the shape of a circle with nine smaller orbs in spirals around it. A year later, in the nearby community of Peach Orchard, another crop circle appeared. It resembled a bicycle wheel. In 2007 a third design materialized in Delaplaine in neighboring Greene County.

★ ★

Reporters and crop circle investigators moved at warp speed to see the phenomena. No one had a definitive explanation for the spectacles, though one crop circle expert mentioned plasma discharge. The locals took all the fuss in stride, and the wheat was harvested without any problems. Nobody was beamed up, and E.T. wasn't hiding in the tool shed. A bigger to-do would have been made if David Duchovny had shown up.

Cosmic graffiti?
CLAY COUNTY COURIER

Bear's Big Adventure
Cord

In 1974 Karen Stogsdill (now Craft) was flying home to Arkansas from Alaska with her two-year-old black Labrador, Bear, who was placed in a portable plywood kennel in the airplane's cargo hold. During a plane change in Seattle, airline personnel discovered that Bear had chewed his way out of his kennel. They put him in another one for the next leg of his flight, but by the time the plane reached Chicago, Bear had again chewed through his crate and was missing. Everyone assumed that he had walked off the plane while someone's back was turned.

Frequent flyer miles finally pay off.
KAREN CRAFT

11

A week later, Karen received a phone call from United Airlines. Bear had been on the plane all along, hiding in a dark, tunnel-like hole. Although ten pounds lighter, he was pronounced fit to fly . . . again. Shipped home in a chew-proof metal crate, he arrived feeling no pain, as he was tranquilized to the max.

Bear became a celebrity, and United Airlines presented him with a plaque in recognition of his amazing accomplishment. He had flown more than 16,000 miles. His itinerary included San Francisco, New York City, Los Angeles, and two trips to Honolulu.

Sadly, a few years later Bear was struck and killed by a farm truck. "He was quite a dog!" Karen said.

He was, indeed, Karen. He was, indeed. When Bear went to that great airport in the sky, it was about the only one he had not already visited.

Dem Bones, Dem Bones, Dem Dry Bones
Fontaine (Greene County)

In the northeastern part of our state is a series of dune fields. These ancient sand dunes, along with the loess deposits that formed nearby Crowley's Ridge, are remnants of the most recent ice age, when it was much drier than today. (The climate, that is, not the county.)

Near the town of Fontaine in the southwest corner of Greene County, a farmer named Frank Sloan noticed Indian artifacts eroding out of the sand atop one of these old dunes. He called on experts from Arkansas State University at Jonesboro to investigate. In 1972 anthropology professor Dan Morris headed an excavation team, and what they found was puzzling at first. Four hundred forty-eight artifacts, some in clusters and others laid out in 6-foot patterns, were discovered within a 39- by 36-foot area. One hundred forty-four of the pieces were Dalton points, a distinctive spear point made by ancient hunter-gatherers at the end of the ice age between 10,500 and 9,500 years ago. Among the tools were thirty adzes, the first large woodworking tool invented by early Americans. All of the tools were in pristine condition, showing little or no signs of wear.

On a hunch, the diggers began sifting through the sand and found a large number of tiny bone fragments. One hundred of them were identifiable as human, and none were identified as nonhuman. Based on the thickness of the skull fragments, the ages of the remains varied from children to adult. Scholars believe that the site was a cemetery comprising twelve to twenty-five graves. The fact that these graves had what appeared to be grave offerings suggests that the mourners had believed in an afterlife. The Sloan Site, as it is now called, is internationally famous as the oldest documented cemetery in the Western Hemisphere. The site is on private property, and none of the artifacts is on public display, according to officials at Arkansas State University in Jonesboro.

No Nudists in the Natural State
Forrest City

According to the Book of Genesis, nakedness was humanity's natural state, an opinion still shared by many anthropologists and exotic dancers. But when one group of modern Arkansans formed a club that literally interpreted the state's earliest nickname, The "Bare" State, they found the long arm of the law reaching straight for their private members.

Or so it must have seemed in 1957, when locals in Forrest City learned that one Gordon Satterfield was running a nudist camp at the nearby Wildwood Lodge. Arrested for indecent exposure and displaying obscene photographs, Satterfield was fined $350. Because the nudism occurred in an enclosed area on private property, however, Satterfield couldn't be charged, since there was no law specifically banning nudism in Arkansas. The resulting public outcry led legislators to draft Senate Bill 95 (Arkansas Code 568-204).

According to lawyers, Arkansas's anti-nudity law may be the only one of its kind in the Western world. It's definitely the only such law in the United States. It forbids unmarried people of the opposite sex

★ ★

from being nude together as a form of social practice. As written, it apparently exempts same-sex groups—a rare case where gays have fewer restrictions than their straight counterparts.

Branded unconstitutional by the American Civil Liberties Union for violating citizens' rights to free speech and freedom of assembly, the law prohibits advocating or promoting nudism—in effect, making it illegal to lobby for changing the law.

Nudist fleeing with only the clothes off his back.

For the record, this text in no way advocates or promotes the practice of nudism. Why risk time in jail where one would no doubt be strip-searched?

Death . . . It's a Living
Heber Springs

As we said in our introduction to this book, we were often disappointed to learn that many of the destinations we considered curious and worthy of research were either no longer in existence or were simply not all that interesting. That's why we crossed our fingers when looking up the Olmstead Funeral and Historical Museum in Heber Springs. We were afraid it would be just another dead end. Turns out we were dead wrong.

Before malls and super-centers, the Olmstead family knew the importance of diversification. Their establishment included a hardware store, post office, livery stable, and funeral parlor. Customers could take care of a lot in one visit. They could nail it or mail it and curry 'em or bury 'em.

The business's founder, T. E. Olmstead, was an embalmer who moved his family to Heber Springs in 1896 and opened the funeral home. A fire in 1909 destroyed the original building, but T. E. rebuilt. That stone edifice, today's museum, is listed on the National Register of Historic Places.

After T. E. died in 1923, the business passed down to his son, Ralph, who started offering burial insurance to clients. For 25 cents a year, clients received $100 worth of coverage, which was the going rate for funerals at that time.

The funeral home has continued through subsequent generations of Olmsteads, who share their family heritage with the public through the museum. The numerous exhibits include antique embalming equipment; old Victrolas that play funereal music on shellac disks; and the prize showpiece, a restored 1896 horse-drawn hearse. Also displayed is a pressurized embalming machine, which Ralph received as a gift in 1939. Handheld cardboard fans with religious pictures are reminders of the mourners who crowded into little country churches during hot summer services. Black velvet drapes that fit in a grip of

The One That Got Away

The Little Red River, one of the best trout fishing streams in America, produced the largest brown trout ever caught. Howard "Rip" Collins from Heber Springs caught the whopper in 1992. It weighed forty pounds, four ounces.

Heber Springs also has bragging rights to fishing records set at Greers Ferry Lake. In 1982 Al Nelson, of neighboring Higden, caught a twenty-two-pound, eleven-ounce walleye. At first glance, he thought he had hooked a small alligator. The catch set a new state record, and in 1996, after much controversy, it was named the world-record walleye. The next year Jerald C. Shaum of Shirley set a world record by catching a twenty-seven-pound, five-ounce hybrid striped bass.

What is it about the waters in and around Heber Springs? Why do they produce such consistently big fish? Originally called Sugar Loaf, the town was built at the site of seven springs that contain minerals with alleged medicinal properties—sulfur and magnesium, for instance. Our sources don't say anything about radioactive mineral water, but such a thing does exist. And remember all those old horror movies about monsters that grew to huge proportions after exposure to radioactivity? It's just a thought. Whatever the cause, Heber Springs is heaven for fishermen.

And it's not just for human fishermen. We heard about a cat named Boots that allegedly was granted a fishing license by the

★ ★

portable floral racks were called "jack in the box."

The Olmstead Funeral and Historical Museum is located at 108 South Fourth Street in Heber Springs. For information about touring the museum, call (501) 250-3890.

Arkansas Game and Fish Commission. Boots, a cat of unspecified breed, was said to have liked nothing better than catching dinner by dipping a paw into the Little Red River with astounding accuracy. Being diligent journalists, we tried seven ways from Sunday to confirm this story as fact, but no one we spoke to in Heber Springs could either verify it or deny it, and the cat wouldn't return our calls. We contacted

A cool catch: Rip Collins with his world-record brown trout.
ARKANSAS GAME AND FISH COMMISSION

the Arkansas Game and Fish Commission, and even though we corresponded via e-mail, we swear we could hear them laughing.

The story probably originated from a cat-owning fisherman who wanted to one-up his buddies. You know how fishermen are.

★ ★

Ships of Fools
Heber Springs

Since the corrugated box was invented in 1890, it has been used to ship most anything and everything. But suppose one were to make a *ship* out of cardboard? That was the idea proposed by newspaper publisher Pat Zellmer in 1987, when the town of Heber Springs, Home of the World Record Brown Trout, began looking for bigger fish to fry. As a result, Heber Springs now holds annual boat races

And the trophy goes to . . . the Soggy Bottom Boys.
ARKANSAS DEPARTMENT OF PARKS AND TOURISM

on Greers Ferry Lake, where the contestants must finish four heats around a semicircular 200-yard course in human-powered boats designed and built from cardboard.

Do-it-yourself projects are not our strong suit, so the idea of cardboard boats seemed all wet, but we thought we'd give it a try. For our own design, we were going to take an empty refrigerator box, cut one side out of it, duct-tape and caulk the seams, and then spray it with about fifty coats of water sealant. We also meant to invest in a couple of high-quality life vests for good measure. After rethinking our options, we decided instead to pack a picnic lunch with something cold to drink and park ourselves safely out of harm's way.

The race is held every July when the City Parks Department hauls in fresh sand, transforming the place into a Redneck Riviera. The boat designs run the gamut from pretty crude to crudely pretty. It's an amazing sight—an armada of miniature Spanish galleons and pint-size Viking dragon ships. One can almost picture them searching for a cardboard monastery to plunder or some pygmy Irish lassies to carry off. There's even a Titanic Prize given to the most dramatic sinking.

This is one boat race you won't want to miss!

For more information about the World Championship Cardboard Boat Races, call the Heber Springs Area Chamber of Commerce at (800) 77-HEBER (43237).

King Crowley, the Great White Hype
Jonesboro

In 1922 Egyptologist Howard Carter found King Tut's tomb in the Valley of the Kings. That discovery and its alleged curse made worldwide headlines and became the stuff of legend. Meanwhile, half a world away near the town of Jonesboro, Arkansas, a different sort of legend was being born.

In 1924 nationally known Arkansas novelist Bernice Babcock was approached by a Jonesboro deaf-mute named Dentler Rowland. Rowland claimed that while walking on his land one day, he had literally

★ ★

stumbled across a small stone carving of a human foot. He dug down to a depth of about 10 feet, where he found a small coffin about 18 inches wide by 3 feet long. Little hand-carved figurines of humans and animals circled the box. They were, Rowland claimed, proof of an unknown civilization, related to the Aztecs of Mexico.

Babcock took the bait and bought the alleged relics for $600. The

King Crowley was the centerpiece in Dentler Rowland's dubious discovery.
UALR PHOTOGRAPH COLLECTION / UALR ARCHIVES

largest piece was a novaculite bust weighing about forty pounds and looking like a decapitated Rock'em Sock'em Robot. Babcock dubbed it "King Crowley" after the Delta landmark, Crowley's Ridge. The eyes, with inlaid silver pupils, bore a remarkable resemblance to brass furniture casters.

Scorned by every reputable expert who saw it, Rowland's collection became the centerpiece of the newly formed Arkansas Museum of Natural History. Babcock ironically started the museum partly to offset the widely held belief expounded by H. L. Mencken and others that Arkansas was a cultural wasteland "where nobody can read, and those who can, don't."

Babcock continued to defend the articles as genuine, reportedly saying that Rowland lacked the skill to carve the crudely fashioned objects, even though he was, by trade, a jeweler and gunsmith. The so-called artifacts remained on display until Babcock's retirement, when she offered to sell them to the museum at cost. Her offer was politely declined. At that point, an anonymous buyer from California arrived and bought the collection, which is probably worth a small fortune today. A few surviving pieces of Rowland's handiwork, known as the Babcock Collection, are now kept in a drawer at the Arkansas State University Museum at Jonesboro.

For more information or to arrange a tour of the museum, call (870) 972-2074 or visit www2.astate.edu/museum or e-mail museum@astate.edu. The museum is located on East Johnson Avenue (US 49) between Melrose Street and University Loop West in Jonesboro.

Mona's Bonas
Jonesboro

When we were kids, we loved Tarzan. What a dad! Did Boy have to go to school? Heck, no. Tarzan didn't bathe or change clothes, and he didn't take any crap off anybody. No matter what kind of a fix he got himself into, all he had to do was let out a Rebel yell and the

★ ★

elephants would stampede in and stomp the offending party flat. Problem solved! If we were Tarzan, we'd never have to wait in line at the supermarket checkout.

Too bad Arkansas doesn't have wild elephants anymore. We say "anymore" because once upon a time in the not-too-distant past, we did (sort of) have wild elephants here.

A few years back, a local man fishing on the Arkansas River near Palarm Creek in southern Faulkner County noticed an unusual object washing out of the gravel along the riverbank. It was a large tooth, with the enamel still in place.

Experts identified the tooth as the molar of a mastodon. These large mammals roamed over North and South America as recently as 6,000 years ago. Unlike their cousins, the modern elephant, these animals were browsers instead of grazers, preferring the forest cover to open grasslands. Rather than being herd animals like their cousins the mammoths, mastodons are believed to have lived as solitary creatures.

The demise of these beasts meant the slow decline of a species of tree called the bois d'arc, or Osage orange. The elastic properties of this wood made it the number-one wood of choice for Indian bow making.

The seeds of the bois d'arc tree are contained inside a bitter, grapefruit-size fruit that the mastodons ate. Later they would pass the undigested seeds in their stools and in the process disperse the trees over a wide area, like a lumbering, defecating version of Johnny Appleseed. By the time Europeans arrived, the tree grew only in a very small area along the Red River, where the Caddo Indians held a monopoly on its export.

To see a facsimile of the mastodon, visit the Arkansas State University Museum at Jonesboro, where a reconstructed skeleton, which the staff named Mona, is the centerpiece of a fascinating display. Don't forget the password: "Ungawa, timba!"

Even prehistoric models could never be thin enough.
ARKANSAS DEPARTMENT OF PARKS AND TOURISM

For more information or to arrange a tour of the museum, call (870) 972-2074 or visit www2.astate.edu/museum. The museum is located on East Johnson Avenue (US 49) between Melrose Street and University Loop West in Jonesboro.

Captain Elmer Stubbs, a Sharpshooter Who Aimed to Please

In the 1880s Captain Elmer Stubbs performed in Wild West shows. Billed as the "Restless Spirit of the Plains," he had steel-gray eyes and a mane of silver hair. He played at Madison Square Garden and was the rifle wing-shot champion of the world. After retiring from show business, he moved to Jonesboro, Arkansas, where he opened a gun shop.

In 1896 Colonel Mark Bodine of the Royal Gun Club of the Transvaal challenged Stubbs to a shooting match for the world championship; Stubbs accepted. Before the main event, Stubbs put on an exhibition with the help of his little girl, Cleo. From a distance of 20 feet, he shot a silver dollar out of the moppet's fingers and an apple off her head. He wasn't up for the Father of the Year Award. He shattered four glass balls as fast as Cleo could throw them in the air. Then, almost as an afterthought, Stubbs easily defeated Bodine.

Ten years later the Stubbs family relocated to Texarkana; the trail goes cold after that. Maybe if his name had been catchier, he would be as famous as Buffalo Bill. Somehow, it's hard to picture Clarice Starling and Hannibal Lecter discussing a villain named Elmer Stubbs.

Le Mans at Lepanto

Lepanto

If Ernest Hemingway were still around, he no doubt would seek the excitement generated by Lepanto's Terrapin Derby and Festival. Sure, Pamplona's Running of the Bulls has speed and reckless abandon, but nothing beats the Terrapin Derby for suspense. It takes about fifteen minutes for the hundreds of competing terrapins to navigate their way over the 60-foot course. Watermelon slices are placed along the goal line to encourage the contestants.

Lepanto has been celebrating the lowly terrapin since 1930, when American Legion Post #26 established the event. In 1937 *The Literary Digest* devoted a full page to coverage of the Terrapin Derby. From 1982 until 1999 the festival was sponsored by the Lepanto Museum. Since then, the Lepanto Fire Department has taken over the reins.

Other entertainment at the festival includes helicopter rides, vendors, crafts, carnival rides and games, music, dancing, and a 5K run-walk. One time-honored custom of the event, the crowning of the Terrapin Derby Queen, was immortalized in Julia Reed's popular book *Queen of the Turtle Derby and Other Southern Phenomena*. The queen joins a procession of elected officials, floats, and antique cars in a mile-long parade down Main Street.

But the true stars of the celebration are the hard-shelled derby athletes. All the competitors wear numbers, and the first three to cross the finish line win prizes. The throng of spectators cheer on their favorites from a healthy distance, lest they get trampled in the stampede. Sometimes it's a tour de force a la Secretariat at the Belmont Stakes. Other times, the victor wins by a hare—uh, hair.

AR 135 and AR 140 intersect at Lepanto in Poinsett County, about 42 miles southeast of Jonesboro. The Terrapin Derby is held the first weekend in October. For more information call Lepanto City Hall at (870) 475-2415 or e-mail cityoflepanto@yahoo.com.

Smoke on the Water
Marion

In that fateful month of April 1865, the steamboat *Sultana* left New Orleans headed north up the Mississippi River, bound for Cairo, Illinois. The *Sultana* had been built to carry only 376 people, but on this voyage it carried 2,400 passengers, the majority of whom were the pitiful shells of men released from Confederate prisoner-of-war camps at Andersonville and Cahaba.

★ ★

At Vicksburg, Mississippi, the steamboat's chief engineer noticed one of the boilers was cracked, and a boilermaker made repairs. The *Sultana* continued upriver to Helena, Arkansas, where a photographer took a picture of the boat and its passengers before they moved on to Memphis. After docking there for four hours, the boat lumbered onward with its heavy load.

At two in the morning on April 27, near Mound City, Arkansas, the *Sultana*'s boiler exploded with a blast so loud that it awakened people in Memphis. It took twenty minutes for the boat to burn to

EXPLOSION OF THE STEAMER "SULTANA," April 28, 1865.

The *Sultana* explosion was the worst maritime disaster in American history.
JOHN N. HASKELL PHOTOGRAPH COLLECTION/UALR ARCHIVES

the waterline. Of the 2,400 passengers, only 780 survived; 250 of those died soon afterward.

A bar formed at the place in the river channel where the boat sank, eventually becoming so large that it changed the river's course. As the bar grew, it landlocked Mound City. Thirty-five years after the accident, people were still finding wood from the boat sticking up out of cotton fields. They would cut up the timbers to use for fire-wood. The sinking of the *Sultana* remains the worst nautical disaster in American history, yet it is largely forgotten.

In 1982 archaeologists discovered deck planks and timbers about 32 feet under an Arkansas soybean field. A marker in Marion, Arkansas, commemorates the *Sultana* tragedy. On April 1, 2000, the Northeast Arkansas Civil War Heritage Trail Committee and the Arkansas Daughters of the American Revolution dedicated the monument in

They Tried to Tell Us We're Too Young

In 2007 the Arkansas Legislature set the minimum age of consent for marriage at eighteen, with younger teens being allowed to wed with parental consent if the bride was pregnant. At least that's what the lawmakers *meant* to say. Then a typographical error was discovered. Act 441 actually said anyone under eighteen and not pregnant could marry with parental consent. Technically, babies could marry under the law. Red-faced legislators envisioned Toys R Us offering bridal registries and newlyweds honeymooning in the sandbox.

The Code Revision Committee quickly amended the loopy legislation, and the governor signed the corrected bill into law.

★ ★

front of 300 people, some of whom were descendants of the *Sultana* passengers. Descendants of people who pulled survivors from the river were also present at the dedication. The marker is located at the intersection of AR 77 and US 64, in front of Marion City Hall.

On April 2, 2009, Arkansas Representative Vic Snyder introduced a congressional resolution remembering the sinking of the *Sultana*.

Like, What? Were You Raised in a Barn?
Maynard

Since the town of Maynard was founded in the 1870s, we know it wasn't named for Maynard G. Krebs. (Anyone who remembers Maynard G. Krebs wins a set of bongos.)

The population of Maynard is normally 381 but swells to as many

Even Aunt Bea couldn't spruce up this jail.
ARKANSAS DEPARTMENT OF PARKS AND TOURISM

as 8,000 people when the Maynard Pioneer Days Craft Fair and Festival is held the third weekend in September.

An interesting attraction for out-of-towners is the Maynard Pioneer Museum and Park on AR 328 at Spring Street. Founded in 1980, the park reflects life as it was in the Randolph County area in the late 1800s and early 1900s. The museum is housed in a nineteenth-century log cabin that was deconstructed at its original site east of town and, log by numbered log, reassembled in the park. The cabin's rooms are furnished as they would have been several generations ago. In 1999 Maynard townsfolk moved another log cabin, piece by piece, to the park. The second cabin is a combination of an old-timey one-room schoolhouse and church.

Maynard Goes Medieval on Crime

Before leaving Maynard, be sure to check out the old city jail, located behind the Maynard Community Center.

Be forewarned: This is not the kind of jail Andy and Barney ran in Mayberry. It's not even as nice as Marshal Dillon's jail in Dodge City. The marshal himself wouldn't be able to lie down crossways in this hell hole—it's only 6 feet by 10 feet, making it possibly the smallest jail in Arkansas.

What's really hard to believe is that the jail was constructed in 1936, after civilization had arrived, or so we thought. The jail door was made from old wagon wheel rims. The structure was used for seventeen years, and the first inmate was a man who helped build it.

★ ★

The museum is open Tuesday through Saturday from May through September. For more information stick your head out the window and holler, or call (870) 647-2701.

Mountain Beanery Scenery
Mountain View

Mountain View, Arkansas, may not be as big as Chicago, but this little Ozark burg could dub itself the Windy City of the South, thanks to an annual event called the Arkansas Bean Festival and Great Championship Outhouse Race.

This festival, held the last weekend in October, celebrates the lowly bean in a big way. Since beans are the musical fruit, the celebration starts appropriately with music concerts Thursday and Friday, with performers offering a mix of folk, bluegrass, Cajun, and other styles of music. Then on Saturday morning, more than two dozen teams compete in a bean cook-off. Using special herbs and spices, the teams prepare nearly a ton of beans in large, antique cast-iron kettles set up on the courthouse square. (No doubt some of the family recipes are so well guarded that only the cook is privy to the secret.) At noon the crowd gathers round, and everyone enjoys a banquet of free beans and cornbread.

Nothing follows beans better than an outhouse, so after lunch

Trivia

While in Randolph County, ask the residents about Arkansas's first school near Ravenden Springs, 30 miles southwest of Maynard. The school, started by Caleb Lindsey in 1817, was in a cave. Classes included Walking Upright and Fire-making One-oh-one.

the Great Championship Outhouse Race gets under way on Jefferson Street. Two contestants propel each outhouse-on-wheels, with one person guiding it and the other one sitting on the throne. The vehicles are known as people-powered potties, but there's a lot of natural gas helping them along. Sometimes they manage to catch a tailwind, too. The fastest team wins a cash prize and the coveted Gold Toilet Seat Trophy.

Each year the festival attracts about 40,000 people who enjoy playing games, square dancing, and shopping for Ozark arts and crafts—nothing too artsy-fartsy, though.

We're used to running to the bathroom, but running after the bathroom?
ARKANSAS DEPARTMENT OF PARKS AND TOURISM

★ ★

If you're looking for something different, head on up to Mountain View for a rootin' tootin' good time.

Known as the Folk Music Capital of the World, Mountain View is about 100 miles north of Little Rock on AR 9. For more information about the town and the Bean Festival and Great Championship Out-house Race, call the Mountain View Chamber of Commerce at (870) 269-8068 or visit www.mountainviewcc.org.

The White River Monster
Newport

Since 1915 people have reported seeing a monster in the White River near Newport, Arkansas. The sightings have been sporadic, and accounts vary as to the size of the creature, but it is said to be any-where from 12 to 30 feet long. The beast is gray with spiny protru-sions on its body. According to some witnesses, the monster bellows like a cow.

One theory for the sightings is that Whitey, as he is affectionately known, may be a northern elephant seal that wandered into the Mississippi River from the Gulf of Mexico and then strayed into the White River. But the average elephant seal's life span is only about fifteen years, so why the sightings over a period of decades?

No clear pictures document Whitey's existence, but he is not without a fan club. After a flurry of sightings in 1973, the Arkansas Legislature created the White River Monster Refuge and passed a resolution that made it a crime to "molest, kill, trample, or harm the White River Monster while he is in the Retreat." Such consideration seems appropriate, since Whitey himself has never hurt anyone.

Weird Weather
Old Davidsonville State Park

In 1948 Hot Springs was the site of a hail storm that produced doughnut-shaped hail (Mmm, doughnuts!). Even stranger was the black snow that had fallen in Yellville in 1940. Similar occurrences were seen in New York in 1889, Indiana in 1895, and Illinois in 1919. Based on the feel and taste of the snow, the culprit appeared to be pollutants in the form of dust or soot picked up in the air upwind of the area where the snowfall occurred.

Today few history books remember our state's worst weather. The year was 1816. As Mary Shelley sat by the fire half a world away in a gloomy chateau on the shores of Lake Geneva, struggling with the plot of a short story that would become the basis for her novel *Frankenstein*, early settlers of Davidsonville and other pioneer Arkansas outposts were grappling with a monster of their own.

The town of Davidsonville had just been established the previous year and was quite prosperous. It was the site of the first post office and courthouse in what was to become the state of Arkansas. In its infancy, however, the community faced an unusual challenge.

The year had begun promisingly enough; the weather was mild, unusually so for January. Even through February, it seemed as if spring would come early. Some people neglected to tend their fires in their hearths. Then March came, and the weather turned cold and stormy.

In May, snow and sleet fell intermittently for two weeks. In June it snowed nearly every day, and it remained frigid and icy in July. The landscape looked bleak. The crops were dead and so were the young birds, frozen in their nests. An inch of sleet fell in August.

As bad as conditions seemed in Arkansas, they were pitiful in New England, where 10 inches of snow and ice covered the ground in July. Wintry conditions continued on into August and September.

The meteorological phenomenon affected the entire Northern Hemisphere. It was triggered by the explosion of Mount Tambora in Indonesia. The volcanic eruption sent billions of tons of dust and ash into the upper atmosphere and made for some spectacular red sunsets, much to the delight of sailors.

Davidsonville bounced back from the "year without a summer," as it was called, but the town was not to survive in the long run. Today Old Davidsonville State Park occupies the land, and visitors can stroll around what was once the old public square and see where homes and businesses once stood. The park is located about 6 miles north of Black Rock on AR 361.

How Big Was He When He Was Little?
Osceola

> There were giants in the earth in those days.
> —Genesis VI: 1–4

Many early Arkansas newspapers touted a theory that the Mound Builders were a mysterious lost race of giants. In 1873 the *Osceola Times* reported the discovery of a 13-foot-tall skeleton. A child's skeleton that was found was said to be "as large as a full-grown man of our day at birth." Perhaps the *Fort Smith Elevator* wasn't going quite all the way to the top floor when in 1884 the newspaper told about an enormous skeleton dug up in the southwestern part of the state. The skull had "huge proportions, receding from the eyebrows so as to make the impression of a brutal nature, like that of a gorilla . . . the man could not have been less than 8 feet in height . . . for the skeleton measured 6 feet from the knee to the top of the skull."

In 1891 Captain J. Hays was digging a ditch on his farm 5 miles south of Okolona when he "unearthed the remains of a monster member of some prehistoric race." We presume the relic's body was proportionately large.

Arkansas newspapers referred to an ancient race of giants eleven times between 1873 and 1943. As late as 1927, the *Arkansas Democrat* declared the Mound Builders to be "a race of giants averaging between 7 and 8 feet in height." In 1930 the newspaper reported that skulls found at Corning were one-quarter larger than modern man's and belonged to "a race of people who may have been at least more than 8 feet in height." A story from 1932 reported a footprint in stone that was 5 inches wide by 15 inches long.

Sadly, since the 1940s no more remains have surfaced. As for the skeletons, they seem to have vanished, along with the public's belief in them.

Everybody's Out of Town
Parkin

During the late Middle Ages, Arkansas was a very different place. Farmland in the river bottoms was among the richest on Earth. A type of soil called bottomland loam was particularly fertile, light, and easily worked with a hoe. This, coupled with Arkansas's long growing seasons (we occupy the same latitude as North Africa), allowed native peoples to produce surpluses of food. Native populations grew to numbers beyond anything ever seen before, all built on a diet of beans and corn. Spanish witnesses of the time called northeastern Arkansas the most heavily populated area they had yet encountered in their travels.

Still, as in Europe and other parts of the world, food production could never keep pace with population growth, and the result was the same—conflict. By 1541 Arkansas's river valleys were divided into warring city-states where citizens crowded into large, walled fortresses covering ten to twenty acres. Some were quite elaborate, according to Spanish descriptions. Surrounded by moats or defensive ditches, their walls were made of interwoven wooden posts and branches and plastered with clay. Lookout towers and slots along the top of the wall allowed archers to shoot attackers.

The archaeological site at Parkin in northeastern Cross County was once such a town. Around the seventh century AD, tribes in the Mississippi River Valley began to lay out their towns in patterns resembling Mexican ceremonial centers. Parkin was no exception. Built and occupied between 1000 and 1550 AD, the walled town covered seventeen acres on the St. Francis River. The interior of the fortification was dominated by a large, flat-topped pyramid-shaped mound, which may have served as a platform for a temple. Below it was an open space, or plaza, where people gathered to watch public ceremonies.

One day in June 1541, Hernando de Soto arrived, and there went the neighborhood. Archaeologists estimate that Parkin was abandoned around 1550. When the French passed through the area 150 years later, not a living soul was to be found.

Parkin Archeological State Park is located at the junction of US 64 and AR 184 North. For more information call (870) 755-2500 or visit www.arkansasstateparks.com/parkinarcheological.

Parkin Archeological State Park goes to pottery.
ARKANSAS DEPARTMENT OF PARKS AND TOURISM

The Importance of Being Ernest

Piggott

The Hemingway-Pfeiffer Museum in Piggott commemorates the time during the 1920s and 1930s when author Ernest Hemingway was a part-time resident there. Hemingway's second wife, Pauline, had grown up in the grand home as part of the prominent, philanthropic Pfeiffer family. Pauline's uncle, Gustavus Pfeiffer, was the couple's benefactor, financing many of the trips that inspired Hemingway, including the African safari that produced *The Green Hills of Africa.*

The house and furnishings look much as they did during the Hemingway era. The ceiling in Pauline's room is particularly interesting because the design has faces hidden in it. No doubt, however, the most popular attraction at the museum is the building behind the house where Hemingway did his writing. Once a barn, the converted writer's studio still contains Hemingway's poker table and his clay pigeons. It was here that he wrote part of *A Farewell to Arms,* a sequel to his unpublished first novel, *A Salutation to Legs.*

Never known as a clotheshorse, Hemingway sometimes drew taunts from children as he walked around Piggott. Armed with rocks, the little devils followed behind the shabby, bearded man as they chanted, "Tramp, tramp, tramp." The Great White Hunter fled in terror to avoid a rock pelting.

Behind the Hemingway-Pfeiffer Museum is the Matilda and Karl Pfeiffer Education Center. Karl was Pauline's brother. He and his wife lived in the Tudor Revival–style house before it opened to the public in 2004. Matilda had a passion for reading and rock collecting, so the center has a library of more than 1,600 books and 1,400 rocks and minerals. Especially memorable is a display of naturally fluorescent rocks that glow in shades of green, orange, and purple under ultraviolet light.

The Hemingway-Pfeiffer Museum is located at 1021 West Cherry Street in Piggott. Hours of operation are 9:00 a.m. to 3:00 p.m. Monday through Friday and noon to 3:00 p.m. on Saturday. Donations are appreciated. For more information call (870) 598-3487.

★ ★

Prim's Rolling Stones
Prim

The little town of Prim in Cleburne County is the site of an unusual geological phenomenon: spherical rocks that vary in size from 1 to 4 feet in diameter. Farmers in the area originally considered them nuisances, a hindrance to plowing, but now see them as potential sources of income. The stones make great decorative lawn accents and can fetch as much as $700 each.

Spherical stones, often called cannonball concretions, occur in many other places around the United States and the world. Other sites in Arkansas generally run in an east-to-west line 100 miles long through the northern part of the state. Spherical boulders have been reported at a White County quarry 40 miles east of Prim and at Alum Cove in Newton County 40 miles to the west. In salt marshes along the coast of England, geologists have found modern concretions growing around spent shell casings and shrapnel left over from World War II.

The Prim rocks formed about 300 million years ago when the area was a river delta. They were created not by mechanical action such as abrasion or being rolled by water but by chemical action. The spheres form and grow from within rocks, like crystals. Cross sections of the spheres reveal growth rings similar to those seen in a pearl; and like a pearl, they appear to form around a nucleus, often of organic matter like fragments of bone, wood, or shell. Their form is revealed when the softer surrounding rock weathers away. Some are joined together in the shape of a large peanut.

Hundreds of these concretions are known to exist, and geologists estimate a thousand or so remain in the Prim area. They erode out of hillsides and roll down the slopes into creekbeds. Most were believed to have rolled to their current positions about 10,000 years ago, when the climate was dryer.

Prim is located 12 miles north of Greers Ferry, heading toward Mountain View on AR 263.

Mick and Keith.
WWW.JULIEJOHNSONSPHOTOGRAPHY.COM

★ ★

Ravenden Raven
Ravenden

The town of Ravenden was established in 1883 and was originally called Ravenden Junction because of a proposed railway junction. When the railroad plans fell through, the town's name was changed to Ravenden. It was sometimes confused with Ravenden Springs, 7 miles to the north. Ravenden just didn't have anything to set it apart.

One day in 1991, members of the Ravenden Volunteer Fire

The bird is the word in Ravenden.
ARKANSAS DEPARTMENT OF PARKS AND TOURISM

Department were sitting around the coffee shop shooting the bull, carrying on about how New York City had the Statue of Liberty and St. Louis had the Gateway Arch. Bobby Clements proposed they build a big statue of a raven to represent Ravenden. One thing led to another, and they decided to do it. After holding a bingo party to raise funds, a group of volunteers got to work. Using rebar wrapped in wire mesh, they created the skeleton of a bird and covered it with fiberglass. At last Ravenden had something to crow about.

Then in 1996 the raven statue was burned down by vandals, possibly a gang of literary types who thought it was a Poe excuse for a statue. The community rallied behind the fricasseed fowl and replaced it with another one, also made of fiberglass. After the bird-brained pyromaniacs struck again, the townspeople vowed to create a more durable model of their mascot.

The third time was, indeed, the charm. The raven arose from the ashes, much like its mythic cousin, the phoenix. This concrete-and-stucco version endures today and would charm even Alfred Hitchcock. The statue is 12 feet tall and stands atop a 2-foot-tall pedestal. Though it might be stretching the truth to say that people flock to see the steroidal statue, it still generates plenty of attention.

The raven is located near the intersection of US 63 and AR 90 in Ravenden.

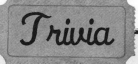

Trivia

While in Ravenden, you can enjoy the cool waters of the nearby Spring River. Fed by Mammoth Spring, 33 miles northwest, the river temperature is a constant, refreshing 58 degrees. That's a little chilly for us, but the rainbow trout seem to love it.

Razorback Rashomon

In 1929 sixteen-year-old Tiller Ruminer of St. James, Arkansas, became engaged to Connie Franklin, a young drifter. As they were trying to find the justice of the peace one night, five men allegedly killed Connie and had their way with Tiller. The men were arrested and put on trial. What happened next is still debated among descendants of key players in the drama. A collective gasp filled the courtroom as Connie Franklin himself strolled in. Most observers agreed he looked mighty good for a dead man. He attempted to prove his identity by playing "Turkey in the Straw" on the harmonica.

Then something weird happened.

It was revealed that the man who had claimed to be Connie Franklin was in reality a married man and former mental patient named Marion Franklin Rogers.

It's pretty hard to convict when the murder victim testifies in favor of the accused, so the jury acquitted the defendants.

Tiller married and raised a family before dying in the early 1990s. Connie was sued by his wife and wrote a book of poetry. In December 1932, suffering from exposure and exhaustion, he died. Really.

Long Live the King
Swifton

US 67 from Bald Knob to Corning was the center of a vital club scene in the mid-1950s, with bars like the Bushwhacker in Clay County or Charlie's Place and the King of Clubs in Swifton. Singers like Elvis Presley, Jerry Lee Lewis, Johnny Cash, and Roy Orbison were paid $10 a night to entertain the "redneck crowd."

At Charlie's Place, the manager kept a tear gas pistol under the bar, and every so often he had to use it to disperse rowdy patrons.

Musicians at the Bushwhacker often spent the night fending off drunks with a whip and chair.

At the King of Clubs, Bob King was a manager who wasn't afraid to step in and mix it up if trouble broke out. "Back in the early days," he said, "if I told brawlers to take it outside, they listened."

Elvis performed there to a packed house in December 1955 with a young Johnny Cash as his opening act.

"Elvis asked if I'd give Johnny $10 to sing a song. I said no, but I'd give him a Swifton kick in the rear if he didn't." (King actually gave Cash twenty bucks to sing three songs, a tidy sum back then. Guess they didn't call him Cash for nothing.)

Jerry Lee Lewis kept the local music stores in business—the club's piano strings usually had to be replaced after his possessed, Pentecostal-preacher gone-wild performances. He would pound the keys with his elbows and feet during his closing number, a tour de force cover of "Thank Heaven for Little Girls." The club bouncer often had to stand by with a fire extinguisher, just in case Jerry Lee's crotch spontaneously combusted.

The King of Clubs and others were breeding pens for rockabilly, a rough-and-ready mix of country and blues that influenced many of the British invasion bands like the Rolling Stones and that other bunch of long-haired, yeah-yeah guys whose name will live forever.

In the end, rockabilly proved too country for blacks and too bluesy for whites.

In 2009 the Arkansas Legislature officially designated US 67 in northeastern Arkansas "Rock 'n' Roll Hwy 67." As for the King of Clubs, the King may have left the building, but the building is still King. Get ready Teddy and go, cat, go to 21517 US 67 North in Swifton.

The Texas Giant Who Lived in Arkansas
Turrell

A giant of a man once called Arkansas home. James Grover Tarver grew to a height of 8 feet 6 inches and weighed as much as 435 pounds.

★ ★

Tarver was born in Franklin, Texas, on September 17, 1885, to average-size parents. As an adult he traveled with Ringling Bros. and Hagenback-Wallace Circuses, gave a command performance for England's King George V, and acted in a silent movie called *Jack and the Beanstalk.* During his circus career, he bought a farm near Turrell, Arkansas, in Crittenden County and lived there during the circus's off-season.

Tarver was billed as "the World's Largest Man" and "the Texas Giant." He was so tall, he had to drive a car from the back seat. His ring was so big, it would encircle a half dollar, and replicas of the ring were handed out as souvenirs. He once said he was a cowboy until he got bigger than his horse.

He Picked a Fine Time to Name His Guitar

One night in the mid-1950s, B. B. King was performing at a club in Twist, Arkansas, when two men, fighting over a woman named Lucille, knocked over a kerosene stove. A fire ensued, and in his haste to escape, King left his guitar inside the burning building. He ran back to retrieve it and narrowly escaped death. From then on, as a reminder never to do such a foolhardy thing again, he named all of his guitars Lucille. When he was eighty-two years old, King told *Parade* magazine, "About fifteen times a lady has said, 'It's either me or Lucille.' That's why I've had fifteen children by fifteen women."

In 1935, after twenty-six years with the circus, he retired to his Arkansas farm, where he stayed until his death in 1958. He is buried in Crittenden Memorial Park Cemetery in Section 5 . . . and 6 . . . and 7.

Mosquito, the Other State Bird
Walcott

Arkansas has a geological anomaly that is unique in the Western Hemisphere. Extending 200 miles from southern Missouri to Helena–West Helena, Arkansas, and rising 200 feet above the Delta floor, Crowley's Ridge is an erosional remnant formed over a fifty-million-year period by the changing courses of the Mississippi and Ohio Rivers. Windblown sediment, called loess, covered the area. The only other land formation in the world like Crowley's Ridge is in Siberia.

Four state parks are located on Crowley's Ridge. Lake Frierson State Park, 10 miles north of Jonesboro on AR 141, has great fishing and beautiful dogwood trees. Lake Poinsett State Park, on AR 163 about 4 miles southeast of Harrisburg, also offers excellent fishing opportunities plus a guided kayak tour. Village Creek State Park, 13 miles north of Forrest City off AR 284, has two lakes and 7 miles of hiking trails. The park that bears the name of the region, Crowley's Ridge State Park, is located on AR 168 at Walcott.

Like most parks in the state, Crowley's Ridge State Park presents special events from time to time. One such event, unfortunately no longer held, was the Mosquito-Calling Contest and Mosquito Cook-Off—a salute to our state bird, the mosquito. (Bet you thought it was the mockingbird.)

The cook-off attracted as much interest as the calling attracted mosquitoes. (A hint for any would-be mosquito caller: Just stand there. They'll come.) Even England's BBC contacted the park about the cook-off.

Park employee Rick Lane said, "We showed people that mosquitoes, like everything else cooked properly, could be put in food. We had them in cookies, gelatin, things like that. They're basically just a protein anyway."

Larry Clifford, assistant park superintendent at the time, won the second annual cook-off with his mosquito cookies. The recipe was simple and is printed here for your edification.

Mosquito Cookies

Prepare some cookie batter.

Catch mosquitoes. (This is not too difficult; see previous instruction on attracting them.)

Swat them to prevent escape.

Mix mosquitoes with brown sugar and syrup.

Boil them. (This should take care of the West Nile virus.)

Dry them, chop them, and add them to cookie batter.

Bake until done.

Bon appétit!

Pie in the Sky
Walnut Ridge

Some of us are afraid of flying. Our very rational fear has something to do with the fact that we were not born with wings. If we should ever find ourselves on a plane that is plummeting to earth, we will die. It's as simple as that. We do wonder what it's like to fly, though. Therapists often treat phobic patients by gradually exposing them to the object of their fears. We found the first step to overcoming a fear of flying could be as easy as dining out. That is, if you dine at the Parachute Inn in Walnut Ridge.

Part of this unique restaurant is in an actual airplane—stationary of course. The seats are real airplane seats arranged around tables. You don't have to worry about boring in-flight movies, pilot fatigue, seat belts, or lost luggage. Overhead compartments provide space for "carry-ons." And best of all, everybody goes first-class here. No coach.

When the owner decided to expand her restaurant, located on the grounds of the Walnut Ridge Airport, she came up with the idea of converting a retired Boeing 727 and adding it to the existing eatery. Some thought it was an idea that would never fly, but when the new addition opened to the public, business took off and soared.

Part of the attraction, of course, is the unusual setting, but it's the good food that keeps customers coming back. Among the popular items on the menu are catfish, seafood, frog legs, a colorful veggie salad, and peach cobbler. The service is great, too. This is no fly-by-night establishment.

Breakfast and lunch are served Tuesday through Friday from 7:30 a.m. until 2:00 p.m. Dinner is served on Friday and Saturday from 5:00 p.m. until the last customer is full.

The Parachute Inn is located at 10 Skywatch Drive in Walnut Ridge. For more information call (870) 886-5918.

You won't want to come in for a landing.
ARKANSAS DEPARTMENT OF PARKS AND TOURISM

The Age-Old Struggle to Get a Head

Wilson

Since 1880, ninety clay head pots (not to be confused with potheads) have been found in northeast Arkansas. These human head effigy vessels are believed to date from the time just prior to or shortly after the arrival of the Spanish in the sixteenth century. Most are stylized or abstract. A notable exception is on display at the Hampson Archeological Museum State Park in Wilson, Arkansas. This priceless piece could arguably be called the most photographed Native American work of art in North America.

Park superintendent Marlon Mowdy explained, "What sets this piece apart from other Late Mississippian period head effigy pots is that it's so extremely lifelike, we believe it could represent an actual human being from that time period; a person of high status and rank as indicated by the numerous ear piercings, the hairstyle, and cultural markings on the face."

Several explanations have been offered as to why and for what purpose the piece was made. It may have been a deathbed portrait similar to a death mask made as a way of honoring and remembering a beloved tribal member. Or it may be a war trophy, the likeness of a decapitated enemy who lost his head in battle. Chronicles from the Hernando de Soto expedition tell about two warring Indian towns, Casqui and Pacaha, in northeast Arkansas. The narratives say that in 1541 the Casqui combined with Spanish forces to lay siege to the Pacaha village but found it almost deserted. The Casqui warriors went to the mortuary temple, reclaimed the trophy heads of their people killed in battle, and replaced them with the heads of citizens from Pacaha who had remained behind.

As dramatic as the headhunting theory for the pot's origin seems, many experts remain unconvinced. As one archaeologist put it, "We simply don't know."

At any rate, if you dig archaeology, head on up to Hampson Archeological Museum State Park, 2 Lake Drive in Wilson. Hours are 8:00 a.m. to 5:00 p.m. Tuesday through Saturday and 1:00 to 5:00 p.m. on Sunday.

For more information call (870) 655-8622 or e-mail hampson archeologicalmuseum@arkansas.com.

The tattoos may indicate an aristocrat.
ARKANSAS DEPARTMENT OF PARKS AND TOURISM

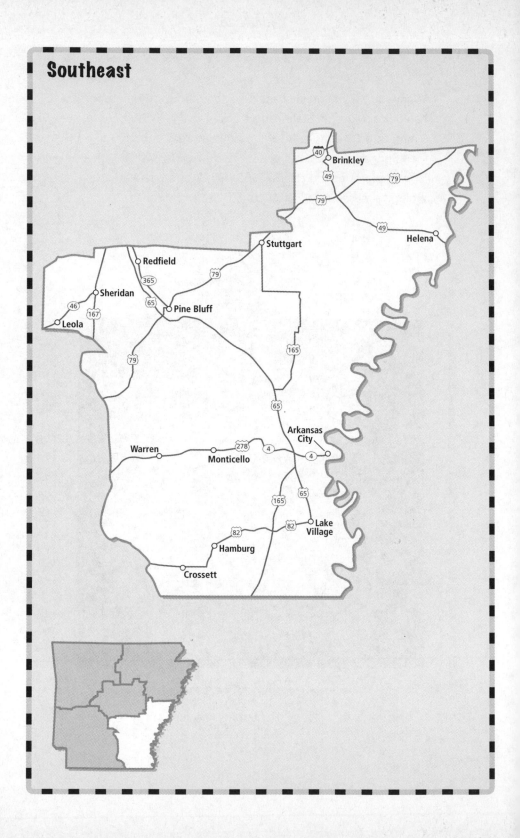

Southeast

Brinkley

Helena

Stuttgart

Redfield

Sheridan

Leola

Pine Bluff

Arkansas
City

Warren

Monticello

Lake
Village

Hamburg

Crossett

2

Southeast

Southeast Arkansas conjures *up images of cotton, rice, and soybean fields. The region put the culture in agriculture, and farming is celebrated in festivals such as the Bradley County Pink Tomato Festival in Warren. Another typical Delta passion and pastime is music, especially the blues. The area has spawned many a hard-living bluesman laid low by good whiskey and bad women. Helena hosts the Arkansas Blues and Heritage Festival (formerly the King Biscuit Blues Fest). The Delta Cultural Center, also in Helena, pays tribute to musicians with links to the region; country music stars such as Johnny Cash and Charlie Rich, gospel greats including Helena's own Roberta Martin, and blues legends such as Louis Jordan, Robert Nighthawk, and Peetie Wheatstraw. Wheatstraw billed himself as "The Devil's Son-in-Law and High Sheriff of Hell." Another musician honored is Levon Helm, who grew up in Turkey Scratch, Arkansas, where renowned bluesman Robert Lockwood Jr. was born.*

While in Helena, we visited a spot some folks call Anti-Gravity Hill, where a car will move all by itself. That's good news in these times of high gas prices. The bad news is the car will only move backward.

Hernando de Soto liked southeast Arkansas so much, he stayed. He's still there, lying at the bottom of Lake Chicot, the largest oxbow lake in North America.

★ ★

Time Will Tell
Arkansas City

County seats are the hubs of all things legal, and county courthouses are often the center of attention and the site of great drama, both historical and personal. Sometimes we say, "Wow, if these walls could talk!" Well, if you listen carefully, you might just hear voices in the Desha County Courthouse . . . even if no one is there.

Some residents of Arkansas City, the Desha County seat, believe their beautiful old Romanesque courthouse, with its distinctive clock and bell tower, is haunted. They strongly suspect the ghost (they call him Willard) was a man hanged for arson sometime around the turn of the twentieth century. It seems Willard—who steadfastly proclaimed his innocence to the end—put a curse on the courthouse, in particular the courthouse clock. Before he died, he said the clock would never work right again . . . and it hasn't.

The clock malfunctions on a regular basis. Sometimes it runs fast; sometimes it runs slow. So what, you ask? Well, how about a clock with a long hand that tells the hour and a short hand that tells the minutes? Or how about a clock that thinks it's a car horn on the blink, disturbing people's sleep with a bell that won't stop ringing?

Believers in Willard's existence include county officials and clerks who have worked in the courthouse. They say even the clocks on office phones don't work properly. They also suspect Willard of slamming doors and making other mischief, but the clock is the main bugaboo. They called in a repairman once. He tinkered with the clock and put new parts in, but that didn't help. Next they brought in Spirit Seekers Paranormal Investigation Research and Intervention Team (SPIRIT), a team of paranormal investigators based in Little Rock. Using video cameras, recorders, motion sensors, and thermal imaging devices, the group investigated the courthouse and came to the conclusion that the building is indeed haunted. Their equipment recorded sounds that could not be explained, and they captured the image of what they call a spirit shadow in an office window.

★ ★

Our minds are open to the possibility of a haunting, but we wondered if Willard was a handsome man or if he had a face that could stop a clock.

The Desha County Courthouse is located at 608 Robert Moore Avenue in Arkansas City. For more information call (870) 877-2426.

They cleaned his clock, so he cursed theirs.
ARKANSAS DEPARTMENT OF PARKS AND TOURISM

The Lazarus Bird

It's the UFO of ornithology, the Bigfoot of Birddom. We speak of the ivory-billed woodpecker, thought by many to have been extinct since the 1940s until a man named Gene Sparling spied the feathered fugitive flying above the Cache River near Brinkley, Arkansas, in 2004. Ornithologists and other bird-watchers flocked to the Cache River National Wildlife Refuge and surrounding area in attempts to verify the sighting. Skeptics, however, say the bird seen by Sparling was just the common pileated woodpecker. Both have red crests (in males), and both have black-and-white wings. Birders distinguish the two by their color pattern. The ivorybill has white on the rear half of its wing; the pileated has white on the front half of the wing. A video of the find is fuzzy and is viewed with the same doubt as the famous 1967 16-millimeter film footage purported to be a Bigfoot in northern California.

John James Audubon wrote that the ivory-billed woodpecker was plentiful in Arkansas when he visited the area in the early 1820s. One hundred years later, however, the bird was a vanishing breed because of hunting and loss of habitat. In 1924 Cornell University ornithologist Arthur Allen and his wife, Elsa, spied a couple of ivorybills in Florida, but two taxidermists heard about the find and did what taxidermists do. In 1944 artist Don Eckelberry saw a lone female ivorybill in her roost among virgin timber in Louisiana. That was the last confirmed sighting until 2004.

The mere possibility of the famed fowl's return caused a flutter among bird lovers everywhere. Brinkley experienced a business boom, with motels and cafes filling up with birders, newsmen, and tourists. Residents jumped on the bandwagon, hawking such items as ivorybill T-shirts and caps, ivorybill burgers and salads, and even an ivorybill haircut.

An anonymous donor has offered a $50,000 reward to the first person who produces a photograph or video of the ivorybill, so while out among the tupelo and cypress trees of the bayous near Brinkley, keep your eyes peeled for peckers. If you find the right one, call the authorities and give 'em the bird.

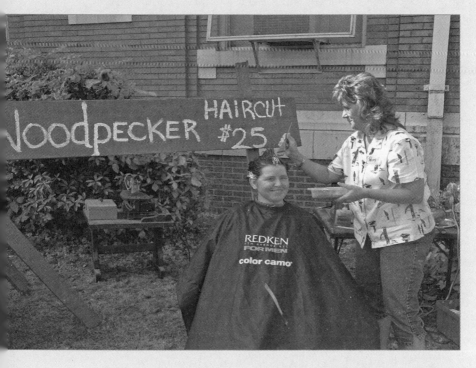

There was a time when a woodpecker haircut would set you apart.
ARKANSAS DEPARTMENT OF PARKS AND TOURISM

This Little Light of Mine
Crossett

For eighty years or longer, the people of Crossett, Arkansas, have witnessed a light that appears and disappears near a crossroads east of town. The oddity was featured in an episode of the 1980s television show *That's Incredible.* A similar mysterious light is said to materialize in Gurdon, Arkansas, but that site is not as easily accessed as Crossett's.

The source of the eerie phenomenon is open to debate. Some say it's a headless ghost looking for his noggin as he lights his path with a lantern. Debunkers claim car lights are to blame and also question why a headless ghost would need a lantern.

We talked to our friend Wade Graham, who grew up in Crossett and has actually seen the puzzling light several times. He verified much of what we had heard and read about it: The light is visible after dark from the intersection of CR 16 and CR 425. Facing south, watchers turn off their headlights and wait; soon the light appears. Wade described it as yellowish, with sometimes a reddish or greenish tint.

"It's mainly stationary," Wade said. "Then it disappears and reappears at another site. I have heard stories about the light appearing almost directly in front of a vehicle, disappearing, and then reappearing right behind the car. It can get pretty creepy."

Believers in a possible supernatural reason for the light point out that it was seen years before cars were common. Even now, the area is fairly remote and not heavily traveled. Could so little traffic produce sightings in the numbers that have been reported? Also, although two headlights might look as if they were one at a distance, eventually they would become two distinct beams as they neared the observer. The Crossett light is always referred to as one.

Wade said, "The closest I've ever been to it is 50 feet, maybe 100 feet at the farthest. I've been close enough to know if it were a vehicle."

The story about the headless ghost does not have a consensus either. Some have heard he was a hobo who lay down to take a nap on the railroad tracks and was decapitated. Another says he was a brakeman who lost his head in a train mishap.

And then there's the claim that it's one big mother of a lightning bug.

Flying Machine Charlie
Dermott

The town of Dermott was named for Dr. Charles McDermott (1808–1884), who acquired the first patent for an airplane when the Wright Brothers were still in knee pants.

McDermott's goal in life was to design a machine that would allow men "to fly from one state to another and back home at night in time to feed the chickens." The endeavor was expensive. At first he used silk to make the wings. As money got scarce, he used less-costly material, finally resorting to paper.

His best effort was a plane with fifteen pairs of wings placed atop one another. Supposedly, hand and leg power would operate the plane. The ability to rub your belly and pat your head at the same time was a prerequisite for this type of flight.

McDermott continued to perfect his invention and offered his gold watch to anyone who could find fault with his design—other than the fact that the machine wouldn't fly. The last plane that McDermott built was the only one that did fly. A storm came through one day and blew the plane into the air before crashing it into a tree.

Great Balls of Fire
Dermott

In 1902 or 1903 J. W. Bernard was plowing on his farm in Dermott when a storm blew up suddenly. Smelling a strong odor and hearing a strange swooshing sound, he turned to see a ball of lightning about the size of a man's head coming between him and his mule.

The glowing ball exploded, knocking man and animal to the ground. Stunned but uninjured, Bernard sat up, still clutching the smoldering remnants of his plow handle. Luckily, his ass was saved; the mule had recovered quickly and galloped to the edge of the field.

Theoretically, the phenomenon of ball lightning occurs when lightning hits a quartz-rich plot of earth and vaporizes the crystal. This creates silicon gas, which rises out of the ground to combine with oxygen and then ignites. Ball lightning is often reported along active fault zones, leading to speculation that seismic shocks may also create the phenomenon. That might explain the mysterious lights seen in the sky during the New Madrid earthquake of 1811–12.

Tall Tales
Hamburg

Arkansas's state tree is the pine, and the granddaddy of them all is located in the Levi Wilcoxon Demonstration Forest (LWDF) near Hamburg in Ashley County. Known as the Walsh Pine, it is named in honor of the late Bruce Walsh, the forestry technician who found the tree. In 2008 it was added to the National Register of Big Trees and designated the National Champion Shortleaf Pine by the conservation organization American Forests. The tree measures 136 feet in height. How tall is that? It's so tall that if the wind blew it down, the top branches would land in Missouri. It's so tall that a falling pinecone takes two days to hit the ground.

As impressive as the Walsh Pine is, it isn't bigger in overall volume than another famous tree that's also located in the LWDF. The Morris Pine is named for Louis Morris, a longtime employee of the Crossett Lumber Company, which once owned the land and established the LWDF in 1939 to promote forestry research in the Upper West Coastal Plain of Arkansas. The current landowner is the Plum Creek Timber Company.

The Morris Pine, a loblolly pine, is arguably more famous than the Walsh Pine. Estimated to be between 300 and 350 years old, the

We're talking a whole lot of toothpicks.
DON BRAGG AND THE USDA FOREST SERVICE

tree stands 117 feet tall and has a circumference of 14.5 feet and a diameter of 4.6 feet. Before the modern era, loblollies routinely grew to a height of 140 feet, and some were even 150 to 170 feet tall. As the old-growth virgin forests were logged out, however, the giants became less common. Today most trees grown for commercial purposes are cut by the time they are thirty-five years old. That's why the Morris Pine is so special. It has survived.

The Morris and Walsh Pines are both located about 3 miles south of Hamburg near the intersection of US 425 and AR 52. For more information call the USDA Forest Service in Monticello at (870) 367-3464.

And if you take your dog with you to visit these remarkable trees, tell him to show some respect.

Our BFF
Helena

For some reason, we Americans love to tease the French, but it's the good-natured ribbing akin to the class clown giving the hall monitor noogies on the head. France is, after all, our oldest ally, siding with us in the American Revolution. In the late 1940s, after fighting alongside each other to defeat Hitler and the Third Reich, France and the United States exchanged gestures of friendship that brought the two countries even closer together.

Though the American government provided humanitarian aid and relief to war-ravaged Europe through the Marshall Plan, the people of the United States wanted to do something on a more personal level. Syndicated newspaper columnist Drew Pearson started a grassroots effort to fill railroad boxcars with food, clothing, and other necessities and ship them to France. The result exceeded expectations—$40 million worth of articles were loaded onto 700 boxcars. The boxcars from Arkansas contained rice, wheat, and canned food. It was the original Meals on Wheels.

French citizens were so moved by the outpouring of compassion and the generous spirit of the American people that they resolved to show their appreciation. A French railroad worker and war veteran, André Picard, came up with the idea of filling a boxcar with gifts of gratitude and shipping it to the United States. The response was so overwhelming that the one boxcar became forty-nine boxcars containing 52,000 gifts with a total weight of 250 tons. The items included tree seedlings, children's drawings, toys, books, letters, wine, works of art, and even a Louis XV carriage. The boxcars arrived in New York City aboard a ship with "Merci, America" written in big

Parlez-vous Français?
BILLY RAY, PHILLIPS COUNTY CHAMBER OF COMMERCE

★ ★

letters on its sides. The boxcars were dispersed to state capitals across the nation and the contents distributed among various charities and institutions. Arkansas received her presents on February 13, 1949, and over 25,000 people showed up at the capitol to see them on display.

Arkansas's Merci Boxcar can be seen at American Legion Post #41 on Porter Street in Helena. A few of the items delivered in the boxcar are on display at the Arkansas Art Center in Little Rock.

Vive la France!

Gravity Takes a Holiday
Helena

Looking for a fun way to spend an afternoon without having to take a shower afterwards? In the mood for a cheap thrill? Do you enjoy breaking the law? Of course you do! After all, this is Arkansas. Who among us has not at some time jaywalked, loitered, or parked in a fire zone? Well, here's one law we bet you haven't broken yet: Newton's law of gravity. But if you're of a mind to break that one, too, you can at Anti-Gravity Hill—just up the road from Pro-Levity Holler.

Actually the hill is in Helena. From AR 185 turn north onto Sulphur Springs Road. When you reach the intersection with US 49, pull up to the stop sign and put your vehicle in neutral. Be sure to remember to take your foot off the brake. Then brace yourself, Linda Lou. If all goes well, you will find yourself rolling backward, uphill, for 150 feet or thereabouts.

Do this as many times as you like—or until the nice policeman shows up and writes you a ticket. By the way, don't tell him we sent you.

So how does it work? Some experts, surveyors and the like, claim that the apparent flouting of natural law is actually an optical illusion caused by the lay of the land. Whenever the horizon is obscured, as it is here, our perception of other things around us is skewed. Normally straight things, such as trees and telephone poles, seem to lean because we no longer have the horizon as a reference point. Down-hill looks like uphill. Hence the song lyrics, "I've been down so long, it looks like up to me."

Gotta Get on Down the Road
Jefferson County

For early travelers in frontier Arkansas, the roads seemed to run in two forms: rough, like those in the River Valley and Delta regions, and nonexistent, like those in the mountains. They weren't so much highways *to* hell as highways *through* hell. The Boston Mountains in Northwest Arkansas were sarcastically named in an attempt to disguise the teeth-shattering ruggedness of the terrain, much in the same spirit that led Eric the Red to call an arctic wasteland Green-land. In early times, many roads were simply trackways cut through the woods; and as befits the Natural State, they retained their rough-hewn character, stumps and all.

Arkansas's road system developed into a patchwork quilt of differ-ent byways of varying quality as each county and township struggled to provide the funding for its own small area. Until 2006 *Overdrive Magazine*'s annual truck drivers' survey consistently ranked Arkansas roads the worst in the nation.

Ironically, Arkansas once had the country's longest stretch of con-crete paved road, at a time when only about 5,000 Arkansans had cars. The road ran from the Pine Bluff city limits northwest 23 miles to Pulaski County. It was called Dollarway Road because its construc-tion cost about $1 per square yard or lineal foot. The project began in November 1913. After it was completed on October 27, 1914, folks came from great distances just to zip along at a hell-bent-for-leather speed of 45 miles per hour.

The name Dollarway Road remains as part of AR 365 in Pine Bluff, but the state highway now covers most of the original road. A short section is located south of Redfield where a park used to be. Reynolds Road, in the community of Jefferson, lies atop another 1.6

★ ★

miles of the original Dollarway roadbed, which you can see in places exposed by potholes.

Dollarway Road is listed on the National Historic Register.

Lucky Lindy Lands at Lake Village
Lake Village

In the 1920s early aviators found the Mississippi Delta much to their liking because the vast expanses of flat terrain made landing planes relatively easy. One day in April 1923 one such airman landed his small plane in a field 2 miles north of Lake Village, near the former Lake Village Country Club. Financial problems had caused the country club to close, but its clubhouse was being used as an inn; the airman took lodging there. The innkeeper, a Mr. Henry, was a friendly fellow, and the airman offered to take him up for an airplane ride in return for his hospitality; Henry declined.

That night the sky was unusually clear, with a full moon, and the aviator decided to make a night flight. Again he asked his host to go up with him, and this time Henry accepted the invitation. The two men took to the skies with the soft glow of the moon lighting their way over the calm waters of the Mississippi River and Lake Chicot. They flew over miles of alfalfa and cotton fields and over the sleeping town below.

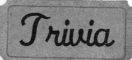

Trivia

Another interesting tidbit pertaining to a Jefferson County thorough-fare: Mr. Charles Calkins told us that Barraque Street in Pine Bluff is the only street by that name in the nation. Antoine Barraque was an early influential settler in the area.

**Nothing captures the spirit of flight quite
like a piece of granite.**
ARKANSAS DEPARTMENT OF PARKS AND TOURISM

The next day, after his guest had departed, Henry told folks about his memorable experience, referring to the aviator as Mr. Limburger. Though his host had gotten the name wrong, the young aviator did go on to become a big cheese when, four years later, Col. Charles A. Lindbergh made his historic trans-Atlantic flight to Paris. The flight over Lake Village was significant for Lindbergh because it was his first night flight. Lindbergh wrote about his stopover in Lake Village in his book *We*. He said he wondered what Henry's reaction "would have been, had he known that I had never flown after dark before."

Lindbergh's first-ever night flight is commemorated by a monument on North Lakeshore Drive, just north of downtown Lake Village.

Hard Wood
Leola

The New Madrid earthquake of 1811–12 was so powerful, it caused whole sections of land in northeast Arkansas to shift and sink. These "sunk lands," as they are called, created shallow lakes with treetops rising above the murky waters.

Many times in the past, the Mississippi River has shifted course, burying stretches of forest along its banks beneath a blanket of mud. In some cases the wood cells in the buried material were replaced by silica from water that leached through the sand and gravel, "petrifying" the wood. Ancient petrified tree trunks were once so common in the area around Piggott that the locals used them as grave markers.

Although many of those trunks are quite large, perhaps the largest piece of petrified wood recovered in Arkansas was found on a farm owned by Carlton and Tudy Dorey in the small town of Leola in Grant County. Geologists told them it was some sort of hickory tree.

The Doreys decided to dig the trunk out of the ground and put it in front of their catfish processing plant. Moving it proved to be problematic because it is 16 feet long and 5 feet in diameter and weighs approximately seventeen tons. After two attempts failed to move it, a large crane was used to accomplish the job.

When the Doreys closed the processing plant in 1998, they moved the giant, hollow log again. They transferred it to the catfish restaurant they own and put a fence around it, so everyone could enjoy the spectacle.

William Prior, a geologist with the state of Arkansas, gave an impromptu stump speech and called the piece of petrified tree "one of the largest I've ever seen, especially in Arkansas." He explained that during an ice age around 1.5 million years ago, a river had flowed through this area. The tree was growing along the bank when it fell into the river and was washed into a gravel bank, where it remained until being found by the Doreys.

This curiosity stumped us.

To see this petrified piece of the past—and to have a mighty fine meal at the Dorey Catfish Restaurant—go to Grant CR 5 in Leola, which is 15 miles southwest of Sheridan. Call (870) 765-2749 or check their Web site (www.doreyfishfarm.com) for more information.

Lady Sings the Boos
Monticello

Ladell Allen was a privileged lady. She was born into a prosperous family and lived in a magnificent house on North Main Street in Monticello. The lovely Victorian mansion with its widow's walk and turrets is thought to be one of the most haunted places in Arkansas, because some say Ladell still resides there . . . even though she's been dead for more than sixty years.

Ladell's life went from idyllic to tragic after she married Boyd Bonner, an irresponsible philanderer who drove his wife to drink. The only good thing to come out of their union was a son, Elliott Allen Bonner, but he succumbed to pneumonia at the age of twenty-eight. Ladell moved back into the family home to care for her ailing mother. The day after Christmas in 1948, Ladell went upstairs to her bedroom and calmly drank punch that she had laced with mercury cyanide. It was a horrible, agonizing death. She lingered for a week.

After the Allen family sold the house in the 1950s, it became an apartment house that catered to students attending the University of Arkansas at Monticello. Since then, many curious incidents have been reported. One man thought he was taking a picture of his wife, but when the film was developed, the spectral figure of another woman was also in the frame. Other tenants would walk in and find their furniture and other objects rearranged. On one occasion, some residents of the house were trying to open a closet, but an invisible force kept pulling the door from the other side. (Guess somebody wasn't ready to come out of the closet.) A female figure, believed to be Ladell, has been seen frequently through an upstairs window.

After Rebecca and Mark Spencer bought the house in 2007, they

★ ★

**With such a beautiful home, no wonder
she doesn't want to leave.**
REBECCA SPENCER

allowed Louisiana Spirits Paranormal Investigations to look into the ghostly goings-on. The group's findings seem to support the stories of supernatural visitations. You can go to their Web site (www.laspirits .com/allenhouse) to hear and see what they captured on tape and camera. Better yet, you can make an appointment to visit the Allen house itself—if the spirit moves you. Special Halloween tours are also available.

The Allen house is located at 705 North Main Street in Monticello. For more information, including details about the house's history and the tours, go to www.allenhousetours.com or call (870) 224-2271. The e-mail address is allenhousetours@aol.com.

Rough and Ready Cemetery
Monticello

Many people haunt cemeteries in search of genealogical information, and some of us like cemeteries because they're such peaceful places. You can hear yourself think there. But the name Rough and Ready gave us pause. We can understand why the residents might be feeling pretty rough, but what they're ready for is anybody's guess.

The Rough and Ready Cemetery at Monticello got its name from a little settlement by the same name that was the site of Drew County's first village and court. Actually, the village existed before the county did. Records dating back to the 1830s reference the name. Historians believe that the community was named Rough and Ready in honor of General Zachary Taylor, who was given that nickname by his men during the campaign against the Seminoles at Okeechobee in December 1835.

Rough and Ready lived up to its name. It was a lively place, full of feudin' and fightin' and boisterous, bawdy taverns. A distillery was located behind the cemetery, so there was no shortage of spirits. At some point around 1849, the town's founding fathers feared its

Trivia

Rough and Ready Hill was the site of the last Civil War skirmish in Arkansas, which took place in late May 1865, several weeks after Lee's surrender at Appomattox. The Rough and Ready Days Festival, held annually in Monticello, commemorates the battle. For more information about the festival, contact the Drew County Chamber of Commerce or the Drew County Historical Museum at (870) 367-6741, or e-mail monticellochamber@sbcglobal.net.

name would conjure up the wrong image, so they established the new community of Monticello, just north of Rough and Ready. They couldn't very well relocate the cemetery, though. It is located 1 mile southeast of the Monticello Civic Center on AR 19.

In 1999 the Rough and Ready Cemetery was named to the National Register of Historic Places. The lovely, tree-shaded place is rich with history. One of the residents is W. H. Bybee, who was once sprung from a Texas prison by none other than Clyde Barrow. Bybee was later killed in a hail of machine-gun fire 12 miles east of Monticello.

The Mouth of the South
Pine Bluff

Former president Richard Nixon once said, "If it hadn't been for Martha, there'd have been no Watergate." He was referring to Pine Bluff native Martha Mitchell, who was married to Nixon's attorney general, John Mitchell.

Born Martha Elizabeth Beall on September 2, 1918, Martha was a vivacious and flamboyant individual who loved to talk from the time she uttered her first words. She was remembered in her high school yearbook with a poem about her loquaciousness.

"I love its gentle warble.

I love its gentle flow.

I love to wind my tongue up,

And I love to let it go."

Martha worked as a teacher and a secretary before marrying her first husband, Clyde Jay Jennings. They were divorced in 1957, and a few months later she married John Mitchell. With her trademark sunglasses and dimpled smile, she added a touch of glamour to an otherwise stuffy presidency.

When John became embroiled in the Watergate scandal, Martha started calling reporters and spilling the beans about the Nixon administration's illegal activities. The late-night calls became fodder for Johnny Carson's monologues and other stand-up material, and

★ ★

Martha was nicknamed "the Mouth of the South." At first the country laughed with her and cheered her on, but then she became a sad, tragic figure and a pariah in some circles. Negative publicity discredited her after she claimed she had been drugged to keep her quiet and the White House leaked stories to the news media about her alleged alcoholism. She and John separated in 1973.

Martha lived to see Nixon's downfall but died of cancer in 1976 before being vindicated and restored to her proper place in the history books. She was buried at Bellwood Cemetery in Pine Bluff. A wreath saying "Martha was right" was prominently displayed at her funeral.

Martha Mitchell's childhood home at 902 West Fourth Avenue in Pine Bluff is on the National Register of Historic Places.

Silenced forever.
ARKANSAS DEPARTMENT OF PARKS AND TOURISM

Seventy-six Trombones—And Then Some
Pine Bluff

One of our favorite comedians was the late, great former trumpet player Jackie Vernon, the master of deadpan delivery. He often used a cornet as a prop, and it was a very strange-looking cornet. It looked as if it had been run over by a bus. Some of the musical instruments found in Pine Bluff's Band Museum reminded us of ol' Jackie's cornet. Especially the sax-o-trumpet, which appears to be as saxually conflicted as it sounds.

The Band Museum's founder is—and we're not making this up—Jerry Horne. (Add that to your list of chefs named Cook and psychiatrists named Nutt.) Horne has been collecting unusual instruments since 1970 and now has about 1,500 of them. He opened the

No Map Required

Every year the Arkansas State Auditor's Office holds the Great Arkansas Treasure Hunt, during which attempts are made to unite or reunite individuals with property that rightfully belongs to them. Since 1979, valuables totaling more than $50 million have been turned over to their owners. The loot may include money from inactive bank accounts, final paychecks not picked up, contents of safe deposit boxes, and utility deposits. Some items, such as pictures, have more sentimental value than monetary. Probably the most unusual items that have gone unclaimed are two sets of cremated human remains.

museum in 1994, and it is the only museum in the nation devoted exclusively to the history of band music and instruments.

If you've ever had a sibling or a child who played in the school band, a tour through this museum may help explain why the rehearsals in your home sometimes sounded as if a bull and cow were mating in the next room. The museum displays such musical mutants as a 1923 double-bell euphonium, a 1927 sarrusaphone, and an 1825 opheiclide, which doesn't even resemble its offspring, the tuba. Other unusual instruments and antiques include the tiny sopranino saxophone and one of the first saxophones ever made by Adolph Sax, who invented the beautiful, soulful instrument in the 1840s and by doing so, created a cross between woodwinds and brass. Hail to thee, Adolph Sax. Our childhoods would have been incomplete without the scratchy, well-worn saxophone recordings of our favorite songs that played as moviegoers entered the old Conway Theatre.

The museum houses memorabilia from the Pine Bluff High School Band, and Horne dedicated the museum to the school's former band director, the late R. B. "Scrubby" Watson, a former vaudevillian. Watson, who seldom tooted his own horn, became the first Arkansan accepted into the American Bandmasters Association.

A soda fountain inside the museum serves ice-cream floats, milk shakes, sundaes, and banana splits.

The Band Museum is located near the intersection of Fifth Avenue and Main Street in downtown Pine Bluff and is open Monday through Friday 10:00 a.m. to 4:00 p.m. For more information call (870) 534-HORN (4676).

A Sign of the Times
Pine Bluff

Contrary to what some jaded people might think, the big "M" at McDonald's does not stand for millions, as in millions of dollars and millions of customers, though the fast-food giant does serve fifty-two million people every day. The double arch is better known worldwide than the Christian cross, according to Eric Schlosser in his best-selling book *Fast Food Nation.*

Brothers Dick and Mac McDonald started with a hot dog stand in California and opened their first McDonald's in 1940. Ray Kroc was just a salesman selling milk-shake mixers when he came along in 1954, but he was soon establishing McDonald's franchises for the brothers. In 1961 he bought the company and rights to the name. When the McDonald brothers went back to their first eatery and

Half the sign but twice as nice.

called it the Big M, Kroc put in a McDonald's practically next door and ran the brothers out of business.

In those early years, a single golden arch beckoned customers to McDonald's. Then as success grew, so did the sign. Very few single arches remain today, and Arkansas has one of them. For forty-five years the arch showed the way to the Royale with cheese on Main Street in Pine Bluff, but that McDonald's closed in 2007. The sign's future seemed uncertain, even though it was added to the National Historic Register in 2006—the only sign of its kind to be honored with such a listing.

Other single arches around the nation have been disappearing from the cultural landscape. In 2008 a single arch in Huntsville, Alabama, was taken down because it was in poor condition and no longer met city code regulations. It was retired to the American Sign Museum in Cincinnati, Ohio.

Arkansas's single arch wasn't put out to stud, though. It was renovated and moved to the new McDonald's location at 2819 South Olive Street in Pine Bluff, where you can see it today.

The Mammoth Orange Cafe
Redfield

From the 1920s through the 1960s, America's love affair with the open road was in full swing. Motor lodges and restaurants were so numerous along the roadside that some establishments resorted to gimmickry in an effort to attract business. These tourist courts and cafes were built to resemble igloos, hot dogs, tepees, and other eye-catching oddities. Some of these still exist along the old highway routes, such as Route 66. One of Arkansas's iconic cafes is located on AR 365 at Redfield between Little Rock and Pine Bluff. It's called the Mammoth Orange Cafe.

Built in 1965, the original cafe structure was shaped to look like a big orange with outdoor seating all the way around the circumference. In the 1970s white cinderblock additions on each side of the

As orange-shaped eating establishments go, this one's the pick of the crop.

orange allowed for interior seating, so the cafe doesn't look quite as much like an orange as it once did, but it's still worth a stop and look-see. Even though it has been around for a long time, the cafe isn't seedy at all.

The cafe carries on in the spirit of the original owner, Mrs. Ernestine Bradshaw, whose friendliness and promise of quality food brought customers back time after time. Mrs. Bradshaw made everyone feel at home and was supportive of her community. The current Mammoth Orange still has pictures of Redfield baseball and basketball teams that the restaurant has sponsored.

After Mrs. Bradshaw died in 2007, her daughter, Cynthia Carter,

★ ★

became owner and operator of the Mammoth Orange. The menu offers the traditional fare enjoyed by hungry travelers in earlier generations—milk shakes, grilled-cheese sandwiches, and hamburgers—but it has a lot more. Catfish is king on Friday, and the tartar sauce is made right there on the premises. Gravy is also homemade at the Mammoth Orange. Everything has a personal touch. They even pound the hamburger meat. The tasty cuisine is reasonably priced, too. They won't put the squeeze on you.

The Mammoth Orange Cafe is located at the intersection of AR 46 (Sheridan Road) and AR 365 in Redfield.

In Hindsight
Sheridan

The Grant County Museum in Sheridan presents a good picture of what it has been like to grow up in small-town America through different eras. One exhibit that's sure to get a conversation going is a replica of an old privy that stands proudly inside the museum—an in-house outhouse. It's a relic from the days when the most popular WP (wipin' paper) was the Sears, Roebuck catalog. Folks who had the catalog were highbrow. Resourceful country women made the versatile catalogs into decorative doorstops, too, by folding the pages. It's a lost art. One thing missing from the museum privy is a copperhead snake coiled up in the corner.

Early modes of transportation are represented at the museum by a covered wagon, a buckboard, and a bicycle made entirely of wood. An Arkla Gas Company exhibit fills an entire room, and military artifacts occupy several rooms. Military vehicles have their own building. Several other outer structures from different eras include a church, a cafe, and a Masonic lodge.

The Grant County Museum is truly impressive. It has so much to see, you may want to visit more than once. It is located at 521 Shackleford Road in Sheridan. Call (870) 942-4496 for precise directions and other information.

The Little Brown Shack out Back

The history of the outhouse is not ancient history. As recently as the late 1950s (and even the early 1960s), outhouses were part of rural life, and though they may seem crude today, they were quite a step up from their forerunner: a bush, a barnyard, or the woods. In 1912, out of 7,500 homes inspected in Arkansas, 53 percent didn't have any form of toilet facilities.

The ol' family reading room.

The habit of humans trudging barefoot to the bushes enabled hookworms to bore into people's feet, and that caused hookworm disease, a serious health problem. Tests conducted in Arkansas in 1913 showed three out of four people in Grant County had hookworms. When doctors started educating people about the horrors of so-called "promiscuous defecation," outhouses started popping up all over the place. Toilets at one Mount Magazine hotel were suspended from trees overlooking the river valley. Bombs away!

* *

A Rose by Any Other Name
Sheridan

According to the Center for Health Statistics in Little Rock, 1996 was a banner year for unusual names bestowed upon newborn babies by their proud and loving parents. Names for girls included Destroy, Disney, Messiah, Omega, Travisty [sic], and Tyranny. Names for boys included Crimson, Nails, Rainsun, Reality, Shady, and Paradice (a born gambler, no doubt).

We became interested in names after reading in the *Arkansas Times* about the death of a lady from Sheridan. She was born February 24, 1914, to William Thomas Pennington and Tommie Thomas Pennington, and her given name was Dew Drop. Now that's an unusual name in and of itself, but her married name was what caused people to smile. When Dew Drop entered into holy matrimony with her sweetheart, Keith, she took his last name as her own. She became Dew Drop Snowball. She was ninety-three when she died on a very hot July 28, 2007.

Cold Duck
Stuttgart

Stuttgart, Arkansas, is known as the Rice and Duck Capital of the World because they grow more rice in Arkansas County than any other county in the United States and because duck hunting is more than a pastime there; it's a passion. Stuttgart hosts the World Championship Duck Calling Contest and Wings over the Prairie Festival every year during Thanksgiving weekend.

Since the first duck calling competition in 1936, only two contestants have won without the use of duck calls, the whistles that lure the feathered prey. Serious duck hunters spare no expense when buying a duck call—the festival's champion takes home more than $15,000 worth of prizes.

Hundreds of duck calls are displayed at the Museum of the Arkansas Grand Prairie, located at 921 East Fourth Street. Other exhibits

Duck caller attracts a gander with her seductive quack.
ARKANSAS DEPARTMENT OF PARKS AND TOURISM

include antique farm equipment, grains from Stuttgart's first rice crop in 1904, an 800-year-old duck effigy pot, a stuffed albino goose, and a green feather coat and matching hat made from the heads of 450 mallards.

Ducks are so plentiful over Stuttgart, they have been known to fall from the sky without a shot being fired. On the afternoon of November 23, 1973, a storm system passed through that had a little bit of everything: hail, heavy rains, funnel-shaped clouds, lightning, and ice-encrusted ducks. Dr. Roland Roth, an expert in avian ecology, documented the meteorological anomaly for the *Wilson Bulletin,* which is published by the Wilson Ornithological Society. Roth surveyed people who had witnessed the spectacle.

One hundred and six waterfowl were counted on the ground, and though it was not an election year, at least nine were lame ducks. Seventy-six were dead ducks. Not even a quack doctor could have helped them. Eighteen of the counted ducks were frozen. A picture in the local newspaper, the *Daily Leader,* showed a female mallard with chunks of ice on her feather tips. Lightning had also singed some of the ducks, as evidenced by their "kinky" feathers. Several of the surviving birds acted dazed and confused, as though they didn't know exactly where they were. They just knew they weren't in Kansas anymore.

Next time you're in Stuttgart, if fowl weather approaches, remember to duck and cover. Then break out the carving knife.

For more information about the Museum of the Arkansas Grand Prairie, call (870) 673-7001. To inquire about the annual festival and duck calling contest, contact the Stuttgart Chamber of Commerce at (870) 673-1602 or go to www.stuttgartarkansas.org.

Pretty in Pink
Warren

Citizens of Bradley County in southeast Arkansas fairly blush with pride when they talk about their pink tomatoes. The cash crop has been a cash cow for the county since the 1920s. The Pink Tomato Festival was established in 1956 to honor the garden favorite.

The festival is held in Warren, the county seat, during the second week of June. Judging by the degree of community involvement and support, everyone has a stake in the success of this time-honored event. It may have struggled in the beginning, but nobody seemed to mind being in the red. They persevered, and today the Pink Tomato Festival welcomes about 30,000 people every year.

The celebration offers fun for one and all, but judges in some of the contests have a tough time choosing winners. All the young ladies in the beauty pageant are tomatoes. The cutest baby and cutest dog contests are held several hours apart, presumably so no one will get the two mixed up. In arts and crafts, quilts have it all sewn up. In athletics, nobody can ketchup with the 5K runners. Talent show contestants have nothing to fear, since rotten tomatoes are strictly prohibited at the festival.

Can the world's largest glass of ice tea be far behind?

Americans eat about twenty-two pounds of tomatoes per person per year. Competitors in the Pink Tomato Festival's tomato-eating contest consume more than their fair share. The "Great Bowls of Fire" Salsa Contest is sure to set off alarms, and the all-tomato lunch may be your only opportunity to sample a chocolate cake made with tomato juice as an ingredient. Big, luscious tomatoes were the main ingredient in the world record–setting bacon, lettuce, and tomato sandwich that was made for the 2009 festival. It measured 168 feet, 5 inches long.

For more information about Bradley County's Pink Tomato Festival, call (870) 226-5225 or send an e-mail to bcc.warren@sbcglobal.net.

This is a great festival, no matter how you slice it.

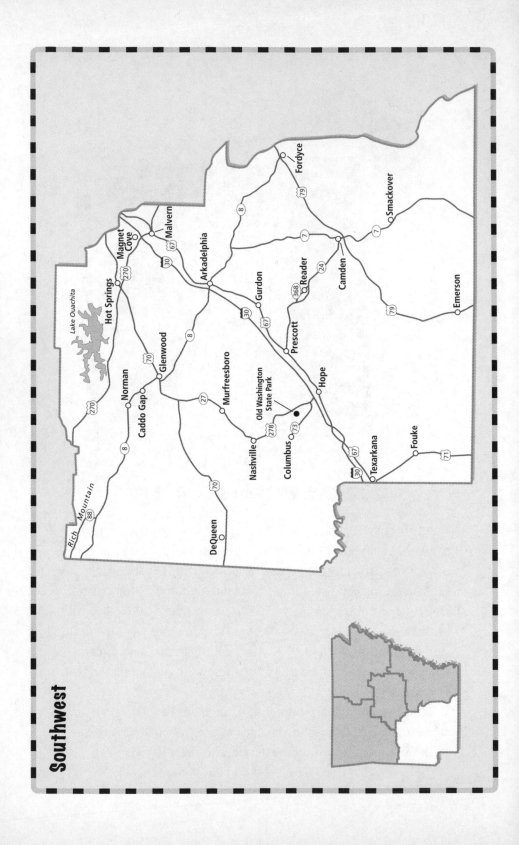

Southwest

3

Southwest

You'll take a *shine to southwest Arkansas. Its many attractions include Murfreesboro's Crater of Diamonds State Park, the only authentic diamond mine in the nation.*

Another precious southwest Arkansas gem is Hot Springs, a place so special that it is the country's only city located within a national park.

Early visitors to Hot Springs were drawn to the therapeutic thermal waters that gave the city its name, but after enjoying the soothing saunas and massages, they looked around for other diversions, and the Spa City never let them down.

One pioneering entertainment entrepreneur was Norm McLeod, founder of Happy Hollow Amusement Park. McLeod was by trade a photographer, but the park he established in 1888 had a petting zoo, shooting gallery, and other attractions. He enjoyed posing people in photographs with live ostriches, stuffed alligators, and bears (live and stuffed).

Animal acts were mainstays in Hot Springs for a long time after McLeod was gone. A baseball-playing hen named Chicky Mantle was a star at the now defunct Clowers' Zoo with IQ, a descendant of the original IQ Zoo.

Hot Springs still has plenty to amuse and entertain, including the annual Documentary Film Festival at the old Malco Theatre, top-notch horseracing at Oaklawn Park, and the grand old architecture of Bathhouse Row.

Boo Boo the Chicken
Arkadelphia

In 2005 Jackie Lynn Calhoun of Arkadelphia bought a chicken for $2.35. He and his family named the chicken Boo Boo because she was easily frightened. One day Jackie found Boo Boo floating face down in a small pool behind the house. Jackie plucked the chicken out of the water and attempted to resuscitate the bird. About that time, Jackie's sister, Marian Morris, dropped in and offered her

Malibu Boo Boo stares into the existential abyss.
JACKIE CALHOUN

assistance. Marian, a retired nurse, performed mouth-to-beak resuscitation on Boo Boo and, lo and behold, it worked.

Word of the miraculous recovery spread far beyond Arkadelphia. Marian and Boo Boo appeared on the *Tonight Show* with Jay Leno, where they were a big hit. The audience cackled. Marian was bleeped once. (We think she said something about giving Boo Boo a blow job.) She explained how the family had kept Boo Boo warm in a cardboard box, which Leno called Arkansas's version of ICU.

Unfortunately, mere weeks after her appearance on national television, Boo Boo died. Contrary to rumors, she was not a victim of fowl play. She had a condition that caused seizures, which is probably why she fell in the water and "died" the first time. Bye-bye, Boo Boo.

Tula, de Soto's Waterloola
Caddo Gap

At Caddo Gap in Montgomery County stands the 9-foot-tall bronze statue of an Indian with his hand raised, as if he's expecting a high-five. First erected in 1937, the statue was blown down during a storm in 1988 and replaced with the current model. The inscription on its base reads, "Here was the capital of the warlike Tula tribe of Indians, who fiercely fought de Soto and his men."

Hernando de Soto arrived in 1541 and roamed from town to town seeking a rich empire to rob. Wherever there was a village to pillage, he found it. After ransacking the chiefdom of Pacaha in the northeast, he skirted the eastern edge of the Ozark Mountains, passing near present-day Batesville and pushing southwest until he got to the Arkansas River near Conway. There he turned northwest up the river's north bank until he reached the kingdom of Cayas and the town of Tanico near present-day Russellville, where news of a large kingdom to the southwest called Tula piqued his interest.

De Soto set out with a small detachment, hoping the place would be worth looting. The townsfolk must have figured he wasn't with Publishers Clearinghouse, because they attacked when he drew near.

The invaders drove the natives back and advanced into town, but the Indians climbed to the rooftops of their homes to shoot arrows down at their foes.

De Soto left, but three days later the opposing forces squared off again. The Indians had learned from the earlier skirmish that the use of mounted lancers gave their enemy an edge, so they adapted their tactics accordingly. They armed themselves with wooden pikes, ordinarily used for hunting buffalo, and wielded them with deadly results. It was a tipping point. Cavalry had been the deciding factor in every fight de Soto had won, but that advantage was fast slipping away. After Tula, he had fewer than forty horses.

Historians now think the battle took place farther north, along the Fourche LaFave River near Bluffton or perhaps by the Arkansas River near Fort Smith. The statue commemorating the event was based on earlier reconstructions of the route at Caddo Gap.

Don't Dis These Able Men

In 1928 *Time* magazine noted an unusual occurrence in that year's Arkansas general election. J. Oscar Humphrey, who had lost both of his arms in a boyhood accident, was elected state auditor, and Earl Page, a man with no legs, was elected commissioner of mines, manufactures, and agriculture. After the Agriculture Commission was abolished, Page was elected state treasurer and won reelection four times; his adversaries didn't have a leg to stand on. After a single defeat in 1934, Humphrey was reelected state auditor a total of twelve more times, always winning handily over his opponents.

To see the statue, go 32 miles southwest from Hot Springs on US 70. Turn north onto AR 8 and travel 7 miles to Indian Valley Road at Caddo Gap. Just follow the signs.

Boolah, boolah; hurray for Tula.

★ ★

Maud Crawford, Where Are You?
Camden

Maud Crawford, the first female lawyer in the history of Camden, disappeared from her home on the night of March 2, 1957. Crawford's husband had gone to the movies, and when he arrived home the lights and television were on, Maud's clothes were in the closet, her car was in the driveway, her purse was in the living room, and the family dog was resting peacefully on the floor. Nothing was missing—except Maud.

Odis Henley, the original Arkansas State Police detective on the case, found evidence implicating Henry Myar "Mike" Berg, a member of the Arkansas State Police Commission. After Henley reported his suspicions to his superiors, he was taken off the case, and his files disappeared as mysteriously as Maud had.

While acting as attorney and guardian for Berg's senile aunt, Rose Newman Berg, Crawford discovered that Mike Berg had illegally transferred Rose's valuable property, worth more than $20 million, to himself. Before Crawford could have the fraudulent deeds decreed null and void, she vanished and so did Rose's will. Mike Berg, who died in 1975, ended up with his aunt's entire fortune.

And there lies a tragic tale of greed and murder. Where Maud lies is anyone's guess. Her body was never found.

Head Out on the Highway
DeQueen

They say everything old becomes new again, and though DeQueen's Easter Island Head is more than fifty years old, it looks pretty fresh compared with pompadours and poodle skirts.

Standing just outside DeQueen along US 70 East, the head is a block of steel-reinforced concrete 16½ feet tall. Local sign painter Harold Mabry built the head on-site in 1959. When asked why he created it, Mabry was coy, saying he wanted to "do something using straight lines and angles."

Locals have had the big head for over fifty years.
BONITA SMITH

Big Bubba Fish

The record holder for the largest catfish caught in modern times is a blue catfish nearly 6 feet long and weighing 150 pounds.

In October 1983 the largest catfish fossil ever found in North America was discovered along the Ouachita River at Camden. Forty to forty-five million years ago, the creature plied the muddy bottoms of what was then a shallow sea. Its skull alone is nearly 3 feet long and, when alive, the fish is estimated to have been more than 10 feet in length and to have weighed about 450 pounds. All one needed for a complete meal was a half ton of hushpuppies and coleslaw.

Today's Mississippi River Valley was at that time a bay off the Gulf of Mexico known as the Mississippi Embayment. The catfish lived along the bay's west coast during a warmer period, when the ocean levels were higher.

The fossil, the first of its kind ever found in Arkansas, is currently being studied by Dr. John G. Lundberg with the Department of Ichthyology at the Academy of Natural Sciences in Philadelphia.

A fish out of water.
JOHN G. LUNDBERG, PHD

Mabry intended it to be one of a pair, calling one *Male Head* and the other *Female Head.* He also planned to build a workshop nearby, perhaps to sell mass-produced miniature versions of the statue as statuettes, bookends, or lamps. The two full-size sculptures would serve as a form of roadside novelty advertising that was so popular in the era. (See the Mammoth Orange Cafe entry.) Photos of smaller, earlier models are clearly labeled "Copyrighted by Harold Mabry." Whatever the case, he never followed through. The male head's female alter ego never got past the planning stage.

Why the shift in plans? We'll venture a guess. *Male Head,* with the elongated oval design of a phallic symbol, bears a striking resemblance to native African and Polynesian fertility icons. Its female counterpart emphasized the triangular motif of the Delta of Venus. Taken alone, *Male Head*'s sexual symbolism could be shrugged off as coincidental, but taken together as a pair, the sexuality would be more obvious. On reflection, Mabry may have realized that rather than attracting customers, the two figures might cause travelers to cover their kids' eyes and step on the gas, erotic art being like kryptonite to most Arkansans.

Who knows? Mabry is gone, but his statue remains. Left undisturbed, it likely will endure for a long, long time, standing like a monolithic stone Kaw-Liga on a lost highway, watching the world go by, awaiting the mate its late creator will never create.

Pass the Peas, Please
Emerson

Located 6 miles north of the Louisiana border in Columbia County, Emerson, Arkansas, is a peaceful little town of 359 people. Make that a peas-full, little town. Delicious purple hull peas are grown in abundance in the area, and the pod pea-ple who live there are crazy about the crop. They'll tell you it's only fitting that the best pea made by Mother Nature is wrapped in the color of royalty. All hail the Lord of Legumes, the Prince of Peas!

Get your rotors running
ARKANSAS DEPARTMENT OF PARKS AND TOURISM

Emerson also reveres the rotary tiller, the garden implement that helps make peas possible; so on the last weekend in June, Emerson hosts the Purple Hull Pea Festival & World Championship Rotary Tiller Race. The festival began in 1990 and was the brainchild of the late Glen Eades, who once said of his fellow Emersonites, "We were so boring, we didn't even have a cop."

The World Championship Rotary Tiller Race is the most exciting under-ten-seconds sporting event on Earth, and in 1995 the competition truly went global when Dominique Niessen came all the way from Holland to compete. The Marquess of Queensbury rules may not apply, but racing barefoot is strictly forbidden. Hey, we don't do *everything* barefoot here in Arkansas!

The rest of the festival is all about the mighty purple hull pea. Contests include pea shelling, pea guessing, and pea cooking competitions. And what goes with purple hull peas? Cornbread, of course,

★ ★

so there's a cornbread cook-off, too. The Emerson folks have beau-
coups of good reci-peas to share—everything from Purple Hull Peas
Thermidor to Purple Hull Peas Creole to Purple Hull Pea Fritters. And
you owe it to yourself to try the Purple Hull Pea Jelly. It's really quite
good. Emersonites are not starved for entertainment, that's for sure.

Arts and crafts are sold at the event make great souvenirs and
gifts; pea-shirts are a real fashion statement.

For more information about the Purple Hull Pea Festival & World
Championship Rotary Tiller Race, go to www.purplehull.com.

Itching for a Good Time
Fordyce

The town of Fordyce annually celebrates its railroad heritage on the
fourth weekend in April with a festival called Fordyce on the Cotton Belt. Food vendors and arts and crafts are plentiful, and events
include a parade, a beauty pageant, and entertainment on the courthouse lawn. Over the years, entertainers have included Johnny Cash
and Jim Ed Brown.

The highlight of the festival for many is a high school reunion, but
not just any old reunion. Like other small towns across the American
South, Fordyce is serious about football, but no other team in the
country can get all over the competition quite like the Fordyce team
can. That's because no other team in the country is called the Redbugs. The annual get-together during the Fordyce on the Cotton Belt
Festival is the Redbug Reunion Rally.

Some sources say the unusual name came about when red bugs
pestered the daylights out of workers who cleared the field for the
first game in the 1920s. Others claim the victims were the football
players. Suffice it to say, somebody realized red bugs are tenacious
little critters, worthy of respect and not to be trifled with. Anybody
who doubts this need only read about the creatures.

Red bug is another name for the chigger, which is actually the lar-
val form of a mite instead of an insect, though they can bug the heck

Don't let these guys get under your skin.
ARKANSAS DEPARTMENT OF PARKS AND TOURISM

out of their hosts. They are called red bugs because of their color. When they bite their host, their saliva liquefies skin cells and the red bug feasts on the pureed product. Who wants to tangle with the human equivalent of that?

The Fordyce Redbugs were the winningest football team in Arkansas from 1956 to 1989, and Fordyce was the boyhood home of Paul "Bear" Bryant, who, when he led the University of Alabama team, was the winningest college football coach in America. Bryant was a Redbug in the 1920s.

For more information about Fordyce, call City Hall at (870) 352-2198 or e-mail cityoffordyce@alltel.net.

★ ★

Trivia

The first direct-dial long-distance telephone call in the nation was made from Fordyce in 1960.

Bigfoot on the Bayou

Fouke

On the early morning of Sunday, May 2, 1971, Bobby Ford of Fouke showed up at the emergency room at St. Michael Hospital in Texarkana. He appeared to be suffering from a mild state of shock as he related a fantastic story.

Ford had been in his new home in Fouke for less than a week when he began hearing strange noises at night, like someone circling the house. Then on the evening of Saturday, May 1, 1971, as his wife slept on the couch, something reached through their open window and pawed her. Ford and his brother rushed to her aid, but the intruder fled, returning around midnight. When Ford walked out on the porch to investigate, the creature grabbed him and hurled him to the ground. He described the beast as being covered in hair, with a foul body odor, and standing about 7 feet tall. It ran away in a stooped posture, swinging its arms like an ape.

Thus the Fouke Monster, also known as the Boggy Creek Monster, entered local folklore as Arkansas's most famous hairy wild man since Ronnie Hawkins. Repeat appearances were somewhat anticlimactic. Three weeks later, three people reported seeing the monster cross US 71. Bloodhounds were brought in to track the beast but failed to pick up a scent.

The monster became a star when it spawned three movies, beginning with *The Legend of Boggy Creek,* a campy cult favorite directed by Arkansas native Charles B. Pierce.

With his movie career in tatters, the Fouke Monster
spirals out of control.

Over the years, the creature appears to have developed rambling fever. Reports of Bigfoot-type creatures have surfaced from places as far away as Mena, Russellville, Jonesboro, Center Ridge, Crossett, and the Palarm Creek bottoms in Pulaski and Faulkner Counties.

Visitors should stop at Peavy's Monster Mart at 104 US 71 North, where you can buy souvenirs featuring the likeness of the Fouke freak. Or travel just up the road and immortalize your trip by having your picture taken as the monster. Just stick your head through the cutout face of the metal silhouette and have someone snap away. It's guaranteed to be a hair-raising experience.

Picking through Stuff
Glenwood

Billy Herrell is a collector of America's collective memories, and he displays them at Billy's House of Guitars and Musical Museum in Glenwood. Herrell has been a musician all his life. In the 1960s he opened for top acts at the Vapors, the hottest club in Hot Springs. When Liberace played there, he gave Herrell a signed picture of a piano that he had drawn himself. An accumulation of many such souvenirs evolved into the museum.

Herrell's father played guitar with Elvis Presley, so he naturally has Elvis memorabilia, including a guitar strap signed by all the members of Presley's band. He has autographs and other items from Colonel Parker, Carl Perkins, Johnny Cash, Jerry Lee Lewis, and Sam Phillips, and the list goes on.

"I crossed paths with a lot of these folks," Herrell said.

A desire to get off the road was instrumental in his decision to open his shop. He did a weekly radio show from there for more than ten years, and a lot of his musician friends came by, many of them donating things to the museum. He still does a monthly show.

"I've got a guitar from Willie Nelson, who kicked off his Spirit Tour here in Glenwood in '96, and we've had Lynyrd Skynyrd do shows with us. You never know who's going to stop by."

★ ★

Confident that Herrell wouldn't string us along, we asked if a pair of glasses at the museum had really belonged to Roy Orbison. He laughed and said, "Put 'em on and see if you can sing 'Only the Lonely.'"

Herrell also has collectibles from vintage TV Westerns such as *Gunsmoke, The Lone Ranger, Zorro,* and *Frontier Doctor.* The biggest eye-catcher is a stagecoach from the days when Roy Rogers reigned as King of the Cowboys.

Herrell's place is down-to-earth and relaxed. "People come around and pick and have jam sessions and just hang out."

A fiddle-playing ninety-three-year-old woman once put on an impromptu concert for about twenty lucky customers who happened to be there.

In a documentary called *American Music: Off the Record and on the Road,* Herrell lamented the demise of mom-and-pop music stores, which were the pattern for his own.

"The Internet and fast-food music stores have pretty much killed all that off," he said.

For more information call Billy Herrell at (870) 356-4301. Your interest will be music to his ears.

Cuckoo over Hoo-Hoo
Gurdon

It was a dark and stormy night in January 1892 when a group of lumbermen, stranded in the tiny town of Gurdon, devised a parody of the world's many fraternal organizations, unaware that their little joke would take on a life of its own. The Concatenated Order of Hoo-Hoo resembled legitimate fraternal orders like the Rosicrucians, Elks, and Freemasons. With outrageous titles, such as Grand Snark of the Universe and Jabberwock (borrowed from Lewis Carroll), the group was clearly meant to send up Freemasonry's pretensions. Where Freemasons claim to have traced their roots back to the building of Solomon's temple, the Hoo-Hoos went them one better, using Egyptian symbols and motifs to imply an even more ancient connection. In rejection of convention and superstition, they used a black cat as their mascot. The term "Hoo-Hoo" was claimed to have been coined by one of the founders to describe the small remaining tuft of hair on the head of the first president, Charles McCarer.

The group has always fancied the number nine. Meetings are held on the ninth day of the ninth month at nine minutes after nine. In the beginning, membership was limited to 9,999, but this was later changed to 99,999. Membership is open to all workers in wood-related businesses. A bronze monument commemorating the Hoo-Hoos features two cats with their tails curled in the shape of nines.

Famous people with ties to the Hoo-Hoos include President Theodore Roosevelt (member number 999) and Elizabeth Taylor, who was named Miss Hoo-Hoo in 1948.

The Hoo-Hoo Museum is located at 207 East Main Street in Gurdon. For more information about the organization or the museum, call (800) 979-9950 or e-mail info@hoo-hoo.org.

World's Largest Watermelons
Hope

Hope, Arkansas, is best known for two things: for being the boyhood home of former President Bill Clinton and for producing the world's largest watermelons. When Bill met Hillary, he allegedly said, "We grow the world's largest watermelons in Hope." Who can resist a pickup line like that?

Hope was named for Hope Loughborough, whose father was the railroad land commissioner, James M. Loughborough. The town became the Hempstead County seat in 1938 after a decades-old struggle to wrest the title from nearby Washington, Arkansas.

Hope first became known for its extra-large watermelons in the early 1900s, when railroad representative C. S. Lawthorp saw a promotional opportunity for shippers, and farmers recognized a catchy marketing gimmick for themselves.

In the mid-1920s Hope started hosting a watermelon festival in

How sweet it is!
ARKANSAS DEPARTMENT OF PARKS AND TOURISM

which the main draw was a competition between farmers to see who could produce the largest watermelon. In 1925 Hugh Laseter won with a 136-pound melon, which was presented to President Calvin Coolidge. Edgar Laseter, Hugh's brother, won the next year with a watermelon that weighed 143.25 pounds. The festival was suspended during the Great Depression and didn't resume until 1977. Since then, the Bright family has dominated the melon competition. In 1979 Ivan Bright and his son, Lloyd, became the first farmers to produce a 200-pound watermelon. Ivan's grandson, Jason, won in 1985 with a melon that tipped the scales at 260 pounds, which held the Guinness world record for several years. In 2005 Lloyd Bright grew a 268.8 pound melon, which put the Bright family back in *Guinness World Records.*

About 50,000 people attend the Hope Watermelon Festival every August. Activities at the four-day event include watermelon eating and seed-spitting contests, as well as a melon-tossing competition. In arts-and-crafts booths, the watermelon image graces everything from kitchen towels and potholders to doorstops to wind chimes. Think Forrest Gump and shrimp recipes. Of course the best part of the festival is eating sweet watermelon, sold whole or by the slice.

For more information about the Watermelon Festival and the town of Hope, contact the Hope-Hempstead County Chamber of Commerce at (870) 777-3640 or e-mail hopemelonfest@yahoo.com.

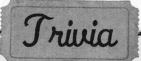

Trivia

While in Hope, be sure to visit our forty-second president's first home at 117 South Hervey Street. It's open for tours Monday through Saturday. Call (870) 777-4455 or e-mail clinton@arkansas.net for more details.

★ ★

Hit Me with Your Best Shot

In 1962 at the Hope Country Club, Larry Bruce scored the first-ever par-5 hole in one. He aimed high over a stand of pines on a dogleg and sent the ball sailing over the treetops. Other par-5 holes in one have been made since then, but the feat is still a rarity. To achieve it, a golfer must sink the ball on a 500-yard drive. The only thing *we* can drive on a golf course is that cute little cart.

Little Big Man in Hot Springs

Hot Springs

Though many gangsters visited Hot Springs over the years, the only one who came to stay was Owney Madden, and nothing went on in the Spa City without his knowledge.

Born in 1892, Madden gained a reputation as a tough guy, growing up on the streets of New York in the area known as Hell's Kitchen. At 5 feet, 6 inches tall, he was called "that little banty rooster out of hell." He was once shot eight times but survived. The gunmen weren't so fortunate.

Madden was imprisoned in 1914 for killing "Little Patsy" Doyle. Now, how could anybody kill someone with such a cute name? With a big gun, that's how. Madden was a crack shot, the best in New York.

After being paroled, he moved to Hot Springs in the 1930s, got married, and set up housekeeping on West Grand Avenue. Though he appeared to be a peaceful, law-abiding citizen, he was the Mob's man in Hot Springs and had a controlling interest in the Southern Club, a gambling house. His guests included Meyer Lansky, Lucky Luciano, and Al Capone.

★ ★

Gambling bit the dust in Hot Springs in the mid-1960s, and so did Madden. He died of natural causes on April 24, 1965.

Better Than a Leg Wax

Hot Springs

Those of us who were raised on a steady diet of old-time horror movies remember *House of Wax* as one of Vincent Price's finest hours. Arkansas's real house of wax is located in Hot Springs at 250 Central Avenue in the building once occupied by the Southern Club. The Josephine Tussaud Wax Museum retains many of the former gambling club's original architectural features and vintage fixtures, but one thing you can bet has been updated is the air-conditioning system.

Modeling figures out of wax has been done for centuries, but it wasn't until Marie Tussaud came along that the art really caught on—and it began in a way worthy of the museum's Chamber of Horrors exhibit. Marie Tussaud was imprisoned in the Bastille during the French Revolution and was forced to make death masks of members of the nobility after their heads had been lopped off by the guillotine. After the Reign of Terror ended, Marie took her collection on tour before opening the permanent museum in London in 1833.

Although the Josephine Tussaud Wax Museum in Hot Springs has no connection to the London museum, it endeavors to carry on in the tradition of the original. It fills 14,000 square feet of space with the wax likenesses of the famous and infamous from show business, royalty, politics, and religion. An exhibit stays as long as the person's recognition waxes and is rotated out as it wanes. Some, such as Alfred Hitchcock, look livelier than their flesh-and-blood counterparts ever did.

The museum opened in 1971 and today displays one hundred wax figures in about forty settings, including the Last Supper and the Crown Jewels of England. Contrary to what you might think, the latter does not show the bonnie Prince Charlie au naturel.

For information about admission prices and hours of operation, call the Josephine Tussaud Wax Museum at (501) 623-5836.

★ ★

Recycling More Than the Christmas Tree
Hot Springs

Every Christmas, Macy's department store in New York City goes out of its way to impress shoppers with elaborate window displays, including scenes from the classic movie *Miracle on 34th Street.* But New York City's got nothing on Hot Springs, Arkansas.

In 1970 Leland Felix decided to do a little something different for Christmas at his place of business, Felix Brace & Limb Co., Inc., in Hot Springs. He made some elves out of broken crutches and put them in a display with Santa and Mrs. Claus. It was the beginning of a tradition.

Every Christmas since then, Felix has displayed the North Pole couple and their little helpers in different theme settings. One year they were printing Christmas cards; another year they were making popcorn balls.

Nearly everything in each Christmas scene is made from discarded items that less-imaginative folk might refer to as junk—everything from broken prosthetic devices to tin cans to cardboard to wheels from bicycles and wheelchairs. One Santa was rescued from a bank's trash heap after a flood. You might say Santa goes green here.

Contributing to the wow factor is the fact that the displays are animated. Motors from a variety of cast-off machines make rocking chairs really rock, dancing elves really dance, and drummers really drum.

Felix's shop was on Central Avenue when he first started present-ing his Christmas gift to the community, and sightseers would back traffic up to Grand Avenue. Crying "traffic hazard," some Scrooges on the city council contemplated sending Santa packing but thought better of it. Tiny Tim might not be old enough to vote a council member out of office, but other Christmas-loving family members are.

In 1976 Felix moved his business to 310 Higdon Ferry Road, where the Christmas displays remain a popular seasonal treat.

X Marks the Spot

Hot Springs

Roller coasters originated as slides on mountains of ice in seventeenth-century Russia. They've come a long way. The latest state-of-the-art roller coaster has been attracting daredevils to Hot Springs ever since Magic Springs & Crystal Falls Theme Park introduced the X-Coaster, the highest upside-down inversion roller coaster in the world. To see another one like it, you would have to go to Germany. Only the two exist.

Costing $4 million and made by Maurer Rides of Munich, the X-Coaster allows riders to experience the inversion without shoulder

This is as close as we're going to get to any roller coaster.

restraints. After a slow vertical ascent of 150 feet, the roller coaster does a backward quarter loop, suspending riders upside down before sending them on a corkscrew roll and then hurtling back down at the heart-pounding speed of 65 miles per hour. The coaster attains a g-force of 5.

The ride holds twelve passengers but can accommodate 500 people an hour. According to a theme park spokesman, the roller coaster's unique design ensures that each row of seats allows a different experience.

In June 2007 a power outage shut down the X-Coaster just as passengers were enjoying the upside-down part of the ride. They were stranded that way for thirty minutes before firemen rescued them by using a ladder truck. A witness at the park said you could tell which people had been on the coaster by their beet-red complexions. Instead of kissing the earth when he landed, one rescued soul anointed the ground with vomit.

The X-coaster has had other ups and downs, what with stoppages for maintenance and such, but it always comes around.

Other amusement rides at the theme park include Big Bad John, Plummet Summit, Wild Thang, and the Gauntlet.

Magic Springs is located at 1701 East Grand Avenue. For more information about prices and hours of operation, call (501) 318-5370 or go to www.magicsprings.com.

The Illusionist
Hot Springs

One of our favorite haunts in Hot Springs is the Malco Theatre at 817 Central Avenue. It was built in 1935 on the site of the former Princess Theatre, which was demolished after a fire. Every October the Malco is host to the Hot Springs Documentary Film Festival, where you can see films that will never play in East Podunk.

We started this by saying the Malco is one of our favorite haunts, and that was a deliberate choice of words. Some say the Malco is haunted. One night there in 1888, a magician named Jerome Schmitar chose an audience member, Clara Sutherland, to assist him with an illusion. He concealed her shapely body under a piece of red silk and allowed the suspense to build before pulling the scarf away. Voilá! Clara had vanished. When Jerome attempted to bring her back, she did not reappear. The stunned magician repeatedly tried to restore Clara to the physical realm, but the lady did not materialize. She was never seen again. Her ghost, however, became part of the lore and lure of the Malco.

(Continued on page 112)

It's only make-believe.
ARKANSAS DEPARTMENT OF PARKS AND TOURISM

World's Shortest St. Patrick's Day Parade

In the 1940s *Ripley's Believe It or Not!* declared Bridge Street in Hot Springs to be the shortest street in the world. Though that title currently belongs to McKinley Street in Bellefontaine, Ohio, Bridge Street now lays claim to another world record. With a length of 98 feet, this stretch of pavement between Central Avenue and Broadway is still short enough to host the World's Shortest St. Patrick's Day Parade.

The event was dreamed up in 2004 by a group of Hot Springs residents who had gathered, appropriately enough, in a bar. The parade drew about 2,000 spectators that first year. By 2008 the exuberant crowd had grown to more than 15,000 people.

It's hard to tell who has more fun, the onlookers or the participants. The processions have included a 6-foot-tall, red-bearded leprechaun; a pack of Irish wolfhounds; a bevy of Irish belly dancers; Michael Fatley's Lards of the Dance; the world's smallest float (a miniature green Volkswagen); the Irish Order of Elvi (a group of Elvis look-alikes who throw Twinkies to the spectators); a contingent of toilets on wheels; and the fire department color guard with a fire engine almost as long as the parade route. The honorable title of Grand Marshal has been bestowed upon such celebrities as Mario Lopez and George Wendt.

Festivities continue after the parade. In 2008 Mini Kiss, a tribute band of little people, performed their rocking version of the Gene Simmons group. A display of green fireworks follows the parade, as does a pub crawl through a number of downtown watering holes, where gallons of green beer flow copiously. Those toilets on wheels could come in handy.

For more information about the World's Shortest St. Patrick's Day Parade, contact the Hot Springs Convention and Visitors Bureau by calling (800) SPA-CITY (772-2489) or e-mailing hscvb@hotsprings.org.

Everybody's Irish at least once a year.
HOT SPRINGS CONVENTION AND VISITORS BUREAU

★ ★

(Continued from page 109)

Fast forward to 1996. Magician Maxwell Blade settles in Hot Springs and makes the Malco his Theatre of Magic. While renovating the building, he discovers Jerome Schmitar's trunk in the basement and learns about the tragedy. It's Kismet. The story of Jerome and Clara blends flawlessly with Maxwell Blade's already riveting act.

But guess what? The story is part of the act. Clara Sutherland and Jerome Schmitar are figments of Maxwell Blade's imagination. He is, after all, an illusionist.

"Everyone loves a mystery," Blade said. "I wanted something different; to incorporate a mystery into the show. The whole thing was just a made-up story, but it got out on the Internet; now it's everywhere."

It is, indeed. Each retelling of the tale adds a new embellishment. Somebody's uncle said his grandfather knew a man whose chiropractor saw Clara's father shoot a man who looked like Jerome. Whew! The story has something that Clara never had—a life of its own. Now if we could just lure it up on stage . . .

See the Maxwell Blade Show in its new venue at 121 Central Avenue in Hot Springs (501-623-6200).

For information about the Hot Springs Documentary Film Festival, call (501) 321-4747.

When Underworld Kings Ruled Hot Springs
Hot Springs

Before Las Vegas was even a gleam in Bugsy Siegel's eye (the one that wasn't shot out), Hot Springs was the gambling mecca of America. It was also a playground for many of America's most notorious gangsters, including Al Capone, Lucky Luciano, and Meyer Lansky.

Known for its soothing hot mineral baths, Hot Springs was a place where gangsters could go to cool off. They buried the hatchet while in town—and not in each other's back. Hot Springs was as neutral as Switzerland. Al Capone stayed in the Arlington Hotel while his

Here's a museum you can't refuse.
ARKANSAS DEPARTMENT OF PARKS AND TOURISM

enemy, Bugs Moran, was registered a block away at the Majestic Hotel.

Now, thanks to Robert Raines, visitors to the Spa City can get a glimpse into that exciting era. Raines is the founder and manager of the first museum in the United States devoted to gangsters. It is located at 113 Central Avenue in a building that has been used as a brothel, a chamber of commerce, and a drive-in mortuary.

To get Raines and the museum off to a good start, the Jonathan M. O'Quinn Classic Cars Collection loaned them Al Capone's Cadillac. During Prohibition, Capone took advantage of a well-known product that was bottled in Hot Springs: Mountain Valley Spring Water. Ol' Scarface bought liquor from Arkansas bootleggers and

★ ★

shipped it back to Chicago in railcars marked with the Mountain Valley brand.

Tommy guns, like those used by Capone's thugs and other mobsters, are on display at the museum, as are vintage gambling artifacts. Audiovisual presentations tell about the various gangsters and the political bosses who allowed vice to flourish. Leo McLaughlin, mayor of Hot Springs from 1927 until 1947, was a flamboyant figure often seen riding in a surrey drawn by his favorite horses, Scotch and Soda.

Another colorful character highlighted at the museum is Maxine Temple Jones, a madam with class and a distinguished clientele. Maxine once said, "Honey, I like an old-fashioned whorehouse that has respect and dignity." She lived well, until mobsters forced her out of business when she refused their offer to join their "syndicate." Nothing as subtle as a horse head in her bed. Both of Maxine's husbands died under mysterious circumstances, and the local authorities suddenly no longer turned a blind eye to her business.

For museum hours and admission prices, call (501) 318-1717 or go to www.tgmoa.com.

Some Like It Hot
Hot Springs

You can probably find a place called Hell's Half Acre in just about any state in the country. Arkansas is no exception. Our piece of Lucifer's land is located in Hot Springs.

It is actually bigger than a half acre, but Hell's One-and-One-Quarter Acre doesn't quite trip off the tongue. The terrain is a barren, rocky no-man's-land surrounded by trees and other vegetation. Why does nothing grow on this particular spot? One theory is that it is the crater of an extinct volcano. We asked a retired state geologist, and he said it may be the top of a very old rock slide. That's a rational, scientific hypothesis.

But of course, logical, simple explanations have a tendency to get shuffled to the back of the mind when a spooky story can be so much more fun. For more than a century, Hell's Half Acre was purported to be the devil's playground where no sane person would dare venture, especially after dark. It was said that even hunting dogs wouldn't go there.

Real estate developers missed an opportunity to turn Hell's Half Acre into a nineteenth-century prison theme park or a nice Japanese rock garden. As it is, the neighborhood has not gone to hell. Quite the opposite. Awhile back, street signs began to appear near Beelzebub's barrio that bore names so heavenly and divinely inspired, they made the whole area sound less like a vortex of evil and more like the Garden of Eden: Promise Land Drive, Manna Court, and Pearly Gate Lane. Resting Place is a little premature for our taste, but it's there.

They say Satan never sleeps. How can he, with the Messiah (Trail) on one side and the Holy Spirit (Loop) on the other? There's also Covenant Trail and Higher Ground (in case the new ark is in Newark when we need it).

The Long and Rocky Road
Lake Ouachita

Early scientists studying Arkansas's rocks noticed something odd: Although rocks in the south of the state and those in the north are the same age, they differ radically in thickness and composition. Seven hundred million years ago, Arkansas was part of Rodinia, a supercontinent made up of all the earth's continents combined. As the supercontinent rifted apart, what is now Arkansas was torn in half along a jagged line running through the north-central part of the state. The missing southern piece was found a few years ago fused to the northwest coast of South America. What remained was a continental shelf with a southern edge somewhere around Heber Springs.

Then, 300 million years ago, the continents recombined to form Pangaea. As North America and South America came together, sediments that had formed in the ocean bottom between the two

★ ★

A Literal Translation

The community of Ink got its unusual name in 1887 when residents filled out a government application to establish a post office. Under the space where the town's name was supposed to be entered, the form said, "Write in Ink," so they did.

Or so the story goes.

The U.S. Postal Service chose the name over two others submitted by the community. The government required three potential place names to avoid duplications. Ink was second on its citizens' list. Their first choice? Melon.

continents were compacted and fused onto North America. The earth's crust buckled like an accordion and formed the Ouachita Mountains, which at that time connected to the Southern Appalachians of Tennessee.

Still-unresolved questions remain, in that many of the rock formations in the south don't appear to be from deep-ocean deposits. Many are thicker in the south and thinner toward the north, indicating they were formed in the deltas of rivers flowing northward. Others contain cobbles (rounded rocks and pebbles tumbled smooth in fast-moving streams) that could only have formed on or very near dry land.

In referring to the Crystal Mountain deposits (some of the state's oldest strata), geologist Cary Crones wrote, "There is some evidence that much of the sandstone without visible bedding and with large rounded grains possibly may be of eolian origin." In other words, windblown particles.

In addition, rock samples collected in the Yucatan match strata found in the Ouachita Mountains. How is this possible? In 1979 geologist George W. Viele theorized that southern Arkansas once belonged to another continental plate. As proof, he cited core drillings made a few miles north of the present-day Gulf of Mexico that contain continental bedrock, indicating the core rock strata that forms southern Arkansas today was part of a "microcontinent." If Viele is correct, it means that part of Central America remained fused to North America after the breakup of Pangaea. Viva El Dorado!

Learn more about the creation of Arkansas by taking the self-guided float trip on Lake Ouachita. For details call Lake Ouachita State Park at (501) 767-9366.

Irresistible Attraction

Magnet Cove

Breaking up is hard to do, and any breakup isn't complete without some fireworks. When North America broke free from South America one hundred million years ago, the land that is now Arkansas was a hotbed of volcanic activity. It formed the Crater of Diamonds in Murfreesboro and the lesser known Magnet Cove, an interesting location in its own right. The name was taken from the lodestone that early pioneers found clinging to their plow blades and shovels. (Read about the effect of this magnetism on compasses in our entry on pole dancing in the Ouachita Mountains.)

Magnet Cove lies 12 miles southeast of Hot Springs on AR 51. The cove, believed to be a volcanic intrusion, is an elliptical area approximately 5 miles in diameter. Although hot magma did not actually reach the surface, hot vapors condensed into veins of ore. More minerals—seventy different types, at last count—are contained within this 5-mile area than in any other spot on Earth. Some of the minerals here are found in only two other locations: the Ural Mountains in west-central Russia and the Tyrolean Alps in western Austria and northern Italy.

★ ★

Magnet Cove has also produced certain types of minerals that scientists had never seen before. In the 1840s Magnet Cove gained recognition among geologists when Professor Charles Shepard wrote about a supposedly new mineral called arkansite; it turned out to be brookite, which was about as new as Grandma's scrub board. Truly new minerals found at Magnet Cove include delindeite and lourens-walsite and a garnet called kimzeyite, which is very high in zirconium. Other minerals present at Magnet Cove are anatase, calcite, and

Early miners noted the remarkable minerals of Magnet Cove.
JOHN N. HASKELL PHOTOGRAPH COLLECTION/UALR ARCHIVES

rutile. One you wouldn't want to look for on an empty stomach is apatite. Industry finds many uses for the minerals. Rutile, for instance, is used in the coating of welding rods and as a paint pigment. Long ago, one inspired use of Magnet Cove's magnetic ore was as love charms; shops in Chicago and New York City bought tons for that purpose.

Most of the land is privately owned, but collecting is allowed around Cove Creek Bridge (AR 51) and the creekbed. A good way to find magnetized ore without breaking your back is to tie a nail to a string and swing it close to the ground. If you do get rockhounding fever at Magnet Cove, please respect the property rights of landowners. Don't trespass!

Sultane's Magnolia Belle
Magnolia

An udderly amazing cow was born in Columbia County in 1926. You don't give just any ol' name to a cow like this. She wasn't Flossie or Bossie and not even just plain Belle. She was Sultane's Magnolia Belle, a Jersey milk cow owned by Magnolia A & M College. On February 11, 1937, she was named the National Champion Jersey Milk Cow, a titillating title she won by producing 1,043 pounds of butterfat.

To help Belle accomplish this feat, Melbourn Walthall milked Belle three times a day for a whole year. Also lending a hand (though maybe not as warm as Mr. Walthall's) were Paul Jetton, A & M's herdsman, and Professor Ves Godley, head of the college's animal husbandry department. The public record does not state who churned all of that butter, but whoever it was deserves a hunka-hunka churning love.

When Lewis W. Morley and R. A. Patterson of the American Jersey Cattle Club bestowed the award upon Belle, the mooving occasion was photographed for posterity. Belle milked her fifteen minutes of fame for all it was worth.

★ ★

Brickfest

Malvern

One of us is directionally challenged. It runs in the family. A cousin literally couldn't find his way out of a phone booth. Really happened. Being without an internal GPS is not always bad, though. Leaving an event in Hot Springs once accidentally brought us to Malvern, and it was a nice detour. The folks there were kind and helpful. One thing you can never say about the people of Malvern is that they're a few bricks shy of a load. That's because their fine city is known as the Brick Capital of the World.

Malvern sprang up as a railroad town in the 1870s, but brick manufacturing companies moved into the area when clay was found to be a plentiful and valuable natural resource there. After fires destroyed much of Malvern in the late 1890s, the town used bricks exclusively to rebuild their businesses. Verna Garvan learned the brick industry from her father, Arthur B. Cook, who had been president of Malvern Brick & Tile Company, but Verna put her own stamp on the business by introducing more colors than the usual red and tan.

Malvern became the world's largest producer of bricks and in 1980 started a yearly celebration known as Brickfest. The event is held the last weekend in June and includes a car, truck, and motor- cycle show; a 5K run; a beauty pageant; and musical entertainment. And, yes, there are the brick contests: a brick toss, brick car derby, best-dressed brick competition, and a scavenger hunt.

Another great product of Malvern is favorite son Billy Bob Thorn- ton, who moved to the Brick Capital when he was a child. Before he became an actor and Oscar-winning screenwriter, he won fame at the tender age of seven months as the heaviest baby in neighboring Clark County. He was thirty pounds of adorability and enjoyed eating sticks of butter as though they were Popsicles. You might say he was built like the proverbial brick outhouse!

For more information about Malvern or Brickfest, call the Malvern Chamber of Commerce at (501) 332-2721.

**And the winner in the Best Dressed Brick
Contest is . . . Miss Hardbody!**
ARKANSAS DEPARTMENT OF PARKS AND TOURISM

★ ★

Hard Rock Heaven
Murfreesboro

One morning in 1906, John Wesley Huddleston, an illiterate farmer, was slopping his hogs southeast of Murfreesboro when he spied a shiny bit of rock lying in the muck. With that stroke of fortune, a man who was considered by many to be an oddball went from kooky character to wealthy eccentric, almost overnight. He was literally sitting atop a diamond mine soon to be known worldwide as the Crater of Diamonds.

Diamonds form 125 miles underground and are propelled to the earth's surface by volcanic vents (or pipes). Such vents are more common than most people realize, although most don't produce diamonds in large quantities. Other, smaller volcanic vents in Arkansas are located near Oppelo and Perryville. Arkansas diamonds are smooth and 28 percent harder than stones found elsewhere. They are the hardest natural substance on Earth.

Huddleston sold his hog farm for $36,000, which he wanted in $10 bills, proving that his diamond discovery did not diminish his peculiarities. Once, when a bull went charging across the movie screen at the Bijou Theatre, Huddleston pulled out a .45 and fired away. He tried to live up to his image as the Diamond King but was regarded more as a zircon. When he attempted to flag down a mail train one day by shouting, "Stop! I'm the Diamond King," he was hit by mail sacks thrown from the train and suffered four broken ribs.

Huddleston's hog farm became Crater of Diamonds State Park, the only diamond mine in the world open to the public. For the price of admission, anyone can dig for diamonds and keep what they find. Hundreds are found every year.

On the third Saturday of June, the park hosts John Huddleston Day. Festival activities include a treasure hunt, three-legged races, an egg toss, and a diamond-digging contest.

The park is located 2.5 miles southeast of Murfreesboro on AR 301. For hours of operation and price of admission, call (870) 285-

★ ★

3113, e-mail craterofdiamonds@arkansas.com, or visit www.craterof diamondsstatepark.com.

Sauropod Promenade
Nashville

In 1983 one of the largest dinosaur trackways in the world was discovered in a gypsum quarry 10 miles south of Nashville, Arkansas. Scientists estimate that the 5,000 to 10,000 tracks were made by

A mother and daughter standing in an actual dinosaur footprint preserved in limestone.
PHOTO BY LOUIE GRAVES IN *THE NASHVILLE* (ARK.) *LEADER*

★ ★

herds of dinosaurs traveling what the scientists believe was a migratory pathway along an ancient beach or salt marsh bordering the ocean 110 million years ago.

The dinosaurs were identified as a species of sauropod called *Pleurocoelus* (pronounced *PLOOR-oh-SEE-lus*). These long-necked animals were plant eaters. They walked on all fours and were about 60 feet in length from head to tail. They had a distinctive gait due to their front legs being longer than their back legs. This was believed to be an adaptation to dryer climate conditions. Elevating the front of their bodies allowed them to compete for diminishing food in the forest by browsing tall treetops, much like giraffes do today. The tracks indicate they walked three and four abreast, adults walking on the outside with the smaller, younger animals traveling in the center for protection against predators. This is a behavior naturalists report seeing today in modern elephant herds.

Nashville celebrates its earliest tourists with the Dinosaur Festival, held every year in May. Activities include a fishing derby, musical entertainment, and even a Bam-Bam and Pebbles look-alike contest.

Though the original trackway is gone, the concrete cast of a dinosaur footprint is located in Nashville City Park. For directions to the park, call Nashville City Hall at (870) 845-1432. Similar casts are on display at several locations around the state, including the University of Arkansas at Fayetteville, the Mid-America Museum at Hot Springs, the Museum of Discovery at Little Rock, and Lyon College at Batesville.

Nashville is located about 140 miles southwest of Little Rock off US 371, US 278, and AR 27.

For more information about the Dinosaur Festival and other area attractions and events, contact the Nashville Chamber of Commerce at (870) 845-1262 or nashvillecc@sbcglobal.net.

The Littlest Library
Norman

The year was 1939, and as the Munchkins were advising a bewildered Dorothy Gale and Toto to "follow the yellow brick road," an Arkansas traveler was following her own dream. As a result, the tiny town of Norman, in Montgomery County, has what many believe is the smallest freestanding public library in the nation.

The building and its contents are the legacy of Marie Pinkerton, who conceived the idea and was able to make her vision a reality with labor and funding provided through the Works Progress Administration (WPA). When Mrs. Pinkerton met with the city council and proposed the idea of starting a town library, she received permission to use a small building that sits in the center of the town square. It originally housed a pump, which was used to bring water from the Caddo River to the town water tower. At 170 square feet, the tiny structure was paneled and shelved in Mission-style oak for a mere $200 and later stocked with 500 books. It was a good home for *The Little Prince,* "Little Red Riding Hood," and *Stuart Little*; and Reader's Digest condensed books fit right in.

In 1993, after a little restoration, both the public square and the library were placed on the National Historic Register. The building was being reroofed when we were there and was temporarily closed, but the townspeople of Norman were busy with plans to seek a listing in *Guinness World Records.*

After browsing in the littlest library, step across the street to Melba's Cafe, where the homemade pies are scrumptious and you're served as though you're the only customer in there. Of course the town's population is about 400 people, so you may very well be the only customer in there. Suffice it to say, you'll never feel small in Norman.

And that's one for the books!

Pole Dancing

You're hiking in the Ouachita Mountains and realize you're lost. You look at your compass and see the needle break-dancing all over the dial. What's happening?

It's called compass spin. Igneous rocks, deep underground, are in a molten liquid state. They are all magnetic. Some, like igneous iron, are extremely magnetic.

Millions of years ago, volcanic forces pushed molten iron through cracks in the earth to the surface. As the molten iron cooled, its molecules aligned with the earth's magnetic poles. Since that time, North America has drifted and rotated. Now the lines of magnetic force in these subsurface bodies no longer line up with the current position of the earth's magnetic poles. The result is a tug-of-war as the steel needle swings between the two opposing forces. In some locations the pull is so strong, it causes the needle to spin in circles.

So how do you find your way in such a place? That's easy. Do what the pioneers did. Relax, take a swig of moonshine, close your eyes, turn around three times, and spit. Then break out the GPS.

Old Mike, the Mortuary Mascot
Prescott

On August 21, 1911, a pencil peddler was found dead of natural causes in Prescott's city park. No one knew his name, and he carried no identification. Cornish Mortuary embalmed him but postponed burial. They put him on display in a glass case and publicized his description in hopes someone would claim him, but nobody did.

The mortuary intended to hold the body for just a few days, but years passed and Old Mike, as he was affectionately called, became a

He was a handsome stinker.
NEVADA COUNTY DEPOT AND MUSEUM

fixture at the funeral home. The staff gave him a fresh set of clothes every few years. After dehydration caused his eyelids to pull back, he received blue-tinted eye caps. He was first-rate advertising for the funeral home. Johnny Carson even mentioned him on TV.

Sue Morris remembers going to Saturday movie matinees with her sister, Sunnee, and then visiting Old Mike. The sisters double-dog dared each other to touch him.

"It was even better if there was a horror movie showing at the Gem [Theatre]," Sue said.

In 1975 state health codes dictated that Old Mike be buried. He was given a proper send-off with casket, red carnations, and tombstone, all courtesy of Cornish Mortuary. He was one lucky stiff.

On the Right Track
Reader

The little community of Reader in south Arkansas is the home of a very successful film celebrity, having shared the silver screen with the likes of Robert Redford, Russell Crowe, and George Clooney. This homegrown talent doesn't give autographs, but that's not because of star temperament. It's because we are referring to a train, or more precisely, two steam locomotives, known as #2 and #4.

The Reader Railroad is the only exclusively steam-powered short-line common carrier standard gauge railroad in the country. It began operations in the 1880s when Lee Reader arrived in Arkansas to start a sawmill and needed a way to transport timber harvested from the forests in the area. The railroad has also been called the Possum Trot Line. We're not sure about the derivation of that name, but we've heard the joke about a train that ran so slow, a possum trotting alongside it would get there first.

Sometime after the railroad's parent company disbanded in the 1950s, the railroad became a tourist attraction. Passengers could take a 5.5-mile ride through the scenic countryside from the Reader Depot to Waterloo in Nevada County and back again—all at the possum pace of 12 miles per hour. Reader became a whistle stop, where people could flag down the train and hop aboard.

The Reader Railroad had its first flirtation with movie stardom when Martin Scorsese, in his directorial debut, used old #2 in the movie *Boxcar Bertha,* starring Barbara Hershey and David Carradine.

The railroad's promising new career was nearly nipped in the bud when it ceased operations in 1991. Some people thought it was the end of the line, but the old girl had a lot of steam left in her and made a comeback that rivaled John Travolta's. The railroad that had started out hauling wood went Hollywood. Altogether, the two loco-motives have been in sixteen movies, many of them critical and box office successes, including *This Property is Condemned, 3:10 to Yuma, Appaloosa,* and *O Brother, Where Art Thou?.*

Though over one hundred years old, the Reader Railroad shows no sign of slowing down. Of course when you move like a possum, slowing down isn't much of an option.

They Crawl by Night
Rich Mountain

Certain types of earthworms have both male and female genitalia, located on opposite ends of their bodies. If by chance during mating season, they fail to find a suitable partner, they merely put on some Barry White and curl up with themselves and set about doing what comes unnaturally (to us). It must really take the pressure off finding a date on Friday night.

Other types of earthworms are not so lucky and become midnight ramblers.

On June 11, 1973, Dr. Bruce Means was digging for salamanders atop Rich Mountain in Polk County when he made a discovery that set his heart to squirming. It was a giant earthworm. *Diplocardia meansi* is the second largest earthworm in the United States and is found only on Rich Mountain, proving the mountain truly is rich. When frightened, the worm is said to secrete a foul-tasting substance that glows in the dark. Don't ask how they discovered the flavor. The creatures migrate on rainy nights in May, when love is in the mud.

Arkansas Sea Serpents

Rick Evans Grandview Prairie Wildlife Management Area

"What is it?" he growled.

When I reached out to touch the odd-shaped rock, he suddenly snatched it back as if he were Gollum guarding his precious ring. He wanted to see me squirm a bit.

"I give up."

He looked annoyed, then whispered, "It's dragon bone. Arkansas sea serpent," he cackled like a demented prospector.

"Yeah, right," I said, thinking 'rock hounds, I'll never understand them,' but it turns out he was correct.

Seventy million years ago, as a warm tropical sea lapped against the shores of southern Arkansas and the salty ocean spray weathered the limestone bluffs, a strange creature sported in the waters off our coast. Looking like a snake pulled through the body of a sea turtle, the plesiosaur was a large carnivorous reptile from the age of dinosaurs. It ranged in length from 15 to 40 feet.

Fossils of these animals were among the first recovered in the nineteenth century. The first complete skeleton was recovered by twenty-two-year-old Mary Anning in England in 1821. Anning, who went on to make a number of other important scientific finds, was largely ignored by the male academic community of her time. She supported herself and her family by selling fossils that she collected from the local sea cliffs, and she is widely believed to be the inspiration for the childhood tongue twister, "She sells seashells by the seashore."

Coincidentally, no sooner had pictures of the scientific reconstruction of the animal been published than reports began to appear of alleged sightings of "sea serpents" resembling the extinct reptile. These culminated with the 1933 publication of grainy photos of the Loch Ness Monster; photos that have since been revealed by the photographer to be pictures of a toy submarine with its periscope covered in a prosthetic plesiosaur head and neck, fashioned from modeling clay.

The south Arkansas sea serpent was no myth, although the majority of the remains are fragmentary. The most common body part found has been the vertebrae. Fossils of the two distinct species—the long-neck elasmosaurs and short-neck plesiosaurs—are found in Cretaceous deposits in Hempstead County.

To view these fossils, visit the Conservation Education Center on the grounds of the Rick Evans Grandview Prairie Wildlife Management Area off AR 73 near Columbus in southwest Arkansas.

For more information call (870) 983-2790 or (870) 983-2740.

Smackover, the Hole Story

Smackover

It was a warm spring day in 1922 near Norphlet, 4 miles southeast of Smackover in Union County. A 112-foot-tall oil derrick towered over the countryside, its slowly spinning drill bit powered by a steam engine like those used in railroad locomotives.

For the crew of Murphy Oil Well No.1, it was business as usual until suddenly they heard a low rumbling coming from deep underground. The drill had struck an enormous natural gas deposit. Within seconds, a huge explosion launched the drill pipe skyward like a missile. Men ran for their lives. The blast obliterated the derrick, shattered eardrums, and rattled windows for miles in all directions. Balls of hard, packed sand rained out of the sky, as sixty-five million cubic feet of gas escaped into the atmosphere. Debris landed as far as 10 miles from the blast site. Pulverized shale struck a pilot in the face as he was flying at an altitude of 7,000 feet—smack in the face over Smackover.

The land around the well began to sink. A crater formed and engulfed the steam engine. The boiler surfaced periodically in peekaboo fashion, spinning around like a circus elephant. It would disappear and then reappear and disappear again.

On the second day the crater caught fire and sent flames 300 feet into the air. In rapid succession, a series of explosions rocked the earth as escaping gas burned out and then reignited.

The gas well explosion is now a landfill.
UALR PHOTOGRAPH COLLECTION / UALR ARCHIVES

★ ★

Underground springs finally put out the fire, leaving behind a bubbling morass 350 feet wide and 100 feet deep. A steady stream of looky-loos traveled over rough log roads to visit what a local preacher called, "the closest thing to . . . hell as I have ever seen." Vendors set

The Goat Woman of Smackover

In 1905 three-year-old Rhena Miller started performing in her father's medicine shows. She could play several musical instruments simultaneously. Later she joined the circus and traveled widely. Then the Great Depression hit, and she was out of a job for the first time in her life.

Rhena and her husband, Charles Meyer, moved to Smackover, Arkansas, where they lived in their circus carriage and Charles sold used tires. Out of her element, Rhena became very withdrawn. Her best friends were her pet goats, the only kids she would ever have. Townsfolk made fun of her, and Charles built a high wall around their home on wheels. His reclusive wife ventured out only at night to stroll around town. Twenty years later, she became her old self again and started entertaining people with her music and her trained goats.

When the Meyers moved a few miles outside Smackover, Rhena became a fixture on AR 7, where she and motorists waved to one another.

After Charles died in 1963, Rhena continued to perform with her goats and appeared on local TV. She died in 1988.

Her circus carriage can be seen at the Arkansas Museum of Natural Resources (870-725-2877), located at 3853 Smackover Highway (AR 7) 1 mile south of Smackover.

up refreshment stands around the rim of the crater to cater to the crowd.

If you would like to know more about Smackover's oil boom, visit the Arkansas Museum of Natural Resources (870-725-2877), located at 3853 Smackover Highway (AR 7), 1 mile south of Smackover. It features an undersea diorama and the replica of a Smackover street during the 1920s. Sound effects and recordings make you feel as if you were there. Outdoor exhibits include vintage derricks. Admission is free, but donations are accepted.

Tale of Two Cities
Texarkana

Texarkana, Arkansas, and Texarkana, Texas, are two cities in one, joined together by a common state border. Each side has its own municipal government, police department, and fire department. Texarkana, Arkansas, is in a wet county, and Texarkana, Texas, is dry. Texas doesn't impose a state income tax, but Arkansas does.

Most people, though, think of Texarkana as one entity, and it is served by one chamber of commerce. The shared name of Texarkana was coined from letters of three states: Texas, Arkansas, and Louisiana. But because the Louisiana border is 30 miles away, we ended up with twin cities instead of triplets.

At 500 State Line Avenue you'll find the only post office in America that stands in two states. Tourists love to have their pictures taken there as they also stand in two states at the same time. A popular picture postcard from Texarkana showed a man and his donkey with the caption, "A man in Arkansas with his ass in Texas." Photographer's Island, in front of the post office, was created just to accommodate all the shutterbugs.

Besides the post office, the federal building also houses two U.S. district courts and is said to be one of the two most photographed courthouses in the country, second only to the Supreme Court in Washington, D.C.

★ ★

The Longhorns and the Razorbacks side by side.
ARKANSAS DEPARTMENT OF PARKS AND TOURISM

Texarkana lives up to its motto, "Twice as Nice"—you can double your pleasure and double your fun by visiting many historical and entertaining attractions on both sides of the border.

Technically in Texas, the Perot Theatre at 219 Main Street is a beautifully restored theater dating back to the silent movie era. It has seen the likes of Will Rogers, Sergei Rachmaninoff, Annie Oakley, and Cary Grant (in his last public appearance). The interior is lavishly decorated; the rare wool carpeting is blue to match the walls, which have gold leaf trim and ornate sculpted designs. Entertainers have marveled at the theater's outstanding acoustics, although Marcel Marceau didn't have much to say about that when he performed there.

Certainly not to be missed is the Ace of Clubs House, also on the Texas side. The original owner, James H. Draughon, built the house in the shape of his winning poker card.

Contact the Texarkana Chamber of Commerce at (903) 792-7191.

Old Times There Are Not Forgotten
Washington

Perhaps no tree is as closely associated with the American South as the magnolia. The name itself positively drips with a honey-dipped Southern drawl. Magnolia trees go back a lot further than the Old South, though. They were around when dinosaurs walked the earth. A well-preserved dino nicknamed Leonardo was found in Montana in 2000, and when scientists examined the contents of his intact digestive system, what should they find but magnolia blossoms. Can't say we blame him. Magnolias certainly smell good enough to eat.

The big magnolia tree at Historic Washington State Park doesn't date back to Leonardo's time, but it is old. Grandison Royston planted seeds for the tree in the 1830s. It's Arkansas's largest Southern Magnolia (*Magnolia grandiflora*), measuring 68 feet tall and 14 feet in circumference.

The Royston Magnolia is just one reason to visit Historic Washington State Park, a living history park that shows what life was like in nineteenth-century Arkansas. Often referred to simply as Old Washington, it sits on the site of the original town of Washington, founded in 1824 on the anniversary of George Washington's birth. It served as the capital of the Confederacy after Little Rock fell to Union forces in 1863 and was an important stop for pioneers traveling on the Southwest Trail.

Visitors can tour restored historic buildings and chat with park guides dressed in period apparel. Strolling along the wooden sidewalks, it's easy to imagine children rolling hoops along the unpaved street and men in bowler hats riding high-wheel bicycles. Surrey rides are available on some days.

How about a nice, cold pitcher of lemonade after that surrey ride?
ARKANSAS DEPARTMENT OF PARKS AND TOURISM

The park, a National Historic Landmark, has many antiques from the 1800s, including spinning wheels, printing equipment, weapons, and blacksmithing tools. It was in Washington, Arkansas, that James Black forged the famous Bowie knife for Alamo hero Jim Bowie. Black's tradition is carried on at the Texarkana College/Bill Moran School of Bladesmithing, the only school in the world devoted to the art of making knives and swords.

Adjacent to the park is Southwest Arkansas Regional Archives, a valuable resource center for genealogists and history buffs. It houses old documents, newspapers, and rare books.

Historic Washington State Park is 113 miles southwest of Little Rock off US 278/AR 4. The visitor center is in the old county courthouse. For more information call (870) 983-2684 or visit www.historicwashingtonstatepark.com.

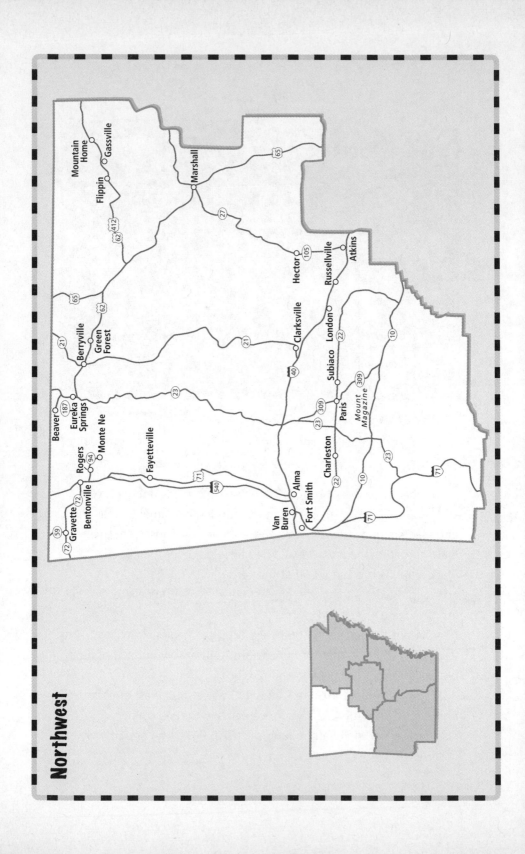

Northwest

4

Northwest

Northwest Arkansas is *a mixture of refinement and backwoods basics. Outside the metropolitan areas are the little communities in the hills and hollers of the Ozark Mountains that helped give Arkansas its hillbilly image—places like Bug Scuffle and Hogeye. Urban areas may appeal more to the intelligentsia, such as Fayetteville's Dr. William J. Baerg, who used himself as a lab rat in spider-bite experiments.*

Fort Smith is a city that still has just enough of its frontier flavor to evoke images of what it was like when "Hanging Judge" Isaac Parker and brothel madam Laura Ziegler took care of the lawless and the lusty. Though Parker died before Ziegler arrived in Fort Smith, the two had something in common. They both looked forward to seeing citizens well hung.

Eureka is a Greek word meaning "I found it," and you can find just about anything in Eureka Springs, the capital city of curiosities, mentioned more times in Ripley's Believe It or Not! *than any other place. One hotel, listed among the ten most haunted hotels in America, was featured on the SyFy show* Ghost Hunters.

Other unusual phenomena in northwest Arkansas include skyquakes, phantom panthers, and inexplicable interference with vehicle engines. Many of these have occurred in or around Fayetteville. Skeptics say such mysteries may be by-products of the city's spirited club scene. We'll have to get back to you on that—after we do more research.

★ ★

Spinach Capital of the World
Alma

The Crawford County town of Alma (originally called Gum Town) proudly proclaims itself the Spinach Capital of the World. They have earned their bragging rights to that title by canning sixty million pounds of spinach a year at the Allen Canning Company. Crystal City, Texas, also contends that it is the Spinach Capital, but only Allen Canning holds the bona fide trademark on Popeye Brand Spinach.

The image of Popeye himself looks out over Alma from the world's largest spinach can. Actually, the can is a water tower that was painted by Fort Smith artist William Bland to look like a can of Popeye

I yam what I yam.
ARKANSAS DEPARTMENT OF PARKS AND TOURISM

Spinach. It is big enough to hold one million gallons of water.

Another homage to Popeye and spinach is in the form of a bronze statue of the sailorman in Alma's downtown park. It replaced a fiberglass-and-papier-mâché statue that had twice been the target of thieves. You can bet Bluto was behind that.

The new and improved Popeye was unveiled in 2007 during Alma's twenty-first annual Spinach Festival. What, you were expecting a Broccoli Bash? The festival is held in mid-April and includes vendors, carnival rides, and music; but the star attraction is Popeye's favorite veggie, featured in recipe contests and eating competitions.

Alma is also known for an incident involving the Barrow Gang, although Bonnie and Clyde were a few miles away in Fort Smith when it happened. Clyde's brother, Buck Barrow, and W. D. Jones robbed the Brown Grocery in Fayetteville on June 23, 1933. While fleeing south on US 71, they shot and killed Alma's town marshal, Henry Humphrey.

Alma is located at the southern end of the Boston Mountain Scenic Loop, which is formed by I-540 and US 71, both National Scenic Byways.

For more information about the Spinach Festival and the town of Alma, call the Alma Area Chamber of Commerce at (479) 632-4127 or e-mail almachamber@centurytel.net.

Pickle Me Elmo
Atkins

Picklefest is a celebration held annually in Atkins, Arkansas, on the second Friday and Saturday in May. The festival honors a great Atkins industry that, alas, is no more. The Atkins Pickle Plant had been in business for fifty-six years before closing in 2002.

The town of Atkins was founded in the 1870s as a railroad town, but it became best known as the Pickle Capital of the World after the Goldsmith Pickle Company of Chicago established a pickle processing plant there in 1946. It was a dilly of a success. The pickle plant was the town's pride and joy, not to mention its biggest employer. At the height of its success, the plant's yearly production amounted to four million cases of pickled products and $50 million in sales. The name Atkins was synonymous with pickles.

The first Picklefest, held in 1991, became an overnight tradition. It featured musical entertainment, arts and crafts, and pageants, as well as contests to see who could eat the most pickles and drink the most pickle juice. Makes us green just thinking about it.

In 1983 Goldsmith sold the plant to Dean Foods; nineteen years later, Dean Foods closed the facility. It was a sad time for the people of Atkins, who had thought of the plant as part of the family. And what about the fate of Picklefest? How could they have the fest without the pickle? Organizers were in a pickle. But where there's a dill, there's a way. It was decided to have pickles shipped to Atkins, and because of the town's ingenuity and resiliency, the festival is still going strong today. One might think the public would have soured on the brine-drinking contest, but no; it too has survived.

A staple at Picklefest is the deep-fried pickle, a culinary treat con-cocted in 1963 by the late Bernell "Fatman" Austin. Austin owned a restaurant across US 64 from the pickle plant and came up with the idea for the fried pickle as a gimmick to drum up business. Poet Allen Ginsberg and novelist Norman Mailer both were said to have enjoyed the delicacy. Though Austin died in 1999, his family continues to provide fried pickles for Picklefest, using their secret family recipe. Is there any food we Southerners won't fry?

For more information about Picklefest, call the Atkins Chamber of Commerce at (479) 641-2000 or the Arkansas Department of Parks and Tourism at (888) 287-2757.

This Castle Is a Keeper

Beaver

A man's home is his castle. How many times have we heard that and wished it to be true? Let's face it; few of us are kings. Most of us are mere peons, and the only monarchs we will ever meet are of the butterfly variety. Smith Treuer may not be royalty, but his home is, quite literally, his castle—he calls it Castle Rogue's Manor.

In the mid-1990s Treuer bought a house and twenty acres near Beaver, Arkansas. He and his partner, Debbie Sederstrom, decided it would be the perfect place for a castle, so they set about creating one. Built on a bluff that was a limestone quarry over one hundred years ago, the castle is still a work in progress. Two guard towers and a cottage have been completed and offer all the modern amenities.

Members of Treuer's family were in the tree-farming business, so he appreciates the natural beauty of wood and has incorporated Arkansas red cedar and black walnut in the making of his castle. Born in Minnesota, Treuer has traveled extensively, and his experiences as a world traveler are reflected in the castle's various European and Asian architectural styles and decor. An aficionado of medieval times, he has possessions associated with that age, including a reproduction of an old English throne, a collection of daggers and swords, and paintings of jousting knights. Other unusual features and furnishings include a molded rhinoceros head, mirrored windows, and exotic gemstones inlaid in dragon sculptures.

The building of Castle Rogue's Manor has been an educational experience for Treuer. He has learned a lot about engineering and about adapting the ordinary to an extraordinary, oversize scale.

Although Treuer and Sederstrom live in the castle, they also rent it out for tours and weddings and donate the use of it for charitable fund-raisers. Information about rates is available online at www.rogues manor.com, which also allows the curious to take a virtual tour of the castle. Treuer's magnificent obsession overlooks the Little Golden Gate Bridge, Leatherwood Creek, and the White River–Table Rock Lake area.

Treuer owns a restaurant in the downtown historic district of Eureka Springs called Rogue's Manor at Sweet Spring. Sederstrom is the chef. Information about the restaurant is also available on the Web site.

For directions to Castle Rogue's Manor and to Rogue's Manor at Sweet Spring, call (800) 250-5827 or (479) 253-4911.

Chew on This for a While
Bentonville

Bentonville native Randy Ober was living in California in the early 1980s when he heard about a tobacco-spitting contest being held in the nearby town of Calico.

"I watched it," he recalled, "and said, 'Heck, I could do that.' The first year I entered, I broke the world record. They put me in the Guinness book, and then I was a celebrity."

While other would-be champs were just plugging away, Ober went on to become a seven-time champion, setting a record in the competition with a spitting distance of 47 feet, 7 inches. He broke his own record with a spit of 53 feet, 3 inches when he accepted a challenge by the Los Angeles Rams during a charity fund-raiser.

Interviewed in 2008, Ober explained the key to his success.

"I would roll my wads up and dry them out on the windowsill, so they would be real hard. They wouldn't come apart that way. Most of [the spitters] would just pull a wad out of a pack and press it together and spit it; and heck, it would just fly apart when they'd spit."

Although Ober was raised in the middle of the Mojave Desert, he remained an Arkie at heart and returned to his home state in 1994. He gave up the life of a spitter when he got saved and became a deacon in his church.

"I didn't think it was a real good image for me," he said. "I don't do any spitting anymore. Heck, I'm sixty-two-years-old."

Still, when spitting is in your blood, temptations do arise.

"I've been wanting to get into that cherry seed–spitting thing," Ober confessed. "They do like 60 feet. Heck, I used to spit tobacco that far."

A Hasty Withdrawal
Bentonville

On June 5, 1893, Henry Starr and his cohorts rode into Bentonville to rob the Peoples Bank. Starr and Frank Cheney arrived first, driving a buggy with extra horses tied behind it. They waited for their accomplices in an alley south of the bank. Shortly, Kid Wilson, Link Cumplin, and two other gang members nonchalantly drifted into town and joined Starr and Cheney in the alley. Leaving one man with the horses, the rest of the heavily armed gang headed for the bank. Starr, Cheney, and Wilson went inside, while Link Cumplin took up his position out front.

Framed by two white iron columns, Cumplin turned to the square and shouted, "Clear the streets!" Then he started shooting, first up one side of the town square and then down the other. He alternated weapons, using a Winchester, a high-powered hunting rifle, and even a six-shooter. Though he held the town at bay for a while, more than half a dozen armed citizens soon stormed the square.

Only minutes had passed since Starr had entered the bank. He held three employees against a wall at gunpoint, while Kid Wilson emptied the cash tills. Frank Cheney ordered a cashier into the vault, telling him to open a safe. The clerk took out part of the money and then slammed the door, saying that was all there was. Cheney pulled a knife and slashed the clerk, who quickly reopened the safe.

A sniper's bullet shattered one of the plate-glass windows, and Cumplin yelled, "It's getting hot out here!"

The robbers gathered the bank officials around them as shields and marched out. They found Cumplin so badly wounded he could barely stand. The hostages scattered as the robbers fought their way down the street. When they reached the alley, they mounted up and rode west. Once they reached safety, they counted their loot, which tallied only $11,000.

Link Cumplin was, in Starr's words, "shot to rags." He had lost one eye, and one arm was shot through twice. Besides that, he was wounded in eight other places. Miraculously he survived, only to die a few months later in the Klondike. Cheney and another gang member also died within the year. Death spared Starr for another twenty-eight years.

The old bank building, now an office complex, is located in the town square off US 71 in Bentonville.

★ ★

Cosmic Cavern
Berryville

Whether you're interested in odd biological specimens or unusual geological formations or just plain ol' nature at its weirdest, Cosmic Cavern at Berryville is sure to intrigue you. The name seems to be a contradiction in terms (outer space versus inner space), but it sounds much better than the first alliterative choice, Claustrophobic Cave. Discovered in 1845, the cave is one of the top-ten show caves in the nation. It has two lakes, and divers have never found the bottom of either one.

Fifty years ago South Lake was stocked with trout, and the fish still thrive there, although some are blind albinos. Ozarks blind cave salamanders also live in Cosmic Cavern. These are animals, not blues musicians. Though the cavern is well lit, tour guides sometimes turn out the lights to heighten the spelunking experience. You get the salamander's point of view, so to speak.

The cave has a constant 62-degree temperature but feels warmer due to high humidity. A walking tour is quite comfortable and easy, and knowledgeable guides offer fascinating information about the various cave formations, including stalactites, stalagmites, and flow-stone. Before we visited Cosmic Cavern, we didn't know a cave from a hole in the ground.

Helictites are the contortionists of cave formations, bending and twisting in gravity-defying fashion. The helictites and the hollow tubes known as soda straws adorn a section of the cave called Silent Splendor. Often transparent, the formations add to the already sur-realistic quality of the surroundings. Although the longest soda straw on record (found in Mexico) is over 29 feet long, one of the straws in the Silent Splendor room at Cosmic Cavern measures an impressive 9 feet.

Cosmic Cavern also offers Wild Cave Tours for the more rugged and adventurous. Hiking boots and hard hats are among the required accessories.

Cosmic Cavern is located at 6386 AR 21 North in Berryville, almost halfway between Eureka Springs, Arkansas, and Branson, Missouri. The cave is open year-round, closing for Thanksgiving and Christmas. For current admission prices and other information, call (870) 749-2298.

The salamanders that live in Cosmic Cavern can't enjoy the beauty of their home because they are blind.
ARKANSAS DEPARTMENT OF PARKS AND TOURISM

The Little Golden Gate Bridge

If you visit the small town of Beaver (population 100), you may leave your heart there. Situated in the scenic Ozark Mountains where Table Rock Lake meets the White River, Beaver has something in common with Tony Bennett's beloved city by the Bay.

In 1949 the Pioneer Construction Company of Malvern completed building a scaled-down version of the mighty bridge in San Francisco. Dubbed the Little Golden Gate, the one-lane bridge is the only suspension bridge in Arkansas still open to vehicular traffic. It was named to the National Register of Historic Places in April 1990.

Popular with amateur and professional photographers alike, the Little Golden Gate was featured in the movie *Elizabethtown,* starring Orlando Bloom and Kirsten Dunst. Though some folks think the yellow paint could be toned down a little bit, residents in the area love the bridge and the fanciful quality it adds to its surroundings. The Beaver Garden Club has been instrumental in beautifying the grounds near the bridge, sometimes planting wildflowers to grace the landscape.

The wooden bridge replaced a concrete bridge that had been there since 1926. Before that, a ferry had carried people back and forth across the river. People on nearby Holiday Island rely on the Little Golden Gate to connect them to the urban area of Fayetteville. The average number of cars using the bridge each day was 660 in 2005.

When catastrophic flooding hit Arkansas in the spring of 2008, fears were that the bridge was doomed. It was literally floating on the swollen river with debris stacked up against it, making it truly a bridge over troubled water. Locals fretted they'd have to put Old

Yeller down, but to everyone's relief, the Arkansas Highway Department brought in an engineer and saved the bridge so that commuters could continue to use it on a limited basis.

The Little Golden Gate Bridge is located on AR 187, 11 miles north of Eureka Springs.

This bridge over the water has had its share of troubles.
DUANE KEPFORD

Boles Boulders
Boles

They lie like great beached whales, these gigantic slabs of rock—different in age and composition from any of the local shale and sandstone outcrops and many miles south of any similar known strata. Named for the little town in Scott County, near Arkansas's western border, the Boles Boulders were a bona fide geological enigma when first discovered by state geologist H. D. Miser in the late 1920s. Such rocks are called erratics because they don't match the surrounding strata. Composed of limestone and dolomite, the largest boulder

An example of erratic boulders near Boles, Arkansas.
ARKANSAS GEOLOGICAL SURVEY, 2009

measures 110 feet by 195 feet. Another one is 50 feet by 369 feet. Their combined weight is, no doubt, hundreds of tons.

Miser speculated at the time that the giant rocks had been rafted on icebergs from Texas during the Carboniferous period. Later, as more evidence accumulated, geologists theorized the boulders had formed in the sea that once covered ancient Arkansas. The boulders broke off the edge of the continental shelf in what is now Crawford County and slid downward, coming to rest in mud at the base of the continental slope.

Erratics have been found in a line through Scott, Perry, and Pulaski Counties, running parallel to the edge of the old North American continental slope. Some geologists think a large section of Pinnacle Mountain in Pulaski County is an erratic. Some smaller erratic boulders and pebbles found in the area around Lake Sylvia in Perry County are composed of extremely old and rare materials, some of which are of volcanic origin—from volcanoes that have long since vanished from the geological record. Others contain rare fossils found nowhere else. Fossilized fossils, if you will.

To see the Boles Boulders for yourself, go south from Boles on US 71. The boulders are on the right side of the highway about 1.6 miles west-southwest of Y City.

"Berth" of a New World Record
Booneville

In 1996 Mona MacDonald Tippins set out to break the world record for most unduplicated miles traveled by train. The existing record was 76,485 miles. Some folks thought her motive was loco, but it was her dream to be in *Guinness World Records*.

The spunky grandmother of four from Booneville traveled throughout Europe, the United States, and Canada. Anywhere trains went, she went. Contending with all kinds of obstacles, she rolled with the punches. A couple of those punches came from a gang of neo-Nazis who blackened one of her eyes. She was mistaken for a spy and,

★ ★

more than once, mistaken for a prostitute. She explained in her book *Tomorrow the Train: Journey to the World Record,* "Youth is not a prerequisite for being a prostitute in Europe."

Mona narrowly escaped train wrecks and endured harsh weather but remained on track. In February 1997 she surpassed the old record while riding the rails in Russia. She had gone through thirty-three countries and once traveled on nineteen trains in thirty-eight hours. Her final, official tally was 79,841 rail miles. She had ridden her way into the record book.

The Battling Beetles of Bug Scuffle

Bug Scuffle

Autumn in the Ozarks is a bonanza of beauty, the hills and hollows ablaze with vibrant hues. Some tourists, however, might argue that the vivid fall foliage takes a backseat to the colorful place names that abound in the region. A double-decker outhouse at Booger Hollow is a great photo-op, though the trading post is now closed. Old Naked Joe and Cow-Faced Hill are also in the area. Hogeye, which is a corruption of the Biblical name Haggai, is in Washington County, not far from the Bug Scuffle Church and Cemetery.

Going to church has always been an important part of life in Arkansas, especially in the small rural communities. In earlier days, church buildings themselves served as gathering places for quilting bees, town meetings, and other social functions. Wherever there were a couple of houses and a business or two, there was bound to be a church.

When the Butterfield Stagecoach Line established a station along its route through northwest Arkansas, a church was also erected there. One day, as the story goes, a circuit-riding preacher was giving a particularly boring sermon, so some of the male parishioners stepped outside. They started watching two dung beetles (also known as tumble tackies) that were fighting over a wad of manure. Being sporting men, the parishioners wagered on the outcome of the bug scuffle.

Though Bug Scuffle cannot be found on any contemporary maps, the church and cemetery are still in existence. The church has about forty active members, and the cemetery has a number of not-so-active members and still accepts new tenants. To get to Bug Scuffle Church, take AR 156 from West Fork to Hogeye and then AR 265 south to Strickler. Turn right onto CR 216 (Bug Scuffle Road) and go 4 miles. The church is on the left.

Stone Walls Do Not a Fortress Make
Canehill

One of Arkansas's most famous stone ruins was first described in 1806, when Daniel Boone, then a spry seventy-two-year-old, visited a place called Black Hill, now known as Canehill, in Washington County. The 6-mile-long hill was the site of several large springs. Atop the hill stood the ruins of a stone enclosure covering one-half acre of land. Made of crude masonry, the structure encompassed several major springs and contained carved stone basins of varying sizes and shapes. Growing through one wall was an oak tree 4 feet thick, indicating centuries of neglect.

The author of an 1854 newspaper item wrote, "In vain do we ask who built that fort? There is no voice to respond, no history to clear away the obscurity that hangs over the whole subject. It is evident that a people far more civilized than the red man once lived here."

What was its purpose? Who built it? It was located along a trade route between the large Native American ceremonial centers in Spiro, Oklahoma, and Cahokia, once North America's largest city. Some sources say local tribes held yearly councils within it and considered it a sacred site.

One thing is certain: Gathered and stacked, the stones of the walls were treated in frontier fashion as an easy source of building material rather than as an archaeological landmark. Today it's hard to fix the site's exact location. By 1832 only a portion of the structure remained, and by 1930 it had been completely leveled.

State Symbols

During the 1837 session of the Arkansas Legislature, two lawmakers squared off in a knife fight on the House floor. One died. Since then, cooler heads have prevailed, even during the naming of state symbols, such as the state bird (mockingbird) and state gem (diamond). Nominees for state historic cooking vessel generated some heat, but the Dutch oven won without blood being shed. In a bipartisan compromise, the tomato was declared both the state fruit and the state vegetable. In 1997 the Stuttgart soil series was named state soil. Yep, we're even proud of our dirt. Can't have tomatoes without it.

The Devil Made Him Do It
Centerton

In 2007 Bruce Kent Williams resigned as mayor of Centerton, Arkansas, after it was revealed that he was really Don LaRose, an Indiana preacher who had been missing since 1980. Turns out, the man had a history of disappearing.

In 1975 he vanished from Maine, New York, but three months later he was discovered living under the identity of Williams, a man who had died in 1958. LaRose/Williams told the news media he was abducted by Satanists, brainwashed with an electric gizmo/memory zapper, and programmed to believe he was Williams. In 1980 LaRose vanished again and resumed his life as Williams. He became a radio announcer in northwest Arkansas, remarried, and became mayor of Centerton in 2001. The charade ended when the LaRose family traced him through a Web site he had created and on which he had recounted his bizarre double life.

After losing his mayoral job, he wrote three books and received invitations to speak at churches and religious functions. He denied ever saying he was abducted by Satanists and thought his kidnappers might have been linked to organized crime. He explained that he developed his Web site as a precaution, lest he be abducted again.

Nary a Prairie So Rare
Charleston

When most of us think of prairies, we conjure up images of the Old West, but once there were a number of prairies here in Arkansas, too. The Grand Prairie covered 1,000 square miles in the Stuttgart area, but only a small portion of it remains today. The Old Conway Prairie, described by Thomas Nuttall in 1819, covered 2,500 acres of lowland in what became Faulkner County. It extended from Cadron Ridge north of Conway to Donnell Ridge in the south. Today a

Chigger heaven.
ARKANSAS DEPARTMENT OF PARKS AND TOURISM

remnant of five acres remains within the Jewel Moore Nature Reserve on the University of Central Arkansas's campus in Conway.

These prairies grew up over areas once covered by ancient lakes. The thick clay deposits that formed in the riverbeds created shale or clay subsoils that drained poorly, thus making it difficult for large trees or shrubs to develop healthy root systems. This enabled grasses, with their shallow root systems, to take hold and flourish, creating savannas in a state that is usually heavily forested. Before the arrival of Europeans, these open areas were maintained by fire, either through lightning strikes or by human design. Native Americans periodically burned these areas in early spring to destroy invasive species and to attract big game.

To get some idea of what Arkansas looked like before most of its prairie was plowed under or turned into subdivisions and strip malls, visit Cherokee Prairie Natural Area near Charleston, Arkansas. If you love grass in the pre–Summer of Love sense of the word, you'll really dig this. (*Note:* Literal digging is prohibited.) The beautiful 566-acre site is one of the largest patches of tallgrass prairie still existing in the state. It contains rare wildflowers, such as the grass-pink orchid and the yellow puccoon. The natural area is about 2 miles north of Charleston at the intersection of AR 217 and AR 60.

It's a Treat to Beat Your Feet on a Johnson County Rock
Clarksville

Human footprints laid down in 200-million-year-old sandstone?

On a slab of local sandstone near the town of Clarksville in Johnson County, there are marks that appear to be three human footprints made by two distinct individuals. The two larger ones look like those of a barefoot man, while the single smaller print appears to be that of a child or woman's stockinged foot.

According to a statement by John Garrett, a schoolteacher named Billy Fritz found the prints on the Garrett family farm around 1832. At one time the prints were thought to have been made in soft

* *

sand that later hardened into rock. Modern experts we consulted considered this possibility unlikely. In the words of a Forest Service employee, "It's just some ol' carving somebody made on a rock."

Shortly after discovery of the prints, the Clarksville newspaper received an anonymous letter that contained a poem the paper later printed. It was purported to be an old Osage legend, a just-so tale explaining the origin of the prints. According to the poem, a French explorer and an Osage princess met and fell in love. An Osage brave rejected by the princess seized the Frenchman, forced him up on a large stone, and began torturing him. The princess fired a golden arrow that struck the rock and caused an earthquake. She jumped up beside her lover, and their footprints were spontaneously created. The Indians took this as a sign they should leave the lovers alone, and everybody lived happily ever after.

The footprints are probably genuine Indian pictographs. The poem appears to be a quaint bit of nineteenth century fake lore created by the mystery poet in order to tether his homespun myth to a particular location. If so, it worked; though it may be humbuggery, it remains afoot in Clarksville.

Those interested in reading the full text of the legend should see "Mysterious Footprints in a Rock at Clarksville" in the fourth volume of the 1942 edition (Number 4) of the *Arkansas Historical Quarterly* or Fred W. Allsopp's *Folklore of Romantic Arkansas*.

Noah's Arkansas

Erbie

In 1903 Waldo Conard was working on his farm in Newton County near Erbie when he decided to explore a sinkhole on his property in hopes of finding zinc ore or lead. He started digging, and as he dug he began to uncover bones. Ten feet down he discovered a fang about 4 inches long. He showed it to a partner, who mailed it along with some of the bones to the American Museum of Natural History in New York. The items came to the attention of paleontologist

Barnum Brown, who was famous for being the first to discover a T.
rex skeleton.

The following spring, Brown arrived in Arkansas and, with the help
of Conard and a few local men, began excavating the site where
Conard had found the fossils. They dug a pit 12 feet long, 7 feet
wide, and 25 feet deep. It was a lot of work, but the reward was
great. Their digging paid off in spades. Mother Nature had used the
fissure as the final resting place for more than sixty-five species of
mammals, birds, reptiles, and amphibians. Three more similar places
in the Buffalo River area would be discovered later. These repositories had been collecting valuable relics for 100,000 years. The caches
included the remains of musk oxen and other Arctic tundra animals
as well as extinct species such as the mammoth, mastodon, and dire
wolf. Also roaming Arkansas and surrounding areas in prehistoric
times were ground sloths the size of grizzly bears, giant short-faced
bears (as tall as 12 feet when standing on their hind legs), and lions
that were larger than African lions and related to the modern jaguar.
Other early Arkansas animals included tapirs, horses, camels, ante-
lopes, peccaries, prairie dogs, giant armadillos, and an extinct species
of cat resembling the cheetah.

The big tooth Conard found was from a previously unknown species of saber-toothed tiger: *Smilodontopsis conardi.* And that, as they
say, is the whole tooth.

The Conard Fissure is located just outside the park boundaries
of the Buffalo National River. From Jasper go north on AR 7 for 3.4
miles. Turn left onto CR 79/Erbie Campground Road and go 6.5
miles. Turn left onto CR 57 and continue 0.7 mile to Erbie.

From Chicken House to *House Beautiful*
Eureka Springs

Some homemakers like to shake things up by rearranging the furniture while their husbands are at work. A friend of ours paints the
rooms in her house more often than we change our sheets. Her

husband's a good sport and never sees red, even when it's staring him in the face.

Elise Fiovanti Quigley was ready for a change in 1943. One day after seeing her husband off to work, she tore their house down and moved their children and belongings into the chicken house. It was her way of saying, "I want my dream house, and I want it now."

Her husband, a model of understanding, set about building the home his wife had designed. When completed, it had thirty-two windows and a 4-foot-wide glassed-in space between the inner and

A real fixer-upper.
ARKANSAS DEPARTMENT OF PARKS AND TOURISM

★ ★

outer walls where she planted tropical plants and other greenery that reached as high as the second-story ceiling.

She covered the exterior of the house with a rock collection she had been accumulating since childhood. A large aquarium was built into the living room wall. Outside, her perennial garden included 400 different varieties of flowers. She added a touch of whimsy by creating fourteen bottle trees made from her husband's bottle collection. She did not drive him to drink. On the contrary, he drove her wherever she wanted to go because she never learned to drive a car. Who would want to go anywhere if you had a home like hers?

Elise died in 1984, but her dream home is still as beautiful as it was when she herself enjoyed its natural splendor. Her descendants live in the house now, and they allow tours between April 1 and October 31. They're closed Sunday and Thursday.

Listed on the National Register of Historic Places, the home has been featured on HGTV, which is very fitting. If she were alive today, Elise would be the network's biggest fan and would probably have her own show.

Quigley's Castle is located 4 miles south of Eureka Springs on AR 23. For more information call (479) 253-8311, e-mail quigleyc@ arkansas.net, or visit www.quigleyscastle.com.

The Truth Is Out There
Eureka Springs

Every April an out-of-this-world event takes place in Eureka Springs. The Ozark UFO Conference is a three-day convention featuring speakers who discuss various aspects of UFO-related phenomena, such as crop circles, alien abductions, and UFO sightings. They're friendly folks. Walk up to any of them and say, "Take me to your leader," and they will introduce you to Lou Farish, the conference organizer for more than twenty years.

Farish said that no one thing drew him to the study of UFOs, but he has been interested in the subject ever since he was dropped off by the mother ship several decades ago. He ran a UFO news clipping service for thirty years, and his antennae still go up at the mention of strange and unusual occurrences.

In a telephone interview, we asked Farish if he thinks the government covers up UFO activity. He said he was inclined to think so.

"Is the government going to disclose things?" he asked. "I doubt it, because there's too much to disclose—and they're responsible for a lot of it."

At that point, the line went dead.

UFO sightings in Arkansas have been numerous, and a few Arkansans have even had close encounters. Whitley Strieber, author of *Communion,* said he was first abducted by aliens as he rode a train through Arkansas.

An account of an older visitation goes back to a rainy night in 1897. Constable John Sumpter Jr. and Deputy Sheriff John McLemore were looking for cattle rustlers in Garland County when they encountered an airship that gave off a brilliant bright light. After the 60-foot-long, cigar-shaped craft landed, two men and a woman emerged from it. Dressed in familiar attire of the era, the threesome offered to take the lawmen aboard the vessel and carry them to a place "where it was not raining." The officers declined and went on their way, as did the strangers.

It's impossible to say how many people have had experiences with UFOs.

As Farish said, "People see things all the time but rarely ever talk about them."

For information about the annual Ozark UFO Conference, call (501) 354-2558.

★ ★

Wind Chime of Mass Distraction
Eureka Springs

In a city that has been listed in *Ripley's Believe It or Not!* nine times, you might think it would be difficult to stand out and make your mark, but artist Ranaga Farbiarz succeeded in doing just that—and in a very big way. The city is Eureka Springs, and Farbiarz's contribution to the local collection of curiosities is a tuned musical wind chime that measures 35 feet, 10 inches tall and weighs 653 pounds. *Guinness World Records* has listed it as the largest tuned wind chime in the world. The previous record holder was a wind chime in Lakeside, California, which was a mere 16 feet, 8 inches tall.

The wind chime was the inspired product of Farbiarz's midlife crisis. He dedicated the wind chime to his late father, Ignatz Farbiarz. Both of Ranaga's parents survived the Holocaust and emigrated from Poland to the United States in 1951.

An important distinction must be made between the tuned musical wind chime and the common wind chime that you find on porches everywhere. With mathematical precision, Farbiarz designed and created the giant wind chime with perfect resonance in mind. It has six pipes made from thick aluminum tubing. The chime's longest and shortest pipes are an octave apart, and since it is tuned to an Oriental pentatonic scale, each octave has five pitches. The longest pipe is 20 feet long and has a deep, rich tone.

For purposes of documentation, it was first hoisted by a bucket truck on November 4, 2004, to the bough of a mighty, 100-foot-tall oak tree, but the wind chime can now be seen hanging from an interior tower at the Celestial Windz Harmonic Bizaar, 381 AR 23 South, Eureka Springs. The Bizaar is billed as "an International Gallery of Contemporary and Primitive Artifacts." Celestial Windz, with its bizarre bazaar spelling, is a trade name for Farbiarz's merchandise of arts, crafts, collectibles, and antiques. One thing is certain—nobody's going to catch any Zs around what Farbiarz calls the "wind chime of mass distraction."

The bells! The bells!
ARKANSAS DEPARTMENT OF PARKS AND TOURISM

★ ★

The Shining, Southern Style
Eureka Springs

Eureka Springs has not one but two famous hotels: the Crescent, built in 1886 as a resort for the upper crust, and the Basin Park Hotel, which opened in 1905. The Basin Park is unique because its position against the side of a mountain allows ground-level access to all floors. Although owned by the same people, the two hotels differ in their pasts and personalities.

The Crescent is the elegant grande dame with a sad past. Norman Baker, a former vaudevillian from Iowa, bought the hotel in 1937 and turned it into a hospital where he claimed to cure cancer patients.

The Crescent Hotel, where you may be mooned by a ghost.
ARKANSAS DEPARTMENT OF PARKS AND TOURISM

★ ★

Baker was a fraud, and because his cure was just water, patients died. The Basin Park, on the other hand, is a swinger with a shady past. In the 1940s and early 1950s, the illegal gambling parlor there attracted mobsters, and the place was raided in 1955. Both hotels have been renovated and share rave reviews from guests. They also share a reputation for being haunted.

The Crescent was featured on Syfy's *Ghost Hunters,* where viewers learned about the many spooky happenings that people have experienced there. Guests have reported strange noises and sensations, as well as actual apparitions. The most famous resident ghost is Michael, a young Irishman who fell to his death during construction of the hotel. His body landed in the area later designated as Room 218, and it is there that his prankish spirit is said to disturb guests as he rummages about for a bottle of Guinness stout. A medicinal spirit of a different sort is the phantom nurse who has been seen pushing a hospital gurney down the corridor.

The Basin Park Hotel is reportedly haunted by a little girl in a yellow dress, a pretty blue-eyed blond young woman, and a cowboy looking for some action.

The two hotels, known as the "Paranormal Pair," are on the itinerary of the Eureka Ghost Tours (479-253-6800). Check it out and check into the Crescent or the Basin Park. No need to bring friends. You won't be lonely.

Hole-Y Water
Eureka Springs

Blue Spring has been a source of wonder for more than 200 years and the biggest boon to the local tourist economy since Daniel Boone, who camped here in 1804. Blue Spring is the second largest spring in Arkansas and one of the largest on Earth. For almost one hundred years, the spring supplied power to assorted mills. Native American artifacts found there date back ten thousand years. The spring flows at a rate of thirty-eight million gallons daily and derives

★ ★

its name from its crystal blue waters that stay a constant 54 degrees year-round. The spring's pool is 70 feet in diameter, funneling down to a 3-foot opening, 20 feet below the surface. It has been plumbed to a depth of 510 feet without touching the bottom.

As far back as the Long Expedition, people have speculated that the source of the Ozark Plateau's many springs was an underground river flowing off the Rocky Mountains. A plaque near the spring states that its source is glacial meltwater from the Pacific Northwest, a claim that most geologists find unlikely. Nonetheless, the species of blind cave fish found living in the spring's lower regions was

A limpid pool of blue.
ARKANSAS DEPARTMENT OF PARKS AND TOURISM

identified by the University of Oklahoma as a northern sculpin. A native of Canada, eh? The spring's normally clear water was muddied by sediment following the great Alaskan earthquake of 1964. Another odd characteristic is the rising and falling of the pool's surface depth in conjunction with the ocean's tides.

Thanks to modern technology, divers have been learning much about Blue Spring in recent years, but the mystical allure of the ancient beauty remains.

Blue Spring is part of the Blue Spring Heritage Center, located on US 62 about 5.5 miles west of Eureka Springs. For information about hours of operation and the price of admission, call (479) 253-9244.

It's such a serene place, you'll never be blue.

Lord, He's Big!
Eureka Springs

Gerald L. K. Smith was publisher of *The Cross and the Flag,* a monthly magazine for racists and anti-Semites. Critics called him "Little Hitler."

From his summer home in Eureka Springs, Smith began considering his legacy in the early 1960s. The result was Christ of the Ozarks (COTO), a supersize Savior perched like a seven-story traffic cop on Magnetic Mountain overlooking Eureka.

Emmet Sullivan, the credited sculptor, claimed the "Christ would be realistic as distinguished from modernistic in design . . . I don't go for all those straight lines. I go for realism." Whatever he may have meant, the final result is more like realism in the imaginary sense. While Smith compared it to the works of Michelangelo, one art critic charitably referred to it as a milk carton with a tennis ball stuck on top. Some locals have called the statue "Gumby Jesus." Dedicated in 1965, it weighs 1,000 tons and towers 67 feet tall, just short of the 70 feet that would have required the builders to mount an aircraft warning beacon on its head. Sullivan later did life-size sculptures for the now-defunct amusement park called Dinosaur World near Beaver

Hey, man, how big was that fish you caught?
ARKANSAS DEPARTMENT OF PARKS AND TOURISM

Lake, where he brought the same attention to detail that he gave to the COTO project. Photos of the T. rex figure there show its legs bending in the wrong direction.

Smith died in 1976 and was buried at the foot of his seven-story tombstone. An estimated 500,000 people visit COTO annually. It was a slow day when we were there, though. We asked a young sightseer for his opinion of the icon. He suggested adding more cement to the nose, mounting a gigantic pair of wire frames on it, and rechristening it Lennon of the Ozarks. Ah, can a Yoko statue be far behind?

To visit Christ of the Ozarks, go about 2 miles from Eureka Springs on US 62 East to Passion Play Road. COTO is open 24/7. Admission is free. All you need is love.

Texaco Bungalow
Eureka Springs

Here's a great destination if you've always wanted to sleep in a gas station. And who hasn't? The Texaco Bungalow in Eureka Springs is a vintage service station turned cozy cottage. Whimsy and comfort blend together for an enjoyable stay. Actually there are two units, the bungalow and the bungalette. If you're of a certain age and remember full-service gas stations, the front of the building will look very familiar. It was the drive-through part of the station where motorists got their gas. Now it's a sunny sitting area. The former garage bay became the bungalette.

In the first half of the twentieth century, mom-and-pop grocery stores often had a couple of gas pumps out front and an oil rack off to the side or back. Motorists filling up their tanks would refresh themselves with Coke, RC Cola, Dr. Pepper, or that most fondly remembered Southern soda pop, Grapette, which, by the way, was bottled in Malvern, Arkansas. Coke was king, but the company's familiar red cooler with its white lettering kept all brands equally chilled. The drinks were as identifiable by their unique bottle shapes as by their logos and names.

Automotive memorabilia from that bygone era are among the decorative features of the Texaco Bungalow. One particularly cute and clever idea is the use of original gas pump handles as doorknobs. It's this attention to detail that makes a stay at the Texaco Bungalow such a delightful and memorable experience.

The Texaco Bungalow is located at 77 Mountain Street (on the

The Battle-ax of Hatchet Hall

Imagine you are enjoying a leisurely pint in your favorite watering hole when in marches a fifty-year-old woman dressed in black. At 6 feet and 175 pounds, she's an imposing figure. She begins singing hymns, then takes out a hatchet and starts destroying the place. No, it isn't a case of the DTs. It's Carry Nation, evangelistic vandal.

Born in Kentucky in 1846, Carry (aka Carrie) was the daughter of wealthy plantation owners George and Mary Moore. She did not have a close relationship with her parents, but that wasn't necessarily bad. Mrs. Moore suffered mental problems, laboring under the delusion that she was lady-in-waiting to Queen Victoria. Eventually she grew tired of waiting and believed herself actually to be Queen Victoria.

Carry married twice, the first time to an alcoholic, but it wasn't until 1900 that Carry started her campaign against the demon rum. Taking hatchet in hand, she visited her wrath upon drinking establishments, smashing windows, mirrors, and of course the bottles and barrels of booze. She nicknamed her hatchets Faith, Hope, and corner of Mountain and White Streets) in Eureka Springs. For information about rates and reservations, call (888) 253-8093 between 8:00 a.m. and 8:00 p.m. Sunday through Saturday or e-mail the hostess, Melissa Greene, at mrsgreene@cox.net. Also check out their Web site at www.texacobungalow.com.

Charity. When she wasn't wielding one of the three virtues, she was giving speeches on the pros of Prohibition. After the lectures, she signed autographs and sold miniature hatchets as souvenirs.

Carry's war on alcohol overshadowed her hatred of fraternal orders, tobacco, coffee, tea, short skirts, corsets, artistic renderings of nudity, dancing, chewing gum, and foreign foods, making her the death of any party.

In 1908 Carry moved (where else?) to a party town, Eureka Springs. She named her house Hatchet Hall and shared it with boarders. She also established a school there called National College. On January 13, 1911, Carry A. Nation was giving her usual temperance oratory at Basin Circle Park in Eureka Springs when she collapsed on stage. She died five months later.

Hatchet Hall was rescued from the wrecking ball in 1935 by artists Louis and Elsie Freund. From 1940 until 1951 it was the Summer School of the Ozarks and was for many years a museum. The building still stands today at 35 Steele Street but is not open to the public. A spring bearing Carry's name is located across the street and is a nice spot for picnics.

★ ★

Trivia

The city of Wichita, Kansas, built a fountain near the site of one of Carry's earliest tirades. A few years later the fountain was destroyed by a runaway beer truck.

Creative Science
Eureka Springs

The Museum of Earth History presents the universe's history based on a literal interpretation of the Book of Genesis. Displays show events or places from Bible history. We couldn't recall any mention of the ice age in the Bible, but why quibble?

In the first exhibit, called "The Creation," we see Adam and Eve strolling through Eden, which looks like a Jurassic nudist park. It also contains the skull of an impressive T. rex named Stan and a large two-legged dinosaur skeleton. "If Eden seems a little less idyllic with a T. rex roaming loose," the guide assured us, "the biblical dinosaurs were vegetarians." But from the looks of the teeth on that skull, there must have been some tense, sleepless nights when the salad bar ran low.

Next comes "The Curse," as in the fall of man, not in the Midol sense. The display features a 17-foot-long T. rex relative against the background of a maroon Day-Glo, Tijuana-style airbrushed mural of a volcano. The fall is the high point. It's all downhill after that.

The Great Flood mural intrigued us. We thought an explanation of exactly how to fit every animal on earth into a space slightly smaller than a modern aircraft carrier might actually be useful, seeing as how we can barely pack a suitcase.

Later a visitor groused about paying the museum's property taxes. "It's a conflict of interest," he said, "giving financial incentives to

The Museum of Earth History, where passion plays a big role.
ARKANSAS DEPARTMENT OF PARKS AND TOURISM

★ ★

a private group that's undermining the public's trust in the educational system."

Having slept through a history class or two, we seem to recall that the church once had the final say on the truthiness of all educational matters, although it escapes us at the moment what those days were called. Oh, yeah . . . the Dark Ages.

Open from April 29 through December 23, the Museum of Earth History is located at 935 Passion Play Road in Eureka Springs. For hours of operation and other information, call (866) 566-3558.

The Ends Justify the Means
Eureka Springs

Why is a caboose like a kumquat? Because you can use either word in a lame joke and still get a laugh. This despite the important role cabooses have played in history.

The word "caboose" comes from the Dutch "kabuis," or ship's galley; the German equivalent is "kabuse." The first cabooses in the 1800s were little more than flatcars with wooden shacks on top, but they served their purpose, which was to protect the train crew from the elements. Cabooses evolved into living quarters and were also a safety feature because the brakeman could spot trouble in areas that the engineer could not see.

Livingston Junction Cabooses in Eureka Springs have given cabooses another assignment—as tourist lodging. They are authentically restored cabooses with all the amenities of modern accommodations.

Caboose #101 is the youngster, built by Burlington Northern Railroad in 1967. It feels a lot roomier than you would think a caboose could be. The space includes a sitting area in the original cupola and a queen-size bed where you can prop up and thumb through the railroad books provided for your reading pleasure. And it doesn't take a trained eye to enjoy the old photographs and other railroad memorabilia decorating the caboose.

★ ★

Caboose #102 was manufactured in 1930 by the Chicago, Burlington, and Quincy Railroad. Riveted rather than welded together, the caboose has beautiful pine paneling and maple flooring. The

The caboose's caboose with a bumper sticker reading, "Railroaders love to couple up."

company operated in the Midwest and West and called itself "the Way of the Zephyrs," a slogan that's still appropriate today—the sleeping accommodations are as restful as a hammock rocked by a gentle breeze.

Bringing up the rear is Caboose #103, the "Frisco," which is decked out in Old West fashion, with lanterns and whiskey barrels used as attractive accents. It lets you get a taste of the Old West without actually having to rough it. Built in 1926, it's one of only a few wooden cabooses still in existence. Original cupola seats convert to daybeds and are quite comfortable, even for those of us with our own wide cabooses.

Overlooking picturesque Livingston Hollow, Livingston Junction Cabooses are located at 927 CR 222 in Eureka Springs. For information about availability and rates, call (888) 87-TRAIN (87246) or e-mail cabooses@ipa.net.

Vamoose to the caboose and let loose!

Venom Within 'Im
Fayetteville

Dr. William J. Baerg liked bugs. He enjoyed studying insects and kept arachnids as pets. Entomology was an easy career choice for him. It certainly had legs: He was head of the entomology department at the University of Arkansas in Fayetteville for thirty-one years.

In 1922 he conducted a study about the effects of black widow spider bites on humans. After first using lab rats as test subjects, he then experimented on himself by allowing a black widow to sink her fangs into him. Time crawled as Baerg recorded his symptoms over the next five days. A "very faint" pain became "rather severe" with "breathing and speech . . . spasmodic." After a few days' recuperation, however, he was back to normal, and the knowledge gained from his ordeal took the sting out of it.

He repeated the experiment with other arachnids over the years, always surviving without any lingering side effects. On the contrary, he lived to the ripe old age of ninety-four. Almost makes us want to stick a hand in a jarful of spiders. Almost. It's a pity Baerg didn't live even longer; he could have seen his work discussed on the World Wide Web.

They Came Out of the Sky!

Fayetteville

At about 4:00 a.m. on February 17, 1930, two Arkansans were driving a team of horses along a country road near the town of Beach Grove. Suddenly everything around them lit up brighter than midday. In the sky, coming at high speed from the northeast, they saw a ball of fire with a long tail. It passed above them and went over the horizon to the southeast. As the men continued on their way, they heard a tremendous explosion and felt a shock wave, like an earthquake. It knocked the horses off their feet. A loud roar reverberated along the object's flight path.

Thus goes an eyewitness account of a meteor crash. The surviving debris came to be known as the Paragould Meteorite. A farmer named W. H. Hodges found the 8-foot-deep crater where the meteorite landed a few miles southwest of Finch, Arkansas, not far from Paragould.

The Paragould Meteorite weighs 816 pounds and is the largest ever found in Arkansas and the third largest meteorite ever recovered in North America. In all, thirteen meteorites have been recovered in our state. Of these, eight are of metallic iron-nickel alloy and four are stone. The remaining one, recovered in Newport in 1923, is a rare mix of both stone and metal. The first meteorite recovered was found in June 1884 in a gully at Joe Right Mountain near Batesville. A second stone was recovered from nearby Sandtown in 1938. Though once thought to be fragments of the same meteor, analysis proved otherwise.

The account of a daytime fall at Lamar, near Clarksville, on March 27, 1886, says, "The noise was heard 75 miles away and was likened to a loud report, followed by a hissing sound, as if hot metal had come in contact with water."

We have a few tips for would-be meteorite hunters. Meteorites are usually heavier than terrestrial rocks, magnetic to some extent, and irregularly shaped but smooth around the edges. Fresh ones are black; old ones are weathered brown. The best place in Arkansas to look for one would be in the mountains. They tend to sink in soft earth, and the moist, acidic soil of deltas and river valleys destroys them.

If you would like to see some samples of meteorites, visit the Arkansas Center for Space and Planetary Sciences at the University of Arkansas in Fayetteville, where several are on display, including the Paragould Meteorite. For more information call (479) 575-7625.

Getting "Nauti" in the Ditch
Fayetteville

On January 20, 2003, a group of college students were hunting fossils around a ditch in Fayetteville when they stumbled onto what is billed as the world's largest nautiloid fossil. Basically it is the remains of what was once a cone-shaped seashell, 8 feet long. The previous record for largest nautiloid fossil is a specimen also found in Fayetteville in 1963. It measures 7 feet. Both these shells belonged to an extinct species of cephalopod related to modern squid that were predators in the warm tropical waters of northern Arkansas 325 million years ago.

The normal size for these creatures is no more than 4 feet, making the Fayetteville fossil the John Holmes of ancient nautili. Geology professor Walter Manger of the University of Arkansas called both specimens pathological giants because squids usually grow, mate, and lay eggs, then die within three or four years. He theorized that parasites had bored into the giants' shells and attacked their sex organs, rendering them sterile. Thus they lived on for decades, growing progressively larger, lending credence to dear old Dad's adage that "children suck the life out of you."

The fossils are on exhibit at the University of Arkansas Museum in Fayetteville.

For directions and other information, call (479) 575-3466.

Alas, I'm but a shell of my former self.
HALEY EMERICK

All's Well That Ends Well

Fayetteville

What do you find at a dowser's convention? A fountain of information on a number of topics. Dowsing isn't just a way of finding the right place to dig a well, especially nowadays, when we buy our water in plastic bottles at the supermarket. Believers think dowsing can also heal psychic and physical ills and provide answers to some of life's troubling questions.

★ ★

Dowsers get together in Fayetteville every April for the Dowsing and Healing Energies Convention. The five-day event offers classes and lectures on dowsing, healing, and other mind phenomena. For some people it's an opportunity to be among others who have similar interests. It can be difficult to discuss arcane subjects with those of a mainstream mentality.

Our late friend, Bob Adams, was a dowser and had been for most of his life. He realized he had the gift when he was about nine years old. It was a watershed moment. He learned the craft from an old dowser who preferred forked peach tree branches as instruments of divination. Bob was more versatile. He used twigs, brazing rods, and bent coat hangers. The weirdest dowsing instrument ever used was arguably a pair of German sausages.

It is thought that some people have heightened sensory perception and that their muscles contract in reaction to electromagnetic frequencies. Veteran dowser and teacher Raymon Grace was a guest speaker at the Dowsing Convention in 2001, where he was asked to de-pollute the water at Blue Spring near Eureka Springs, which he purportedly did by scrambling and adjusting the frequency of the pollutants and the water.

Dowsers also use pendulums, getting answers by watching which way a pendulum swings over a map or in response to yes/no questions. A pendulum can be a ring on a string or a rock on a rope, but crystals seem to be the most popular choice. People who sell gemstones and crystals often attend dowsing conventions, whether they're believers or not. Everybody believes in the buck, and if you've priced crystals lately, you know they don't always come cheap, even if you dig for the crystals yourself at one of the fee-pay quartz mines in the Ouachita Mountains. (For more information see Mike and Darcy Howard's book, *Collecting Crystals*.)

To learn more about the Dowsing and Healing Energies Convention, call the Ozark Research Institute at (479) 582-9197 or visit www.ozarkresearch.org. Be sure to walk softly and carry a big stick.

A dowser using his special waterhound stick.

★ ★

Sound It Out

Some people unfamiliar with Arkansas pronounce the state's name *Ar-KANSAS,* not realizing that by doing so, they're actually breaking the law. The 1881 Arkansas Legislature enacted Civil Code 1-4-105, which decreed that the state's name should be pronounced *AR-kan-saw.* Not long after that ruling, Federal Judge Henry Clay Caldwell was holding court and overseeing jury selection when a potential juror said he was a "postmaster at Harrisburg, *Ar-KANSAS.*" Judge Caldwell rebuked him sternly. "No citizen who . . . hasn't sense enough to pronounce [the state's] name correctly is qualified for jury service in my court. Get out, you ignoramus!"

Flippin Fantabulous
Flippin

You know how some days you feel like flippin' out? Maybe you just need to cool off. We know how you can do both. Go to Sodie's Fountain and Grill in Flippin, Arkansas.

Once a staple in every small town's pharmacy, soda fountains have gone the way of train depots. Sodie's has that covered, too, because the eatery is located in a replica of an old train depot. Stop in and have a milk shake in a real glass for a change.

Though Sodie's is an asset for the town, we can't say it put Flippin on the map. It was already there, thanks in part to a little real estate deal called Whitewater, which involved questionable investments in 230 acres of wooded land on the White River just outside Flippin. Some called the ensuing commotion a controversy, some said scandal, while others thought it a small passage of gas through the national digestive tract.

Years later, journalists from the *New York Times* revisited Whitewater and the little town of Flippin (population 1,357). It was a plum assignment—a vacation in a laid-back locale with side trips to scenic areas. The big-city boys made good-natured sport of Flippin's appellation and some other colorful Arkansas place names, including one that was new to us, and we're Arkansas natives. Stumptoe, we promise to write about you next time.

Flippin folk take all of the joshing in stride. They have something called the Flippin Pride Team (FPT), an organization that promotes community spirit. To raise money for improvement projects, the FPT has published two books called *Flippin Good Recipes*, volumes I and II. You gotta love a town with such a good sense of humor. When they have company over for a dinner of roasted opossum and fried bullfrog, they're sure to have the table decked out in bouquets from a Flippin florist.

After a feast like that, you need to walk it off with a stroll around town. For a good game of soccer or softball, head for Hickey Park; or sightsee and visit historic buildings such as the Old Flippin City Jail, which truth be told looks like something Cool Hand Luke was put in to get his head straight after his mama died.

Flippin is located on US 412/62, south of Bull Shoals Lake.

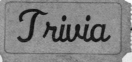

Trivia

Flippin is also the home of Ranger Boats. The famous brand of bass boat originated there in 1968.

★ ★

Man Shot by Pigg
Fort Smith

At 2:00 a.m. on September 12, 1913, E. M. Pigg was sleeping peacefully in his Fort Smith home when he was awakened by noises outside. And no, it wasn't the Big Bad Wolf. It was a very inebriated Clifford Johnson, trying to find someone to show him the way to go home—to Wister, Oklahoma. He was really loaded. Unfortunately, so was Pigg's revolver. Pigg thought Johnson was a burglar and shot him in the neck. The wound wasn't fatal, but when Johnson went home from the hospital, he took the bullet with him, still lodged in his neck. Doctors considered surgery too dangerous, considering the bullet's location.

Pigg was brought up on charges, and the resultant trial required Johnson's testimony. On the train trip from Wister back to Fort Smith, Johnson was feeling a bit sluggish. Suddenly he was stricken with a fit of coughing, and what should he cough up but the bullet. Discharge from an abscess on the outer lining of his throat had dislodged the bullet.

The trial ended with Pigg being fined $50 for aggravated assault. No doubt he was glad to say adieu to Johnson, who was a real pain in the neck. And from then on, Johnson had quite a story to tell when he and friends got together to shoot the breeze.

Good Golly, It's a Trolley
Fort Smith

Fort Smith's first public transportation system, established in 1883, consisted of three mule-drawn railcars. Ten years later, electric trolley cars were introduced in the city. They were open platform cars that exposed passengers to the elements. Then enclosed trolleys came along and by 1920, they even had under-seat heaters. That made a ride downright cozy.

In the 1920s the company that operated the Fort Smith trolleys hit a rough patch caused by legal problems and low profits. Fewer people used public transportation because more of them were buying cars. The Great Depression was the finishing blow. The Fort Smith streetcars made their last run on November 15, 1933. The tracks were ripped up, and the trolleys were dismantled and sold off piecemeal. Trolley #224 ended up as a diner in Ashdown, Arkansas, where it was called the Streetcar Cafe.

In 1979 Charles Winters wrote the history of the Fort Smith trolley system, and that caused a resurgence of interest in the old streetcars.

"Clang, clang, clang," went the trolley.
ARKANSAS DEPARTMENT OF PARKS AND TOURISM

★ ★

Someone learned that car #224 was for sale. The nonprofit Fort Smith Streetcar Restoration Association was formed and bought old #224. That was just the beginning. More of the old streetcars were found and returned, but they needed a home, so the Restoration Association established the Fort Smith Trolley Museum at 100 South Fourth Street.

This is a working museum, so visitors can see how the trolleys are restored. Museum exhibits include a Frisco steam engine, three cabooses, three boxcars, and three combustible locomotives. Also shown is a former Fort Smith bus that was used in the filming of two movies, *Biloxi Blues* and *Tuskegee Airmen.* Railroad and streetcar memorabilia fill up display cases.

And a special note to cat lovers. The trolley museum has several resident cats, most with rail-related names. Frisco was named for Frisco Freight System and KCS (Casey, for short) for the Kansas City Southern Railway.

For more information about the Fort Smith Trolley Museum, call (479) 783-0205 or e-mail info@fstm.org.

A Feather in His Cap
Fort Smith

Del Hampton would make a mother proud. A mother hen, that is. The Fort Smith resident has been the National Chicken Clucking Champion eleven times.

Hampton thought about entering in 1997 when he first heard about the competition, held annually in Wayne, Nebraska. He had a knack for mimicry as a result of watching Looney Tunes when he was a kid. To prepare for the contest, he did his homework and studied the competitors. After all, he didn't want to lay an egg.

He didn't win his first cluck-off, but it was a learning experience. As a burlesque queen tells a young stripper in the musical *Gypsy,* "You gotta have a gimmick, if you wanna have a chance." Heeding that advice, Hampton started using props and acting like a chicken as he clucked. The gimmick worked, and he went on to become numero uno in the pecking order of chicken cluckers everywhere.

Wonder if he gets up with the chickens, too.

Where the King Got Clipped

Fort Smith

The fifty-five-acre Chaffee Crossing Museum District in Fort Smith has what is probably the most famous barbershop since Floyd's in Mayberry. The barbershop is in Building 803 on the former Fort Chaffee Army Base.

Fort Chaffee, originally called Camp Chaffee, was established a mere three months before the attack on Pearl Harbor on December 7, 1941. During World War II the installation was used as a training facility for combat troops and as a German prisoner of war camp. The army base also served as a relocation camp for Vietnamese refugees in the mid-1970s and for Cuban refugees from the Mariel Boatlift in 1980–82. Fort Chaffee was closed in 1995, and the property was divided between the Arkansas National Guard (66,000 acres) and Chaffee Crossing, a 7,000-acre planned community.

The museum district includes the Vietnam Veterans Museum, the Enchanted Doll Museum, and the Chaffee Barbershop Museum. The barbershop is famous for being the place where Elvis Presley got his first military haircut when he was inducted into the U.S. Army on March 24, 1958. The restored barbershop building features a life-size cutout of Elvis in the barber chair. Other vintage barber chairs, scissors, and combs share the space. The museum also has the script from the Elvis movie *King Creole,* which finished filming the day before Elvis joined the army. We must say this is a cut above most museums. The only things missing are a pile of hair on the floor and a barbershop quartet of Elvis impersonators.

The Chaffee Barbershop Museum is located at 7313 Terry Street in Fort Smith. For more information call (479) 769-0402.

The Vietnam Veterans Museum contains a variety of Vietnam War

★ ★

memorabilia, including military gear and firearms juxtaposed incongruously with love letters of lonely soldiers. The museum is located at 12112 Redwood Drive (479-478-0110).

The Enchanted Doll Museum, at 7201 Terry Street (479-478-0225), houses about 5,000 dolls, including a set of the characters from *Gone with the Wind,* a Shirley Temple cutie pie, and life-size figures of Ken and Barbie. The doll museum is adjacent to the Enchanted Wedding Chapel. Maybe Ken will finally make an honest woman out of Barbie.

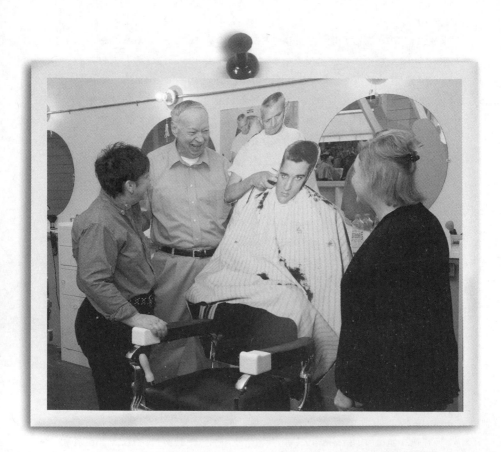

Hair today, gone forever.
ARKANSAS DEPARTMENT OF PARKS AND TOURISM

They Call Me Mister Peanut
Fort Smith

In the nineteenth and early twentieth centuries, the poor rural population of the American South subsisted on a diet of molasses and cornmeal. They seldom grew peanuts, and if they did, they fed the legumes to the hogs. People can be real goobers sometimes. Had the humans eaten the peanuts, they could have prevented the scourge of the South, which is what the National Institute of Health called pellagra. Niacin is a natural remedy for pellagra, and peanuts are high in niacin.

Peanuts had become more in demand as food for people by 1906 when Amedeo Obici and Mario Peruzzi established the Planters Peanut Company. In 1916 Planters sponsored a contest offering $5 to the person who came up with the best idea for a company symbol. A schoolboy named Antonio Gentile won with his drawing of an anthropomorphic peanut that had arms and legs. A professional artist duded the figure up with monocle, top hat, and cane. Mr. Peanut was born and became one of the most recognizable and enduring icons in advertising history. The public went nuts over the aristocratic character.

For many years a 30-foot-tall Mr. Peanut sign was a familiar landmark in Peabody, Massachusetts, but in 1988 it was moved to Fort

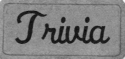

Trivia

Besides peanuts, other good sources of niacin include brown rice, seafood, and yeast. After the flood of 1927, the Red Cross used powdered yeast to combat a deadly plague of pellagra in Marked Tree, Arkansas.

Smith, Arkansas, where it stands today in front of the Planters Peanut Plant. Try saying that three times in a hurry. The sign is so big, it could crush an elephant. Smaller replicas of Mr. Peanut adorn the fence in front of the plant, which is located at 4020 Planters Road (US 71) in Forth Smith.

Oh, Lordy, the Flies!
Fort Smith

Those who read their papers on the fly may have missed an article that ran in the *Fort Smith Times Record* on May 25, 1913. The vast number of flies in the city had become a public health concern. Rather than bring out the S.W.A.T team, the townsfolk decided to hold a contest for the local schoolchildren to see who could kill the most flies. First prize was $10. Second place was worth five bucks, and 50 cents would go to all the runners-up.

The contest created quite a buzz, and the kids had a field day. They gave more thought to their fly-killin' strategies than they ever had to reading', writin', and 'rithmetic. Their means included flypaper, fly swatters, and traps of both the store-bought and homemade varieties. A list of the baits read like a menu that would gag a maggot: fish heads, rotten eggs, rancid meat, and everybody's favorite cafeteria fare, boiled cabbage.

The contest winner, Clarence Laws, had put his traps in tactical locations sure to produce a high body count—livery stables, eating establishments, and outhouses. Clarence killed 220,000 flies. His nearest competitor, Ray Williams, did himself proud with 200,000 dead flies. Women's lib being in its infancy, the little girl who killed 15,000 flies does not have her name immortalized in print.

During the competition, 1,500,000 flies bought the farm. Too bad they weren't alive to enjoy it.

Miss Laura's

Cover the children's ears, Mother. We're going to talk about a cathouse, and it ain't for felines.

The best bordello in Arkansas was undoubtedly Miss Laura's. In 1898 Vermont-native Laura Ziegler moved to Fort Smith and bought the Riverfront Hotel at 123 First Street. She took out a $3,000 bank loan to renovate the building, and Miss Laura's Social Club opened for business in 1903.

Miss Laura was an entrepreneur who specialized in customer service. Her salon of pleasantries became known as the "Grandest Bordello of the West." It was one of several brothels in a strip that lay between the Arkansas River and the railroad tracks. The Row, as it was called, went legit in 1907 when the city passed an ordinance legalizing prostitution in the red light district. Miss Laura already ran a clean establishment, but the ordinance mandated that all bawdy houses be inspected by health officials regularly. No males under the age of twenty-one and no females under eighteen were allowed inside.

Miss Laura's was high class all the way, and prices reflected her special status as "Queen of the Row." Gentlemen paid $3 for an assignation instead of the dollar charged by most other houses of ill repute. It could be said that a patron at Miss Laura's got a lot of bang for his three bucks.

In 1911 Laura Ziegler turned a tidy profit by selling her lucrative venture to Bertha Gail Dean for $47,000.

In 1924 the city repealed the 1907 ordinance, but Miss Laura's didn't just lie down and take it. Business was better than ever, and the good times rolled until the 1940s, when members of the U.S. Army from nearby Fort Chaffee became the last to be serviced at the bordello.

Today Miss Laura's is the only former house of ill repute listed on the National Register of Historic Places. Tastefully decorated with lovely Victorian furnishings, the building now houses the Fort Smith Visitor Center and a gift shop that sells souvenirs. At a garage sale in another Arkansas city, we found a bath towel that had originally been purchased at Miss Laura's. Embroidered on the towel was the motto: "Miss Laura's, where the customer always comes first."

★ ★

No Noose Is Good Noose

Fort Smith

For history buffs with a penchant for the macabre, here's a great place to hang around: the reconstructed gallows at the Fort Smith National Historic Site, where seventy-nine men met their maker during the tenure of Judge Isaac Parker, the notorious "Hanging Judge." From 1875 to 1896 Parker presided over the U.S. Court for the Western District of Arkansas, which included most of the Indian Territory in what is now Oklahoma. Visitors can tour the old "Hell on the Border" jail and the restored courtroom where Parker meted out justice to some of the worst desperadoes of the Wild West. Cherokee Bill showed no remorse for the murders he had committed. When asked if he had any last words, he replied, "No! I came here to die, not make a speech."

Judge Parker was a commanding figure on the bench and often made biased, inflammatory speeches when instructing juries. His arbitrariness led the U.S. Supreme Court to reverse thirty-one of the death sentences imposed by Parker. Outlaw Henry Starr was one of the lucky men spared. Starr wrote in his autobiography, "The judge with his usual ornate vanity gave me a twenty-minute lecture but failed in his object. That fellow never could scare me. He sentenced me to the hemp, but I never batted an eye."

On display just outside the courtroom are pictures of George Maledon, the "Prince of Hangmen," who took great pride in dispatching the condemned quickly and painlessly.

"I have never hanged a man who came back to have the job done over," Maledon once said. "The big knot is the secret of a good execution. That big knot throws his head sidewise and cracks his neck in a jiffy."

The scaffold was built to accommodate twelve doomed men, but only six were ever hanged at one time. Today park rangers present programs on the anniversaries of executions and hang a noose on the gallows for each man hanged on that date.

To reach the Fort Smith National Historic Site, turn south off

Garrison Avenue (US 64) onto Fourth Street and then take a right
onto Garland Avenue. The main parking lot is at the end of the
block. For information about fees and other details, call (479) 783-
3961 or go to www.nps.gov/fosm.

Legendary Loot
Gravette

According to legend, about 350 years ago Spanish soldiers journeyed
north from Mexico, carrying with them gold and other valuables.
When winter weather became too inhospitable, they sought shelter
in a cave in what is now Benton County. Smoke from their campfire
wafted up through a hole in the cave and was seen by a band of
Indians who had been tracking the Spaniards. The Indians attacked,
but the Spaniards had enough warning to move back into the deep
recesses of the cave, where they hid their loot. After all the soldiers
were killed, a contingent of their fellow countrymen came looking
for them. With the help of friendlier Indians, the second group of
soldiers found the cave and the remains of their former comrades.
They also discovered the valuables but did not have enough horses to
carry all the loot back home. They hid the treasure but left signs and
symbols to mark the location and made maps of the hiding place. For
unknown reasons, the soldiers did not return.

In 1885 an elderly man from Madrid came to the area with maps
and clues that led him to the cave. It had been sealed with a large
rock that bore the engraved image of a deer's hoof. The old man
died, however, without finding any treasure.

Is it just a legend? Probably, but Old Spanish Treasure Cave is
an actual place, located 2 miles north of Gravette off AR 59. It is
privately owned, and attempts are still being made to locate the
treasure, which today would be worth more than $40 million. Some
think that the New Madrid earthquake of 1811–12 may have caused
a cave-in, which buried the treasure even better than the Spaniards
had. So far, only artifacts have been unearthed, including helmets,

★ ★

armor, weapons, and coins. The quest continues, though. The owner's treasure-hunting team found new symbols in a previously undiscovered part of the cave, and the hope is that the new clues will finally lead to the fortune.

Meanwhile, Old Spanish Treasure Cave is a tourist attraction where visitors can pan for gemstones and explore the eighteen passageways that branch off from the cave's main chamber. In prehistoric times the cave was undersea, and fossils of brachiopods, crinoids, and trilobites can be seen there.

For more information call (479) 787-6508 or go to www.spanish-treasure-cave.com.

A Towering Achievement
Green Forest

In 2007 the citizens of Green Forest in Carroll County were surprised to learn that their seventy-year-old water tower had been named to the National Register of Historic Places. When people think of the National Register, they usually think of grand old homes and buildings designed by famous architects. But a water tower?

Turns out, the Green Forest water tower is historically significant. It was erected in 1937 as part of a project by the Public Works Administration (PWA), not to be confused with the WPA (Works Progress Administration), though both were funded by President Franklin Roosevelt's New Deal program and intended to help the country recover from the Great Depression. Green Forest, like many small towns of that era, did not have adequate water and sewer systems, a situation that posed potential health problems. The benefits of the PWA project, therefore, were twofold. The program provided jobs during a difficult time and enabled the community to serve basic needs.

The tower came to mean different things to different people. In days before air-conditioning, the tower's overflow created a waterfall where kids cooled off in the summertime. It has been the site of flirtations and marriage proposals. The 155-foot-tall structure is an

A lot of water has flowed under the bridge since Green Forest got its tower.
SANDRA RUSSELL, CITY OF GREEN FOREST

irresistible magnet for daring climbers, a welcome sight for towns-folk returning home, and a landmark that beckons to strangers. The tower's whistle still lets people know when it's time to eat lunch, sounding at noon every day of the week except Sunday. It used to whistle on the Sabbath, too, until a preacher complained about interruptions in church services. (It would be rude to awaken napping parishioners.) The tower also makes one heck of a birdbath according to a former city official, whose son once retrieved a bushel basket of bird bones from the depths of the tower.

The 2,700 residents of Green Forest are rightfully proud of their noteworthy landmark. It is one of only 236 PWA projects in Arkansas named to the National Register. The upkeep of Green Forest's water tower includes regular maintenance and fairly frequent paint jobs, but it still looks much like it did in days gone by.

Green Forest is about 22 miles northwest of Harrison on US 62.

Lurch, the Watusi Steer

Janice Wolf is one of those people seemingly born to help the disadvantaged, abused, abandoned, and neglected. In Janice's case, though, her wards are members of the animal kingdom. She is the founder of the Rocky Ridge Refuge near Gassville (on the back side of Monkey Run). There she tends to the needs of several dozen animals, many of whom suffer from disabilities—the blind, the deaf, and the lame.

Managing the refuge hasn't been easy for Janice, but she is the kind of woman who takes the bull by the horns, which brings us to the most celebrated resident of Rocky Ridge: Lurch, the Watusi steer.

From the start, Lurch was special. He wasn't disabled or homeless, but when Janice saw him, it was love at first sight. Lurch was only five weeks old when he went to live with Janice in 1995. Just three years later he had the largest horns in the world. When Lurch was listed in *Guinness World Records,* his horns measured 7 feet, 6 inches from tip to tip and were 38 inches in circumference. They weighed one hundred pounds each. When we heard about Lurch, we could have told a lot of horny jokes, but that wouldn't have been fair to Lurch. He was, after all, a steer—and that's no bull.

Lurch became an international star. Besides the Guinness book, he was in *Ripley's Believe It or Not!,* appeared on *The Ellen DeGeneres Show,* and was a sensation in the Japanese media. People traveled from near and far to see Lurch. Despite his fame, he never got a big head. Only his horns were big. His sweet disposition made him a favorite with the other Rocky Ridge residents.

Sadly, as we were preparing this book, we received word that Lurch had cancer. Ironically, the disease had stricken him at the base of one of his horns. At this writing, we do not know Lurch's ultimate fate, but we do believe that no matter the time of his demise, he will be remembered long afterward. Upon learning about Lurch's diagnosis, Ripley Entertainment contacted Janice regarding a desire to preserve and display Lurch's body in its California museum.

If you want to visit Janice and her animal family, please call first. The number is (870) 430-5783. Check out their Web site at www.rockyridgerefuge.com.

A star was horned.
JANICE WOLF

★ ★

Where the Heck Is Hector?

Hector

The town of Hector has an ordinance that stipulates a fine of $100 if a person's dog bites someone, destroys property, or doesn't have proper identification. Nothing unusual about that. It may be ironic, though, since the town was named for a dog.

With a population hovering around 500, Hector is located in Pope County about 17 miles northeast of Russellville. The first business in the town was a tannery, established around 1875. Then a doctor opened an office and drug store. Soon the town was flourishing, and

The canine sector of Hector.

in 1885 the people of the community decided they needed a post office. They succeeded in securing one but found they also needed a name. After much controversy and arguing over what the town should be called, President Grover Cleveland was asked to suggest a name. It's hard to picture the president of the United States taking the time nowadays to do such a thing, but Cleveland even answered the White House phone himself. Of course the telephone was still a new-fangled gadget at that time. Anyway, Cleveland christened the Arkansas hamlet Hector in honor of his bulldog. Cleveland also had a poodle or a Pekingese, depending on the source, but Hector was his favorite.

The canine Hector seems to be best remembered as a connoisseur of boiled eggs. The tradition of an Easter egg roll on the White House lawn was already established by the time Hector occupied the presidential home, and it was said he enjoyed the event immensely.

The town of Hector celebrates its heritage each year in May with Hector Dog Days, a festival that includes carnival rides and a parade. Admission is free. We promise that if you are looking for a good time, you won't be barking up the wrong tree here. For more information contact Hector City Hall at (479) 284-5371.

A Ghost with Latta-Tude

London

The "Vanishing Hitchhiker" is an enduring urban legend that has been around since before the automobile. Arkansas has at least two ghostly hitchhikers. One has been reported on Woodson Lateral Road in Woodson, about 19 miles south of Little Rock. The other hails rides on US 64 near London in Pope County. Her name is Laura Starr Latta.

Laura's ghost, dressed in a white wedding gown, sometimes gets a ride but always disappears before traveling very far from her final unresting place in Price Cemetery. Some motorists drive right through her. Maybe she mistakes car lights for *the* light.

Laura was a real person, born September 19, 1879. She was killed on August 22, 1899, either right before or right after her wedding. Some versions of the legend say she was killed in a wagon accident; others claim she was slain. Most agree that she died violently and that her wedding gown had blood on it. Blood is a tough stain to remove. Heloise suggests a mixture of water and meat tenderizer.

Only Laura's monogrammed footstone and part of her headstone mark her grave. Over the years, it became almost a rite of passage for local youths to vandalize or steal the headstone. It has been recovered from a college dorm room and from a car wash. The last such incident resulted in the marker being broken, so part of it is now kept in a secret place, safe from harm.

One way? Usually.

★ ★

In shades of *Candyman,* the tombstone's inscription is said to bring misfortune to anyone reading it aloud, which is practically a posthypnotic suggestion to do just that. Bet you can't help yourself.

"Gentle stranger, passing by,

As you are now, once was I.

As I am now, so you must be.

Prepare yourself to follow me."

Price Cemetery is located 0.5 mile west of London, on the north side of US 64. We understand Laura is more likely to make an appearance on the anniversary of her death. We don't know the appropriate gift for such an occasion, but flowers are always nice.

Snakes on the Brain
Marion County

Where's Samuel L. Jackson when you need him? Marion County resident Chuck Miller could have used Samuel L.'s snake-wrangling charms during the summers of 2005 and 2006, when hundreds of copperheads made Miller's hilltop property their favorite hangout. There were more snakes than you could shake a stick at. And you'd better be sure that's a stick before picking it up.

Miller's snakes started appearing in large numbers in 2005. They would show up around 8:00 p.m. and hang out under a cedar tree for about an hour before departing. It was a nightly ritual. Snakes don't usually congregate like that during the hot summer months. Explanations for the uncharacteristic behavior included theories that the snakes were either following scent trails of fellow snakes or they were being enticed by cicadas, which are delectable morsels in the snake diet.

Copperheads are one of four poisonous snakes found in Arkansas, the others being the rattlesnake, coral snake, and water moccasin. (Snake survival hint: If a snake chases you, do not run in a serpentine manner. Snakes invented the maneuver. Why do you think they call it serpentine?)

★ ★

Granny Rode My Fanny

In 1859 a community near Harrison crossed over into Twilight Zone territory. A young woman from the Gaddy family accused a neighbor, Granny Inman, of witchcraft. Blind in one eye, Granny lived on Lick Branch, east of Alpena.

A trial convened in the Primitive Baptist Church at Alpena. Miss Gaddy testified that Granny had come to her house one night, thrown a saddle and bridle on her, and ridden her all over Carroll County. Granny then mated Miss Gaddy with a Spanish jack. That's a mule with papers.

Granny was convicted and excommunicated from the church, which was like being ousted from a lunatic asylum by the inmates.

Drive Me Out to the Drive-in
Marshall

Drive-in movie theaters once were considered déclassé, the poor country relations of the walk-ins, forever taking a backseat to their uptown cousins. But as any drive-in aficionado will tell you, the back-seat isn't such a bad place to be. You don't have to worry about nosey ushers, and you can dress however you like (or undress, for that matter). Honk your horn if the film breaks; no one cares. In fact, they'll join you. Bring your own food; bring lawn chairs; smoke, drink hooch, smooch, and sit on the tailgate of your pickup.

Several factors killed the drive-in theater. American car culture changed. Muscle-car behemoths were replaced by tiny compacts with bucket seats. No room to fool around meant teens were forced to sit and watch the often God-awful movies. The other "Three Horsemen of the Drive-In Apocalypse" were cable television, the VCR, and rising real estate prices. Drive-ins weren't profitable enough to cover their escalating property taxes.

Arkansas had five drive-in movie theaters in 1948. Ten years later the number peaked at fifty-seven, but by 1991 only five remained; only three of those survive today. The Ozark Mountains, however, remain a refuge from the rushing changes of the outside world, so the three surviving drive-ins are all in the mountains.

The family-owned Kenda Drive-In has a 72-foot-wide screen and is located in Marshall on US 65. Opened in 1966, the Kenda is the only drive-in in the country with a viewing lounge next to the snack bar. Movie soundtracks still play through the old-style metal speakers. The drive-in was named for the original owners' daughter, who was a baby at the time. She is now the manager. The Kenda is open year-round, every night except Wednesday and Thursday. For more information call (870) 448-5400.

Mountain View's Stone Drive-In has a viewing season that runs from March through November. It's also family owned, and sound also comes from the old-style metal speakers. Call (870) 269-3227.

The 112 Drive-In, at 3352 AR 112 between Springdale and Fayetteville, is open from mid-March through mid-November. Sound is broadcast in newfangled FM stereo. Call (479) 442-4542.

Don't forget mosquito repellent.

See the Arkansas Sea
Marshall

There is a road cut 2 miles south of Marshall on US 65. Found in its rock are the remains of life from the old North American continental shelf of 350 million years ago. They are fossils formed from the compacted bodies of an underwater forest, not of vegetation but of carnivorous animals called crinoids. A swimmer in those shallow, tropical waters would pass over gardens of these animals. They resembled brilliantly colored flowers attached to the sea floor by

long, thin, segmented stems, but the petals of their blossoms were
tentacles. Fish caught in these tendrils were slowly eaten. Later the
"lillies" excreted the digested remains as pellets that were consumed
by snails and trilobites grubbing at the base of the stalk. As they say,
"It's a living."

Archimedes, another animal that appeared to be a plant, filtered
plankton from the waters with small, lacy nets radiating off a cork-
screw-shaped trunk. Brachiopods, looking like brightly striped clams,
were joined to the sea bottom. A predatory nautilus, masqueraded

A slice of history.
ARKANSAS DEPARTMENT OF PARKS AND TOURISM

as a small squid tucked inside a 3-foot-long, chambered cone-shaped shell. With its hard parrot-like beak, the nautilus would seize the head of a crinoid and devour the prey.

But a new hunter had appeared on the scene. Its teeth, found in the Pitkin limestone, tell the tale. The ancestor of the modern shark had teeth that were thick and rounded and adapted for crushing bone and shell. In the ongoing contest between heavier armor versus bigger, stronger jaws and teeth, the sharks won.

Crinoids, brachiopods, and the nautili no longer live in the open sea. They have survived today as living fossils by retreating and adapting to areas of the ocean where most other creatures can't live—in deep ocean trenches and the like.

A tiny brachiopod known as *Lingula* appeared in the fossil record in the Moorefield shale; they now live in the no-man's land of the sea, estuaries where the water is brackish—too fresh for most salt-water animals and too salty for most freshwater creatures. They foreshadowed the future, for the ocean was retreating. Northern Arkansas was becoming a river delta as the dome of the Ozark Plateau rose and the sea slipped away, leaving only bone and fossil to mark its passing.

Monte Ne, the Greatest Thing That Never Was
Monte Ne

In 1900 William Hope "Coin" Harvey established a resort town called Monte Ne in northwest Arkansas. The community featured Arkansas's first indoor swimming pool, and two of its hotels were the largest log hotels in the world.

Somewhat an eccentric, Harvey predicted the doom of civilization and proposed the construction of a time capsule that would help future human beings reverse-engineer themselves back to the stage they were in before the fall. The plan called for an obelisk of steel-reinforced concrete 135 feet tall with walls 8 to 10 feet thick. Inside would be examples of modern technology, including a Model T Ford, a phonograph, a printing press, a radio, and safety pins. Engineers reckoned that the pyramid, as Harvey called it, would last a million years.

Unfortunately, Harvey may have been a visionary, but he was no business manager. One would think that a resort owner who believed the end was coming soon would encourage his guests to live it up and spend money like Roman emperors, but not Coin. Once when guests partied past his curfew, they found themselves literally in the dark because he had shut off the electricity. The next morning most of the guests took permanent leave of his hospitality.

Harvey went forward with his pyramid project and began building an amphitheatre, which would serve both as a foyer and as a buttress to stabilize the hillside below the tower's foundation.

In 1931, at the age of eighty, Coin became the first Arkansan to run for president. The Liberty Party's national convention was held at Monte Ne, but it was the last hurrah for Harvey and his resort. Because of his mismanagement and other contributing factors, Monte Ne was failing; construction of the pyramid and amphitheatre was halted. In a last desperate attempt to save the time capsule, he requested donations from the five richest men in the country. None of them replied.

Coin died in 1936 and was buried at Monte Ne. His mausoleum and ruins of a three-story stone tower sit on a hill overlooking Beaver Lake. The rest of Monte Ne was swallowed by the lake when Beaver Dam was built in the early 1960s. Every once in a while, though, the water recedes and Monte Ne rises like an Ozark Atlantis, the lost dream of a philosopher king.

Monte Ne is located 5 miles southeast of Rogers off AR 94.

For more information about Monte Ne, visit Russell T. Johnson's Web site, www.arkansasroadstories.com, where you'll find a plethora of piquant postings about peculiarities particular to Arkansas.

★ ★

Mount Magazine, Up from the Bottom
Mount Magazine

About thirty-five million years ago, an underground stress caused a collapse in the center of the Sawatch Range of the Rocky Mountains. Guess they don't make mountains like they used to. The headwaters of the modern Arkansas River began flowing near the town of Leadville, Colorado. Due to gravitational forces, erosion acts more strongly on mountains than valleys, wearing them away much more quickly. As the river flowed southeast and entered an area called the Arkhoma Basin, it began eating away most of the valley floor like liquid termites, isolating patches of ground as the current switched course, flowing on one side of them and then the other. When the land and nearby mountains were leveled, these patches, like proverbial molehills, began to tower thousands of feet above the surrounding plain.

Mount Magazine, along with Nebo and Petit Jean, are popularly called mountains but are actually plateaus, erosional remnants of the former landscape. It's ironic that Mount Magazine, which is Arkansas's tallest "mountain" at 2,753 feet, was once part of the valley floor.

Mount Magazine has a distinctive geological feature: a boulder train—a long straight line of large rocks trailing along the base of the mountain's north slope. It is believed to have been created during the last ice age, when subfreezing temperatures allowed snow to remain on the hillside year-round, eventually forming an alpine snowpack that pushed the stones down the slope and into their characteristic positions. Similar boulder trains are found on the north slopes of Petit Jean Mountain and Poteau Mountain.

Mount Magazine's isolation, above the surrounding countryside, created a refuge for plants and animals that exist in few other places in the world, and it's the only known habitat for some. The maple-leaf oak, a tree with identity issues, is found here and only on a few neighboring mountains. First discovered by botanist E. J. Palmer in 1924, the tree has leaves that resemble a maple tree, and yet it's an

★ ★

oak—although in size it's barely large enough to be a tree at all. Its origin remains a mystery. Mount Magazine is also home to many rare or endangered species of butterflies; tourists flutter in to enjoy the delicate beauties at the annual Butterfly Festival held in June.

Mount Magazine is on AR 309 near Paris in Logan County.

The Miniature Museum of Merritt & Tiny Town Tours
Mountain Home

Edna M. Merritt is a lady who thinks big. Her museum of miniatures in Mountain Home is a testament to that. It contains more than 200,000 items, even though the building is only 30 by 90 feet. The first room is jam-packed with food items made out of beads and buttons—literally hundreds of pies, cakes, and pita bread. But that's just the first room. Visitors follow Christmas lights on the Tiny Town Tour. Merritt has done 500 individual miniature rooms with more than sixty dollhouses, more than sixty stores, dioramas, and an 11-foot-long farmers' market. She has two 11-foot-long Christmas villages and a house that is 11 feet long and three stories high. One entire village is made of metal dollhouses.

Merritt also puts her original artwork and poetry in miniature books. She plans to do 520 all together, which her daughter will compile into one big book. Merritt hopes the books will raise funds for a foundation to keep the miniature museum open after she is gone.

Every visitor to the museum receives an original black-and-white print and inspirational poem to take home.

Merritt started doing miniatures in her sixties, after a diagnosis of lupus began to limit recreational activities with her family. The hobby kept her mind off her physical pain and helped pass the time pleasantly. Her first creation was a tiny six-room dollhouse with furnishings that measured less than an inch. At Christmastime her family bought her a dollhouse kit; they put most of it together but left the roof for her to complete. When she went to work on it, she realized most kits have just two rooms.

★ ★

"So," she said, "at sixty-five I got out my husband's saw and hammer and nails, and I added a two-story addition. I thought, 'My father was a carpenter, my brother was a carpenter, and my Lord was a carpenter. And at sixty-five, I'm a carpenter.'"

She has been building ever since, and her accomplishment is no small feat. She opened her museum when she was seventy-one years old, and it has been featured in *Dollhouse Miniatures Magazine* and a book called *Eccentric America.*

The Miniature Museum of Merritt & Tiny Town Tours is located at 402 Cranfield Road in Mountain Home. It is open Monday through Saturday, 10:00 a.m. until 4:00 p.m.; closed on Monday during winter. For more information call (870) 492-5222.

Eric the Redneck
Paris

Norse sagas tell that in the year 1009, Leif Eriksson, otherwise known as Leif the Lucky (apparently a babe magnet), sailed from Greenland with an expedition of ships to explore lands to the west. All the ships made it back home by 1012 except one owned by an Icelander named Thorfinn Karlsefni. This ship turned south to circumnavigate Vinland and disappeared, never to be heard from again.

In 1982, Paris, Arkansas, resident David Reider was turkey hunting near Chinquapin Creek, about 6 miles south of the Arkansas River in Logan County. There he discovered a rock measuring 24 by 18 by 12 inches with some unusual symbols carved on it. Like similar rocks found in Arkansas and eastern Oklahoma, it is said to be inscribed with Norse runes, a type of alphabet used by ancient Scandinavians.

The first and most famous of these stones was found near Heavener, Oklahoma, just across the Arkansas border near the Poteau River, a tributary of the Arkansas River. Gloria Farley, a native of Heavener, named it the Heavener Runestone. Farley spent her life researching and traveling along the Arkansas River Valley (on the road to rune, one might say). She documented and recorded ancient rock carvings and rock paintings known as petroglyphs and pictographs.

Attempts to translate the inscriptions yielded conflicting results. Then in 1975, Alf Monge, a Norwegian cryptographer who successfully cracked Japanese codes during World War II, got a copy of the Oklahoma carvings. Believing the inscriptions to be a form of substitution code, which uses letters to stand for numbers, Monge was able to translate the carving. It read, "November 11, 1012." Other stones recovered in the area carry dates between 1012 and 1024. Two stones, written in the same code but found in New England, are dated 1009. Monge concluded that the same man had made all the carvings at various points as he traveled.

This supports a theory put forward by Norse historian Fredrick J. Pohl, who believes that Karlsefni's lost ship possibly traveled south along the coast of North America, then sailed up the Mississippi River and into the Arkansas River before finally reaching the Poteau River near present-day Fort Smith.

To see Arkansas's runestone, visit the Logan County Museum in Paris. Call (479) 963-3936 for hours of operation.

Bet or Not? Better Not!
Rogers

One of the great fictional characters of all time was based on a native of Rogers, Arkansas. The character was Sky Masterson in Damon Runyon's *Guys and Dolls*; the man was Titanic Thompson.

Born Alvin Clarence Thomas in 1892, Thompson was a gambler, hustler, and con man who enjoyed making outlandish wagers. He once bet that he could throw a peanut over the Lion Oil building in El Dorado. The men taking him up on the proposition didn't know Thompson had filled the peanut shell with ball bearings. And once in Chicago, he bet a group of golfers that he could hit a 500-yard drive; he just didn't say he'd do it over a frozen lake. He was such a good golfer and pool player he could have gone legit, but he said he could make more money as a grifter.

Thompson got his nickname in a pool hall in Joplin, Missouri, when a man asked his name and a player said, "It oughta be Titanic, the way he's been sinking everybody." He shucked the name Thomas for Thompson and was Titanic Thompson from then on.

He died in a nursing home in Texas in 1974.

Get the Lead Out!

Rush

The mining town of Rush in Marion County may have gotten its name from the rushing waters of tiny Rush Creek that bordered the town site. More likely, the name came from other towns just like it—boomtowns that sprang up like toadstools in the wake of gem or mineral strikes, where miners rushed to the sites to tear at Mother Earth's vitals until her riches played out, whereupon they rushed off like greedy gigolos to pursue the newest, richest strike elsewhere.

In 1882 miners built the first smelter at Rush to refine the ore they had found. They hoped it was silver, but it turned out to be lead. The disappointed miners offered to trade their entire claim, smelter and all, to a passerby for a case of canned oysters but were turned down. Finally, in 1891 a man named Jim McCabe bought the claim and opened the Morning Star Mine. The venture got a boost when a chunk of nearly pure zinc weighing close to six tons was found there. Nicknamed Jumbo, it was taken to Chicago and displayed at the 1893 World's Fair.

Over the next thirty years, the population of Rush swelled to 5,000, and a total of seventeen mines opened. Like other mining towns, however, it had a few "miner" problems. It was often called Ragtown because so many townsfolk were living in tents, since most of the trees in the area had been cut and used to fire the smelters. Poor sanitation practices caused outbreaks of typhus, cholera, and dysentery. Violence was another by-product.

Rush reached its peak during World War I. After the war ended,

★ ★

the government sold off surplus stockpiles of metal, causing the price of zinc to plummet. The mines closed, and the town never recovered.

Listed on the National Register of Historic Places, Rush is now a ghost town, short on town; the ghosts are pretty scarce, too.

A part of the Buffalo National River system, Rush is about 125 miles north of Little Rock. From US 65 take AR 27 north to AR 14. Go north and turn right onto CR 635. Rush is about 4 miles up the road.

Welcome to the Jungle
Russellville

A dragonfly the size of an eagle is looking for something to munch. A cockroach the size of a Chihuahua is running away with my lunch. No, wait. He is my lunch. Lightning quick, my tongue darts out and seizes him. Mmm . . . so tasty. My giant salamander mate lies naked and slimy like a prehistoric pin-up on a nearby log, while our smaller relatives crawl past us. We hiss at them, "Eat you later," before slithering into a cozy mud hole.

"Pay attention!" A sharp nudge in the ribs from my partner's elbow brings me back to the present.

The chunk of sandstone before us resembles a short, flattened section of a telephone pole. Running parallel to its surface are tiny round pits. It's a piece of a petrified root, and the indentations along its surface are where the rootlets once attached. This scarring, said to resemble stigmata, gives the fossil its name, *Stigmaria*. They belonged to the *Lepidodendron* and *Sigillaria* trees, which looked something like an over-size palm. Some were 150 feet tall. These trees grew in the coal swamps of the Arkansas River Valley 300 million years ago. The decayed leaves of these and other plants from that era now make up the coal beds of this region.

Scientists believe it was the sequestering of carbon in the form of coal during the Pennsylvanian period coupled with the lush plant life that caused oxygen levels in the atmosphere to soar to as much as 33 percent (today's levels are about 20 percent), allowing insects and arachnids and salamanders to grow extremely large. Centipedes reached a length of 6 feet. Spiders' bodies were the size of a modern man's head, and salamanders were almost 7 feet long.

Fossils from this period outcrop in road cuts and shale pits along US 64 and I-40. Anyone interested in collecting may contact the Arkansas Geological Survey (501-296-1877) for directions to specific locations. Excellent specimens of *Stigmaria* may be seen at Arkansas Tech University's Department of Physical Sciences in Russellville. To

Arkansas history has roots older than the hills.

★ ★

arrange a tour, call (479) 968-0293. Other examples may be seen at the visitor centers at Petit Jean State Park (501-727-5441) and Mount Magazine State Park (877-665-6343).

Making a Mountain Out of a Coal Hill

The Arkansas coal swamps formed when the dome of the Ozark plateau rose in the north and the ocean drained away. The swamps' demise followed the collision of Central America in the south and the creation of the Ouachita Mountains. As the continents combined to form one great super-continent, 90 percent of all life on earth perished. For the next 100 million years, Arkansas would remain sealed in the center of this huge land mass, far from the climate-tempering ocean breezes. Like the interior of modern Australia or Antarctica, it was a desert.

Many geologists believe the Ouachitas at that point were as tall as the modern Swiss Alps and were part of what was then the longest known mountain range in Earth's history. They rose in northern Mexico and extended through Texas, Oklahoma, and Arkansas where they connected with the southern Appalachians of Tennessee and stretched on up the east coast and into northern Europe, which was then fused to the northeastern United States. Today fragments of this ancient range are found in Britain, Scandinavia, in the Hartz Mountains in Germany, and as far away as Eastern Europe.

★ ★

An Order of Monk Sauce
Subiaco

Subiaco Abbey and Academy in Logan County has the distinction of being Arkansas's only "full-fledged Benedictine monastery of men," as Fr. Hugh Assenmacher put it.

Subiaco's monks are known for making the best habanero pepper sauce this side of Mexico. They also make a mean batch of peanut brittle. Both items can be bought through their Web site: www.subi .org. While shopping around, we noticed something called the Trojan Shop, and we wondered why a group of Benedictine monks would need Trojans. Then we realized that was the name of their academy's ball team.

In 1943 Subiaco Academy hired a science teacher by the name of Dr. French. He was, in fact, Ferdinand Waldo Demara, aka the Great Imposter—so called for his uncanny ability to pass himself off as a professional in a variety of fields: college dean, surgeon, assistant warden, to name a few. For his role at Subiaco, he had forged a confirmation certificate, signing it Right Reverend Francis J. Spellman, soon to be Cardinal Spellman. On a snowy January day after he had been at Subiaco for several weeks, Demara was called to the abbot's office, where he was confronted about one of his other fraudulent papers. He talked his way out of immediate trouble but knew it was only a matter of hours before the jig was up. That night he stole a car from the monastery's garage and made his escape. Sort of. Unfortunately for him, he was going up against the worst snowstorm to hit Arkansas in thirty years.

Demara eased the car out of the garage, barely making a sound, but then the wheels started spinning on the snow. A light came on in the monastery. He pressed harder on the gas pedal and the wheels squealed. More lights came on in the monastery. When he saw a monk trudging toward him through the snow, Demara gunned it; the car shot forward.

"I can't stop this thing," he shouted out the window as the monk leaped away a second before disaster.

Demara careened down AR 22, bouncing from one snowbank to another and nearly hitting a car in Charleston. Suddenly a police cruiser appeared. Demara slammed on the brakes. His car became airborne but eventually landed upside-down. He survived unscathed, and Subiaco said they would not press charges, provided Demara be out of Arkansas before the next sunset. He agreed.

Digging Up Bones
Van Buren

Van Buren, Arkansas, is a cool place. We went there on our honeymoon but somehow overlooked a side trip to the graveyard.

When Van Buren was incorporated in the 1840s, the town fathers realized they needed a final resting place for their dearly departed. They picked a plot of ground on the crest of a hill and aptly named it Fairview. It was a logical location, seeing as how the site already contained a grave, an ancient one from the looks of it. No one could account for its origin.

The Van Buren mystery grave is not just a pile of rocks marking the departure of someone hastily buried along the trail. Two slabs of sandstone, 4 inches thick and 6 feet long, rise 2 feet out of the ground. According to a longtime caretaker, the slabs continue for another 6 to 8 feet below the surface of the earth. Quarrying, hauling, and maneuvering the heavy stones into position would have been no mean feat. They weigh several hundred pounds. The grave once had a footstone as well as a large slab cover, but both were removed over the years and now serve as bases for other nearby graves.

The headstone itself is a single piece of sandstone, 33 inches tall. The top of the stone is fashioned into a crude circle. Until a few years ago, one side of the circle contained the carving of a man's head. The other side of the headstone had an emblem of two Xs joined together. In recent years, vandals have obliterated these carvings.

Who is buried here? Who made this? And why go to all this trouble and then leave the person's name and date of death off the headstone?

Treasure hunters in the 1930s got legal permission to dig into the grave but uncovered only bones and tacks, which they reburied. If the grave were to be exhumed today, modern forensic techniques might solve the mystery once and for all. However, this is unlikely to happen because the Arkansas antiquity law forbids digging up a grave in a cemetery other than in the event of a crime.

What of the cryptic symbols on the headstone? Unfortunately, dead men tell no tales.

If you want to pay your respects to whomever lies in the mystery grave, Fairview Cemetery is bounded by AR 59 (Fayetteville Street), McKibben Avenue, and Poplar Street.

Ancient Arkansas Travelers
White Rock Mountain

For more than two decades, writer/lecturer Gloria Farley traveled the Arkansas River Valley looking for proof of pre-Columbian visits by Norse explorers. (See Eric the Redneck.) Most mainstream archaeologists scoff at Farley's theory, but as odd as this premise may sound, there is a certain logic behind her choice of search areas. Any voyager skirting the coast of North America would reach the Mississippi River and recognize it as a major water route into the interior, just as later explorers did.

As a result of Farley's fame as a promoter of the Heavener Runestone, people gave her leads on the locations of other stone artifacts. It soon became clear that many of these relics featured other forms of writing unknown to her.

When these symbols were shown to Dr. Barry Fell of Harvard University, he identified them as a type of writing called Celtic Ogam, used by the ancient Celts of Europe. The languages written on the stones varied and contained words and phrases in dialects of Gaelic as well as Iberian Punic, a form of Phoenician spoken in ancient Spain.

Fell speculated that after Egypt fell to the Persians in 525 BC, they closed the eastern Mediterranean Sea to Carthaginian trading, so the Carthaginians turned westward and established trading posts in North and South America. The Carthaginians secretly imported furs, hides, copper, and silver from the Americas until the Romans destroyed Carthage in 146 BC. Voyages continued by the Celts in France until their conquest by Julius Caesar in 55 BC. After that, the Romans had no navy for 400 years because they no longer had any rivals. In the interim, knowledge of the trade routes to America was lost.

One of the stones discovered in Arkansas was found 30 feet up on the side of a cliff at Cass and contained a Gaelic phrase written in Ogam script. Translated it read, "Moral: Unmolested is the Journeying of a Stranger Who is Content with Poverty."

A stone carving found in the woods near Maysville in 1970 is believed to be a type of Ogam script used from 200 to 100 BC. Fell translated it to read, "Surly, Son of Stag without Antlers." A similar rock, found atop White Rock Mountain in Franklin County, is alleged to be an Iberian Celtic gravestone.

5

Central

Central Arkansas is *the state's central nervous system. The capital city, Little Rock, keeps things running and is often the first impression given visitors when they arrive in the state. It's a friendly, outgoing place and generous to a fault. They once let Hollywood blow up the State Capitol!*

North Little Rock's landmark Old Mill was featured in the opening sequence of Gone with the Wind. *In 2005 actress and North Little Rock native Joey Lauren Adams made her directorial debut when she filmed* Come Early Morning *in her hometown. Your humble servants worked as extras on the movie. We were bookends to Ashley Judd and Scott Wilson in the church scenes. Watch for the upper arm that comes into view during our good friend Ashley's close-up.*

Thirty miles north of the river cities, the formerly straitlaced town of Conway has begun to transform itself into the wettest dry city in the state. They're just getting back to their roots, though. An old tavern site with a funny name inspired a Conway festival known as Toad Suck Daze, in which one event is a toad race. Conway also gained a modicum of fame in the 1950s with an amphibian of a different sort. After an encounter with a fisherman, the Lake Conway Monster hooked the public's imagination and became part of local lore.

Other central Arkansas highlights include an elephant farm (Guy) and possible proof of prehistoric aliens (Petit Jean Mountain).

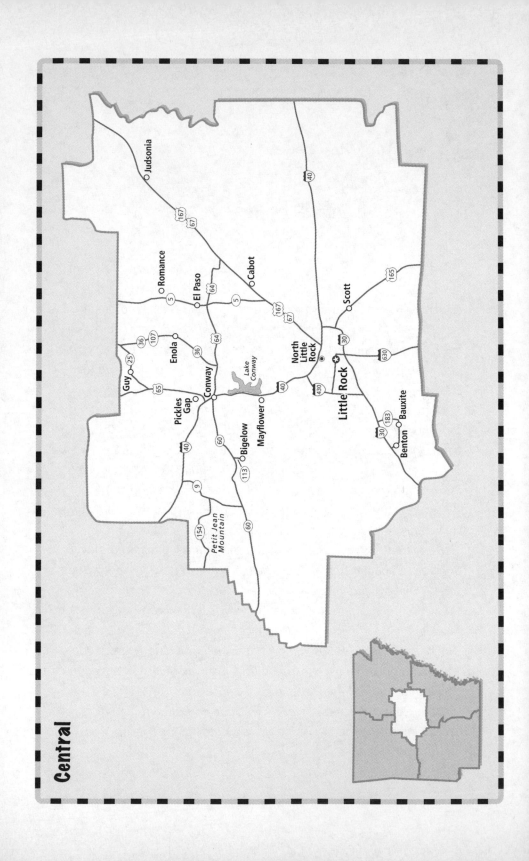

Central

★ ★

Brown Is the Color of My True Love's Teeth
Bauxite

Bauxite ore is the main source of aluminum, and from 1900 to 1964 the main source of bauxite was the little town in central Arkansas that bear's the mineral's name. At the height of mining production, Bauxite's population swelled to 7,000 people. The Alcoa Reynolds Company was based there, and during World War II Bauxite provided 90 percent of the aluminum used in building planes. Postwar America, however, found it cheaper to mine the ore overseas.

Today, with fewer than 500 citizens, the town is a shadow of its former self, but its heritage is remembered at the Bauxite Historical

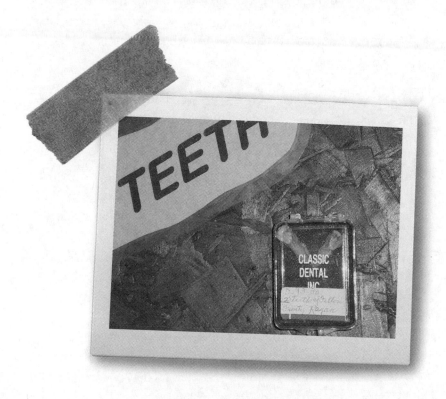

The "before" picture for a whitening strips ad.

★ ★

Association Museum, where you can see numerous artifacts from the community's glory days. A couple of oddities stand out. One is an aluminum lamé ball gown created by Paris designer Jean Desses for Miss Arkansas to wear at the Aluminum Bowl in 1956.

The most bizarre items on exhibit are mottled and brown-stained human teeth—examples of a dental condition that plagued the miners and other Bauxite residents during the town's early years. Minerals in the drinking water caused the discoloration. The effect was something you'd expect to see in the smile of a person with a longtime habit of dipping snuff or chewing tobacco. The Tooth Fairy refused to visit Bauxite, just on principle. Everybody has standards.

The dilemma of the dark teeth, however, had a bright side. The "bauxite teeth," as they came to be known, were actually harder and less likely to decay than normal teeth. Many people afflicted with

He Never Met a Bank He Didn't Rob

During the 1960s, Saline County resident Joe Broadway developed a bad habit. He held up the same bank in Bauxite on four separate occasions.

He started one of the robberies by asking the bank manager, "Do you remember me?"

When the manager said, "I sure do," Broadway quipped, "Well, you know what I'm here for then."

Broadway's streak of luck ran out when he was caught and sent to prison in the 1970s. After his parole in 1979, he moved out of state. We're pretty sure he never returned to Arkansas. They would have seen him in Bauxite. You can bank on that.

the condition still had all their teeth when they died, which was a bit unusual in small, rural towns at that time. Around 1930 the town changed its source of drinking water, and eventually the Tooth Fairy returned.

To get to the Bauxite Historical Association Museum, take I-30 south from Little Rock toward Texarkana. Take exit 123 and follow AR 183 south about 5 miles to the Bauxite Post Office. (Watch for the flag flying above it.) Turn left there onto School Street. Go 1 short block and turn right onto Benton Street, where you'll see the museum to your immediate left at 6707 Benton Street. Museum hours are 10:00 a.m. to 2:00 p.m. on Wednesday and 1:30 to 4:00 p.m. on Sunday, but it's always best to call first (501-557-9858).

The Best Little Orehouse in Arkansas
Benton

The building at 218 South Market Street in Benton isn't just a pretty patchwork of various-colored blocks and mortar. It is truly a unique architectural phenomenon because it's made of bauxite. *Ripley's Believe It or Not!* listed the structure as the only one of its kind in the world.

Known as the Gann House or the Gann Museum, the building was constructed in 1893 as a gift for Dr. Dewell Gann Sr. from his grateful but impoverished patients. They had no money to pay him for his much-needed and appreciated services, but they had access to plenty of bauxite, an ore that was mined in the Saline County area.

Engineers didn't think the bauxite would hold up as a building material, but time has proven them wrong. Harder to believe in today's world is the close doctor-patient relationships existing in that bygone era. Imagine building an office or house for your physician! Then again, you probably have—or at least put his first-born through college.

Dr. Dewell Gann Jr. donated the building to the city of Benton, which used the structure as a library before turning it into the current

★ ★

museum. It still has the feel of an old-fashioned doctor's office and houses some of Dr. Gann Sr.'s belongings, such as his desk. The gabled building, with its fancy wood trimming, has two entrances. It was constructed, after all, during the Victorian era, when genteel ladies would positively get the vapors if they were exposed to the likes of railroad workers and field hands, who also visited the good doctor.

Other exhibits in the museum include a fine collection of Niloak pottery. Niloak spelled backward is kaolin, a high-grade clay. Niloak

Don't knock the house of rock.
ARKANSAS DEPARTMENT OF PARKS AND TOURISM

pottery is an artistic pottery that was created in Benton in 1910 by Charles Dean "Bullet" Hyten and Arthur Dovey.

The museum also contains Sebert Magby's beautiful wood carvings with depictions of historical significance, such as scenes from the life and death of the Confederacy's "boy martyr," David O. Dodd. For all you aficionados of macabre trivia, the man who carried out the execution of Dodd was assistant provost marshal, Lieutenant DeKay.

The Gann Museum's most impressive artifact is the building itself, and that's why it's listed on the National Register of Historic Places.

For museum hours of operation and other information, call (501) 778-5513.

I'm Just Wild about Hairy

Benton

A large, hairy creature was reportedly roaming the woods in northeastern Arkansas as early as 1834. A newspaper article from 1851 claimed that two herdsmen were shocked to find their cattle stampeded by "an animal bearing the unmistakable likeness of humanity." The wild man was of enormous stature with long locks of hair hanging past his shoulders, and his body was completely covered in hair. He stopped and gazed at the herdsmen then turned and ran away at great speed, making leaps and bounds of 12 to 14 feet and leaving footprints 13 inches long.

In his 1941 book *Ozark Country,* Otto Ernest Rayburn wrote about a man called "the Giant of the Hills" who lived in Saline County after the Civil War. Apparently mute, he stood 7 feet tall and wore no clothing, as his body was covered in long, thick hair. Though the wild man was never known to harm anyone, locals using hounds tracked him to a cave in the Ouachita Mountains and roped him.

Locked in the log stockade in Benton, he stripped off the clothing given him and escaped. Trackers followed his trail into Texas, where he got away. Perhaps he was looking for a woman. They say everything is bigger in Texas.

★ ★

Bigelow, a Big Town Laid Low
Bigelow

Bigelow is in Perry County, 13 miles west of Conway. It was originally known by the biblical name Esau, but the name was changed to Bigelow in 1911. At its peak around 1910, Bigelow was the largest town between Little Rock and Fort Smith and had an estimated population of 10,000. It had a train depot, telephone exchange, a newspaper, four hotels, three general stores, two dry-cleaning services, a bank, a drugstore, a hardware store, a jewelry store, an icehouse, a barbershop, a butcher shop, a bakery, a movie theater, and an opera house where concerts and plays were performed by acts from as far away as St. Louis and Kansas City. Ringling Bros. & Barnum and Bailey Circus played there before packed crowds.

Today Bigelow is a like a butterfly that has somehow morphed back into a caterpillar. Only 400 people live there now. A convenience store and self-service gas station make up its entire business district.

What happened? To sum it up in two words: economic collapse. Bigelow was a lumber mill town during the golden era of laissez-faire economics. Unhindered by government control, the timber companies cut every usable tree and didn't replant any. Finally there was nothing left to cut, at which point the timber companies cut and ran, closing down the mills in 1921.

We drove the maze of winding gravel roads that were once city streets. Peeking from the woods, old sagging houses swayed into ruin; elsewhere, stone foundations and crumbling chimneys were smothered in poison ivy and sawbrier. We stopped at the city park, where a clean breeze blew in from the river. A KEEP OUT sign dangled from a barbed-wire fence. Beyond it, in the center of a sun-dappled meadow, cows grazed in the shade of a lone, ancient oak tree. As we enjoyed the unsullied country vista, the advantages of urban development seemed highly overrated.

To visit Bigelow, take AR 60 west from Conway and turn south onto AR 113.

Hallowed Ground
Cabot

The only all-Confederate cemetery in Arkansas is located near Cabot. Though it may sound very elite, this is an exclusive club that no one wanted to join. The soldiers buried there all died not from battle wounds but from disease, and these 428 account for less than a third of the total number who perished.

During the fall and winter of 1862–63, about 1,500 Confederate soldiers died in a typhoid and measles epidemic at Camp Nelson. The camp was a staging location for Rebel troops gathering from Arkansas and Texas. It was named for Brig. Gen. Allison Nelson, commander of the 10th Texas Infantry, who had died in Little Rock at the very beginning of the epidemic. The scourge followed the soldiers to their new bivouac 2 miles east of the Austin community in Lonoke County. The death toll at Camp Nelson dwarfed the number of casualties suffered the following summer during the fight for control of Little Rock. That number was 201, Union and Confederate losses combined.

Before Camp Nelson survivors left the area, they buried the dead, some in communal trenches, others in graves that were mostly unmarked. There they lay nearly forgotten until 1898, when a group of Arkansas Confederate veterans started tending the site where Camp Nelson had been. They found hundreds of poorly marked graves in the woods, and when a veteran named James M. Gately donated some land a few miles southeast of Cabot, the old soldiers disinterred their fallen comrades and reburied them at Camp Nelson Confederate Cemetery.

In 1905 the Arkansas Legislature allocated $1,000 for construction of a monument in honor of the dead. Dedicated with pomp and circumstance on October 4, 1906, the 12-foot-tall obelisk was made of Batesville marble and weighed about ten tons. Granite headstones marked the graves, and a sturdy wire fence enclosed the cemetery. But as the aged veterans started dying, the cemetery deteriorated and the forest reclaimed it.

★ ★

Heaven's gate.
ARKANSAS DEPARTMENT OF PARKS AND TOURISM

For decades the cemetery languished for lack of attention. Then in the 1980s, local residents, including civic groups and the Reserve Officers' Training Corps (ROTC), restored the cemetery, which is now listed on the National Register of Historic Places.

To visit Camp Nelson Confederate Cemetery in Cabot, turn north off AR 321 onto Cherry Road and go about 0.5 mile to Rye Drive. Turn right; the cemetery will be on your left.

Roadside Rodins
Conway

You don't expect to see art along the roadside, unless it's Elvis on black velvet being sold from the back of a van. That's why motorists driving through Conway may do a double take when they pass two outdoor displays of artwork by two very talented individuals. Finton Shaw's Sculpture Garden is located on the old Morrilton highway (US 64), near the Faulkner County–Conway County line. Shaw's friend and fellow artist, Gene Hatfield, has a yard full of abstract art at his home on Donaghey Avenue near the University of Central Arkansas, where he taught art for many years. To create his sculptures, the

Artists Finton Shaw and Gene Hatfield test drive one of Shaw's creations.

★ ★

retired professor uses everything from car parts to metal bed frames.

Hatfield is a beloved institution, not only as an artist but also as a patron of the arts, always ready with encouraging words for up-and-comers. He is not without critics, however. Some look at his lawn and see junk welded together instead of art. In 2002 Hatfield's detractors bent the ear of city officials and sicced the yard Nazis on him. (You might remember that Dennis Rader, aka the BTK killer, was a city code enforcement officer.) The city told Hatfield to take down his lawn art or face heavy fines. His friends and fans rallied to his side and staged a demonstration to show their support. The city backed down, and the art stayed.

Like Hatfield, Shaw has made waves and prevailed. "The bulk of my art is about the human condition," he says.

Shaw's work is often provocative, blending political commentary with eroticism. One sculpture, a nude called *Deseree,* is made of fired clay. A realistic sculpture of terra-cotta, wood, and steel is called *The Penis and the Bullet.* Other pieces are more abstract and made from found objects such as bicycle wheels, clocks, and musical instruments. Shaw is always more than happy to interpret his work. A visitor once singled out a particular conglomeration of pipes and dials for special praise. Shaw smiled but could not take credit for the creation. It was, he explained, his gas meter.

Conway's Clairvoyant
Conway

From the 1930s through the 1980s, Faye George was Conway's resident fortune-teller. She gave consultations in her modest but neat beige brick house on College Avenue. The living room doubled as a waiting room and was seldom empty. She had a reputation that spread far beyond Arkansas.

George knew early in life that she was different. Once while riding with her mother on a bus as a little girl, Faye wondered aloud why a fellow passenger had a suitcase full of left shoes. The surprised man replied that he was a shoe salesman and gave the gifted child his contact information. He wanted to keep in touch.

George had detractors who said all those psychology degrees on the wall in her office showed she just knew how to read people, not their futures, but she also had believers in high places. Winthrop Rockefeller, soon to be Governor Rockefeller, sought her insight about confidential matters.

One visitor arrived incognito behind a large hat and veil, hinting unnecessarily, "Do you not remember *The Little Foxes*?" The mystery woman was none other than Bette Davis.

By 1990 George had become a total recluse, leaving folks to wonder what frightful thing she saw beyond her door.

Driving Blind

An old newspaper item piqued our interest while we were collecting curiosities, and we would like to learn more about this story. If any of our readers can fill in the blanks, we would love to hear from you.

In 1931 a man named Jack "Daredevil" Allen got behind the wheel of a Ford car at Smith Auto Company in Conway, Arkansas. Chief of Police Sam Donnell blindfolded Allen and handcuffed him to the steering wheel. Allen then proceeded to drive for seventy-six hours without stopping. When the endurance drive ended, Allen slept for thirty hours in the show window of Westmoreland's Department Store in Conway. A floor lamp was given away to the lucky person who had come closest to guessing correctly the number of miles "Daredevil" had driven.

The question that begs to be answered: How did he drive blindfolded? And while they were at it, why didn't they give him a few shots of whiskey just to make things interesting?

★ ★

The Froggy Creek Monster
Conway

This whopper of a fish story began in February 1952. George Dillon of Mayflower was running a trotline a few hundred yards southeast of the Narrows Bridge on Lake Conway in Faulkner County when his line snagged. Raising it up he saw a "thing" that had broad shoulders and the green-spotted skin of a frog. Its head resembled a monkey's. Blue lips bordered its mouth, where the fishhook was embedded. Suddenly the creature began to thrash. A webbed hand with long, claw-tipped fingers emerged from the water, and a powerful forearm gripped the side of the boat, causing the vessel to lurch. Dillon dropped the line, and the animal broke free and swam out of sight.

A report of Dillon's experience was printed in the local newspaper, and within a few days the national wire services picked up the story. The following Sunday, a massive traffic jam blocked the one-lane road leading to the spillway. Sightseers came from as far away as Texas, hoping to see the monster.

An unnamed authority with the Board of Health theorized that the animal was a salamander, like the Chinese giant salamanders. Weighing upwards of sixty pounds, these nocturnal creatures nest beneath rock ledges along riverbanks in China and Japan. They are now on the verge of extinction due to dam construction. It seems that when stretches of river are converted to lakes, the rising water levels render normal nesting sites inaccessible.

Was the Lake Conway Monster a hoax? Could it have been someone's exotic pet released into the wild? Or perhaps an unknown species similar to the Asian salamanders?

As time passed, the Lake Conway Monster began to recede from public memory, but it was not altogether forgotten. In the minds of many Arkansans their amphibious Elvis may have left the building, but his legend lived on, if only in B-movie heaven. Two years after the Lake Conway incident, Hollywood released *Creature from the Black*

Lagoon. The movie featured a fictional aquatic villain that bore more than a passing resemblance to Dillon's homegrown original. Arkansas native Julie Adams starred as the object of the creature's affection.

Those interested in visiting the site of the sighting should take the Mayflower exit off I-40 and go east on AR 89 for about 0.5 mile. Turn right onto Dam Road and follow it for 2 miles.

Dazed and Confused
Conway

According to legend, the community on the Arkansas River near Conway called Toad Suck got its unusual name when riverboat crews stopped there and proceeded to drink themselves silly at the local tavern. They were said to "suck on their whiskey bottles 'til their cirrhotic livers caused them to swell up like toads."

Each year on the first weekend in May, Conway hosts an event called Toad Suck Daze. The real Toad Suck was across the river in Perry County, but why let geographical accuracy stand in the way of a good time?

Attractions include carnival rides, musical entertainment, a vintage car exhibition, arts and crafts, and plenty of food. Some of the vittles sound like something even the Clampetts wouldn't serve at dinnertime. Crawfish fried pie, for instance. As one vendor put it, "You never know until you fry it." Fried cheesecake and fried Oreos have both been on the menu. But at least the food is portable. Polish-sausage-on-a-stick, meatballs-on-a-stick, and chicken-on-a-stick have all been available. What next? Fried lard on a stick? Toad à la mode? Can you say "coronary-bypass-on-a-stick?"

The cornerstone of the festival, though, is the toad race. Children and adults capture and train the sometimes-reluctant amphibians. No prodding or poking is allowed, but clapping and yelling get the job done. The human coaches include politicians, who become toadies themselves during an election year.

Perhaps inspired by *They Shoot Horses, Don't They?*, there's

★ ★

Shop at the Toad Store for a ribbeting experience.

Stuck-on-a-Truck, an endurance contest in which competitors vie to
see who can keep a hand on a truck for the longest time. The victor
wins the vehicle and the privilege of driving himself to the asylum
in a bright, shiny new pick-up. Sleep deprivation causes some pretty
weird hallucinations. One person thought they were all at Wal-Mart.
Another thought he was being pulled behind a boat. And then there
was the man who said he had to leave because he was going to a
Tupperware party. It was rumored that one contestant thought he

had been abducted by gigantic, toad-like aliens and forced to compete in a sack race for their amusement. Unfortunately, the fellow who thought he was having pains in his side wasn't hallucinating. He was rushed to the hospital for an emergency appendectomy. Yowza, yowza, yowza!

For more information about Toad Suck Daze, contact the Conway Area Chamber of Commerce at (501) 327-7788.

Nobody Burst Her Bubble
Conway

In 2004 twelve-year-old Kelsey Lea of Conway blew away the competition in a bubble gum–blowing contest sponsored by Wal-Mart and Dubble Bubble, the world's first bubble gum.

Officials in the annual competition use the Bubble Meter, a cardboard caliper, to measure the size of the bubbles. Lea won the preliminary competition with a 20-inch bubble. She was also victorious in the national round, which was broadcast live on NBC's *Today Show*. She walked away with a $10,000 savings bond, a $5,000 donation to her favorite charity, and the right to compete internationally. With her mother, Lesley Lea, as chaperone, Kelsey went to London, England, where she challenged the British Dubble Bubble champion on the BBC and won the title there.

The secret to success in the bubble-blowing biz is practice, practice, practice. You have to stick to it . . . like bubble gum sticks to new shoes.

Prairie Pimples
Conway

Are they the bane of a pubescent prairie dog's existence, erupting at the worst possible time and sending them scurrying to their holes in tears? Hardly. Prairie pimples, or mima mounds, are odd geographical features around 2 or 3 feet high with a diameter of 40 to 50 feet.

These low mounds associated with prairies (and sometimes found in wooded areas as well) are puzzling. Explanations of their origin range from abandoned prairie dog burrows to former anthills to natural gas bubbles beneath the ground. The theory that they were once Indian mounds sounds plausible because Indians did use preexisting mounds as foundations for their houses, but that would account for only a fraction of the total. There are thousands, maybe millions of prairie mounds, all of them west of the Mississippi River and all having formed between 4000 and 1000 BC. How did they form?

One explanation, championed by geologist James Harrison Quinn, points toward a climate shift between 7000 and 3000 BC. Called the Hypsithermal Archaic period, it was an era of prolonged drought, the worst being the 2,500-year period between 7000 and 4500 BC. Within one hundred years, the forests died and Arkansas lowlands reverted to desert, forcing native peoples to head for the hills— the Ozarks and Ouachitas, where water was available from natural springs. They lived among the rock overhangs now often referred to as bluff dwellings.

A time traveler from today would hardly recognize the Arkansas River Valley from that period. Petit Jean Mountain, Mount Nebo, and Mount Magazine would have appeared as treeless mesas, while patches of cacti and desert scrub would have clung to the rocky valley floor. In gently rolling hills or flat areas with little ground cover, wind blew away the topsoil and deposited it at the base of desert shrubs, eventually forming a mound. Over the course of time, the climate became warmer and wetter and the forests returned. Thus prairie pimples could more accurately be called desert pimples.

The mounds are found in abundance statewide. Typical examples may be seen along the walking trail at the Jewel E. Moore Nature Reserve, located off Farris Road in the southwestern corner of the University of Central Arkansas campus in Conway.

The World According to Gar

Conway

We stopped by to sample the organic veggies at the Hendrix College cafeteria in Conway and afterwards walked over to the D. W. Reynolds Life Sciences Building to see a Hendrix legend.

A vivid memory from childhood is the sight of gargantuan fish hanging from the cottonwood trees on the south bank of the Arkansas River, where we used to wait to board the Toad Suck Ferry in Perry County. To a small child, the alligator gar seemed the stuff of nightmares. We shuddered as we listened to old anglers recounting lurid stories of the carnivorous fish's ferocity, how a toddler in the Delta was attacked and killed by a large gar stranded in the flooding of the 1927 overflow.

Those tales, like a number of big fish stories, appear to be rooted more in imagination, but here are some unusual facts: The alligator gar is the second largest freshwater game fish in North America, growing up to 8 feet in length. Record books say that the biggest alligator gar caught on a rod and reel was taken from the Rio Grande in Texas in 1951, but an even larger gar was "hogged" in Arkansas in 1931 either on the St. Francis River or Horseshoe Lake. Sources differ on the location. That fish weighed 279 pounds. Alligator gars can live as long as seventy-five years, and they contain air bladders that enable them to gulp air and remain alive out of water for hours at a time. The big fish seem to have died out in the Arkansas River due to changes in their habitat.

The alligator gar at Hendrix College was caught in 1913 after floodwaters receded on the St. Francis River. Estimated to be more than fifty years old, it was 7 feet, 5 inches long and weighed 161 pounds. It was stuffed and mounted in St. Louis and returned to Arkansas, where it became a big draw at the Meriwether Hardware Store in Paragould. After the store closed in 1962, the gar was brought to Hendrix by Professor Robert W. Meriwether, grandson of the hardware store's proprietor.

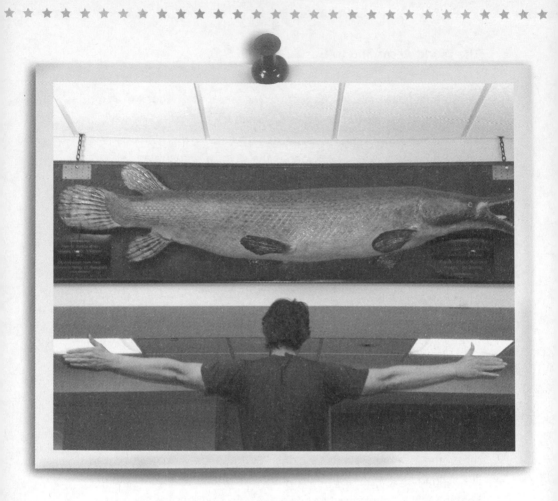

Hey, fish, how big was that man you caught?

Today you can see it hanging in the east foyer of Hendrix's Life Sciences Building. We would categorize its decorative style as "Grotesque Tacky," but on reflection, this stuffed fish is much more widely known and regarded than we are and is likely to remain so long after we're gone.

Hendrix College is located between Harkrider Street and the 1600 block of Washington Avenue in Conway.

Night of the UFOs
Conway

In the mid-1960s, Verna Shoemake and her husband, Lewis, lived on Conway Boulevard near the Faulkner County Fairground. One night, as she got out of bed to investigate an odd rustling sound, Verna wondered why it was so light outside. She looked through the window toward the fairground and there, hovering just above the tree-tops, was an object as big as a house and shaped like a kite.

Mrs. Shoemake's UFO experience, odd as it was, couldn't eclipse an event that occurred on the night of August 16, 1966. Flurries of UFO sightings were reported all across the state. In Fort Smith, 1,500 people joined radio newsman John Garner, as he broadcast live coverage of the spectacle; UFOs, with lights of various colors, moving erratically in the sky. Paragould and Pine Bluff residents reported the same. The next night, it was Little Rock's turn. Air Force spokesmen said they didn't know what the objects were, but just because nobody could identify them didn't mean they were unidentifiable.

For several nights afterward, people sat in lawn chairs in open spaces and watched the sky, but the UFOs were MIA.

Harkrider Hand Jive
Conway

Capt. William A. Harkrider, an early settler, owned a saloon and store in Cadron Gap where US 64 and AR 25 now intersect. In 1863, as he led Confederate troops at the battle of Chickamauga, he was shot in the right leg and passed out. When he regained consciousness, he was too weak to move and lay in a field for three days until Union troops found him.

His leg was shattered, and gangrene had developed. As Union soldiers prepared to load him aboard a wagon bound for the death house, he begged them to get a doctor to amputate his leg, but the soldiers ignored him. In one last desperate attempt to save himself,

★ ★

Driving Miss Fannie

Fannie Turner of Little Rock didn't pass her written driver's test the first time she took it, nor the second time, nor the third, nor the fourth, fifth, tenth, nor twentieth. You'd think she would have given up by, say, the fiftieth, but no. She took Winston Churchill's advice, "Never, ever, ever, ever give in." She was a driven woman. Finally, on October 15, 1978, Fannie passed the test. She had taken it a grand total of 104 times.

he began flashing Masonic hand signs. A Union lieutenant recognized the coded messages and responded by taking Harkrider to a field hospital, where they removed his leg 6 inches above the knee.

Harkrider went on to become a big supporter of Hendrix College (located on Harkrider Street, naturally). Willing to refight the Civil War at a moment's notice, he died in 1899, an un-reconstructed Rebel to the end.

Rockin' at the Crossroads
El Paso

To world travelers, the intersection of AR 5 and US 64 may seem like the middle of nowhere, but it's actually a bustling crossroads where motorists can stop for a while, fill their tanks, fill their bellies, and do some shopping.

Smitty's Trading Post has been drawing customers to the crossroads for more than ten years with their emporium of the eclectic. Their sign says it all: IF WE AIN'T GOT IT, YOU DON'T NEED IT. These necessities include a 4,000-pound gorilla statue that we went ape over and a life-size likeness of Elvis that left us all shook up.

The Smith family started the trading post because Mrs. Smith, better known as Doc, had always liked working flea markets but wanted more regular hours and needed to be close to home. Her husband, Smitty, liked unusual eye-catchers such as the gorilla and Elvis, things you don't see everywhere, so the trading post was born.

The bulk of the merchandise is always changing, but some items stay longer than others. For several years Arkansas's largest rocking

This calls for a very big porch.

★ ★

chair was a fixture at the trading post. Doc couldn't tell us much about the chair because it was Smitty's purchase, and sadly, Smitty passed away in 2006. Doc told us what she did know:

> Smitty asked around till he got a hold of a name of someone who knew someone's cousin's brother-in-law, who might could build such a monster. It took about four weeks to build and was made somewhere in southern Arkansas by a man and his two sons. Nobody local wanted to take on the task, but he finally got in touch with Bob. I want to say his name is Bob.

So, Bob, if you are lucky enough to read this homage to your work, we'd love to hear from you. Not just to give you credit for your creation in future printings of our book but also because we might have another job for you. We writers are sedentary sorts, and with age, our posteriors need ever more sitting room.

For more information about Smitty's Trading Post, such as hours of operation, call (501) 796-8126.

Tornado Alley
Enders

Arkansas weather can get downright freaky sometimes. According to the National Weather Service, three separate tornadoes once hit the same church on the same day. It happened in the Enders community near Guy on Thanksgiving Day, November 25, 1926. Even though this information came from the Weather Service, we doubted it until we talked to Bobby New.

New is the man to see if you want to know about tornadoes in Arkansas. He's a retired professional land surveyor who has studied tornadoes and seen the damage they can wreak. The Cleburne County resident has noticed a pattern in the paths that tornadoes take through Arkansas.

Two areas in Arkansas seem to be more prone to tornado activity.

One route roughly follows a northeast line along US 67. The other goes through central and north-central Arkansas, and New thinks that route follows the old Cherokee Boundary, which starts at Point Remove near Morrilton and ends near Batesville.

"The topography of this area is conducive to tornadoes," New said, explaining that the lay of the land allows for many collisions of warm and cold air. He went on to say, "My theory is that the Cherokee Boundary Line was set as a result of a tornado that came through, a strong one." (A big natural disaster creating a natural dividing line.) "If you take ten tornadoes and average out the directions they run, you'll find they pretty well parallel the Cherokee Boundary."

His mother told him about the storm that went through on Thanksgiving 1926.

"She said the hail with that tornado was like pint fruit jars falling from the sky. The tornado originated somewhere around Guy, and it came through a community called Enders and blew the Methodist Church down. My grandfather was in the sawmill business, and he furnished the lumber to rebuild that church."

New also told us about the Elmer and Pearl Kennedy family who lived 5 miles north of Quitman in the community of Pryor Mountain. A tornado demolished their house in 1938, and they rebuilt on the same spot. Another tornado destroyed that house in 1955. They decided not to tempt Fate again and rebuilt elsewhere. Had they put the third house in the same place, a tornado in 2005 would have blown that one away, too. And yes, it happened where the Cherokee Boundary crosses AR 16.

By the Seat of Its Pants

Faulkner County

Faulkner County was created in 1873, and one of the first orders of business was to name a location for the new county seat. Governor Elisha Baxter appointed a board that selected Conway Station. This

★ ★

decision did not sit well with older residents of the newly formed county who were settled around the communities of Greenbrier, Vilonia, and Holland. They thought the county seat should be located in the center of the county. They petitioned for an election to have the county seat moved to a new town called Arnoldsburg that they were going to establish 3 miles south of Holland.

The other faction was led by Asa Robinson, the founder of Conway Station, who thought his new town would better serve the county's needs due to its proximity to the railroad. Former Chief Engineer Robinson owned most of the land where Conway Station was located.

The pro-center voters out in the county felt the election was a foregone conclusion because they had the numbers on their side, and many of the older residents felt that Robinson, a Connecticut Yankee, was little more than an upstart. (The nerve of the man! As if we

Trivia

Sometime around the latter part of the nineteenth century, settlers in the small farming community of Wooster (as in "Why did the wooster cwoss the woad?") noticed some unusual holes in a patch of boulders 3 miles west of town. Their origin and purpose remained a mystery until the 1960s when M.R. Harrington, curator of the Southwest Museum in Los Angeles, identified them as "grouped-based rock mortars" of the type used by the native peoples to grind acorns and grains into meal. Ranging in size from 6 to 12 inches deep and 12 to 17 inches across, the mortars all lay within a 20 foot radius of each other. Women arranged the mortars close together, so they could visit while they went about their work. When identified, the mortars were believed to be the only such grouping of their kind outside the Pacific Northwest.

asked him to build a railroad across our state. Indeed!) On Election Day the choice on the ticket was between Holland and Conway. The earlier proposal that the new town be named Arnoldsburg (whoever Arnold was) seems to have stumped many of the voters. They cast their ballots for "the center" rather than Holland, and as a result those votes were not counted. It is claimed that if they *had* been counted, Holland not Conway would be the county seat today.

In the end, brand-name confusion prevailed, and while Conway's population of 57,000 people now spend their lives waiting for the trains to pass and crossing guards to go up, Holland's 600 citizens cluster around a wide place in the road, bypassed by history's highway.

Coming to Terms with Pachyderms
Guy

For a unique experience, visit Riddle's Elephant and Wildlife Sanctuary near Guy, Arkansas. Think how much thinner you'll look standing near the gentle giants!

Scott and Heidi Riddle established the sanctuary in 1990 on 330 acres of hills and grassland. The sanctuary is home to about a dozen elephants, both Asian and African. They come from circuses, zoos, and private owners. Though few elephants are born in captivity, the Riddle Farm has a successful breeding program. Two residents, Maximus and Miss Bets, were both born there. At birth they weighed 282 pounds and 263 pounds, respectively.

The Riddles collaborate with veterinarians and research scientists from around the world to improve the chances of survival and quality of life for the largest animal on land.

The sanctuary hosts a yearly International School for Elephant Management, in which students learn about elephant care, including nutrition and reproduction. How to prepare elephants for semen collections is a stimulating class and necessary to prevent broken arms.

The sanctuary also offers the Elephant Experience Weekend. For

**When he trumpets, the Ozark foothills
sound like a savanna in Africa.**
ARKANSAS DEPARTMENT OF PARKS AND TOURISM

$700 you can help feed, water, and bathe the elephants; watch them in their daily routines; or help give a pachyderm pedicure.

The sanctuary is open to the public on the first Saturday of every month between 11:00 a.m. and 3:00 p.m., but it's always best to call first. The admission price depends on how much you want to donate to the nonprofit facility. For a contribution of $35 to $100, you can "adopt" an elephant and help pay for its upkeep. In return, you receive a photo of your elephant, a subscription to the sanctuary newsletter, and a bumper sticker that says, "Ask Me about My Elephant."

For more information about Riddle's Elephant and Wildlife Sanctuary, go to www.elephantsanctuary.org. To contact them, e-mail elephantsanctuary@alltel.net or call (501) 589-3291.

Be Our Guest . . . Forever
Hardin Hill (near Enola)

Decapitation was just one more hazard faced by early travelers in our lovely state.

In 1840 forty-year-old Jonathan Hardin settled in what is now Faulkner County between Enola and McGintytown. There, near a major crossroads, he built an inn atop Hardin Hill. The nearby East Fork of Cadron Creek connected to a drainage ditch that ran along the base of the hill where the corrals were. Many travelers who stopped overnight at the inn were cattlemen on their way to and from the market in Little Rock. For some of these men, flush with money on their return trip, Hardin Inn was an inn without an out—they were never seen or heard from again.

Locals believed that Hardin robbed and murdered travelers, cut their heads off, threw the heads in the drainage ditch, and buried the bodies in nearby Hardin Cemetery. True or not, the story has a poetic "House of Usher" gloom to it. None of Jonathan's sons lived past middle age, and he outlived them all but one. Hardin and his second wife, Elizabeth, are buried in Hardin Cemetery. Their graves are the only ones with tombstones. The rest of the thirty-five or more graves are marked merely by fieldstones.

We have heard rumors that bodies were found floating in a well at a stage-stop south of Hardin Hill where US 64 and AR 36 now intersect. Coincidentally, the family of Hardin's second wife, Elizabeth Greathouse, owned a home nearby, which he visited frequently.

Hardin was said to have buried money on his property. By the 1930s the former site of the old inn had become a large hole because of digging by treasure hunters. When we visited the cemetery, we saw that Hardin's tombstone had been vandalized and nearby graves excavated.

The drainage ditch was said to be "hainted," and children avoided it. Even today, the area spooks people. We interviewed a lady who said she saw three mysterious cloaked figures there one evening when she was driving home. They seemed to float across the road, higher than her car. One stopped, turned its head slowly, and looked directly at her with a surprised look in its amber eyes. It then disappeared with the others beyond the trees.

Hardin Cemetery is off Marcus Hill Road about 100 yards from Clinton Mountain Road.

A Story That Was Hard to Swallow
Judsonia

Arkansas had already made headlines with the rediscovery of the thought-to-be-extinct ivory-billed woodpecker when a bird of a different feather was found in Judsonia in 2008. A true rara avis, it was a pair of conjoined barn swallows that had fallen out of the nest. Odds of finding such a curiosity were calculated at more than a million to one. The baby birds did not survive; one died the day after being found, and the sibling was euthanized. X-rays did not show any shared organs, and though it was first thought they had only three legs, a fourth leg was later found tucked under the skin that connected the birds.

Arkansas sent the deceased duo to the Smithsonian Institution to be studied by experts in ornithology. Alas, preliminary reports cast doubt on the authenticity of the twosome. Seems the birds weren't conjoined twins after all. It is thought that one of them may have had an open wound to which the other became attached. In other words, they were stuck on each other.

Yankee Soldiers Down South, Way Down
Judsonia

The Evergreen Cemetery in Judsonia has a lot of stories to tell. We stopped there initially to see the Grand Army of the Republic (GAR) monument that honors the dead Yankee soldiers buried there. Some books call them Federal casualties, but in actuality the soldiers didn't die as a result of combat. They were men who had no family ties left up north and chose to remain in the Judsonia area after the end of the Civil War. Sixteen of them are buried there near the monument that was erected and dedicated in 1894. It is the only memorial to Union troops in Arkansas and is thought to be the only GAR memorial in the South. The inscription reads simply, "In Memory of the Defenders of the Union, 1861–1865."

While we were at the cemetery, we noticed several graves with the same date of death on the headstones and wondered aloud about the cause of so many deaths on the same day. Later, while researching another story, we stumbled upon the reason for all those deaths. The date was March 21, 1952—the day of the deadliest tornado outbreak ever to hit the state of Arkansas. One hundred and twelve fatalities were recorded, and about half of them were suffered in Judsonia and Bald Knob, 5 miles away.

Altogether seventeen tornadoes raked across the state that day, and twelve of the twisters were deadly. Survivors crawled out of the rubble to see trees turned into kindling wood and debris scattered for miles. The storm uprooted huge old trees at the Evergreen Cemetery, where many of the storm victims would be buried. One service was a

In Memory Of The
Defenders Of The
UNION
1861. — 1866.

Enemies became friends.

mass funeral for eleven. Cemeteries hold a lot of history and a lot of heartache.

Evergreen Cemetery is located on Judson Avenue (AR 385) in Judsonia.

2004, a Space Odyssey
Little Rock

We've come a long way since the days when we described space aliens as little green men from Mars. We now know they're gray. Larry King said so. Seriously, though, virtual reality technology is now so advanced, you can experience the wonders of space without leaving the security of terra firma.

The EpiSphere, located at the Aerospace Education Center in Little Rock, is a combination planetarium and theater. When it opened in 2004, it was the only single-projector, full-dome digital video system on Earth. London now has one, too, but Little Rock's was the first. Images are projected onto the full dome, so the impression is one of being surrounded by celestial bodies in outer space. We were awed by the creation of the Milky Way, and we brought out the hankies when a star died.

The seats in the EpiSphere are from race cars, and during some of the more active presentations, it feels as though seat belts are needed. Visitors can experience the excitement of zooming through wormholes or riding a tornado. We haven't tried those yet, but the tornado sounds like a thrill a minute, if you like the spin cycle.

The EpiSphere can accommodate 150 people. The distinctive dome is constructed of 225 sheets of aluminum, which we assume keeps out all the harmful space alien mind-controlling rays.

Also at the Aerospace Education Center, you'll find the IMAX Theater, which was the first in the state. The screen is eight stories high. Films about dinosaurs are particularly impressive, but at eight stories, even the GEICO gecko comes off looking like Godzilla.

Other attractions at the Aerospace Center include the Arkansas

★ ★

Aviation Hall of Fame and an aircraft collection that features a genuine Sopwith Camel, a vintage World War I fighter plane. It's the only one in the country, and only six others are left in the entire world. Darn you, Red Baron!

The Aerospace Education Center is at 3301 East Roosevelt Road, near the Little Rock Airport. For more information call (501) 376-4629.

Ghostly Government
Little Rock

The Arkansas State Capitol building is a three-quarter-scale replica of the National Capitol in Washington, D.C. Construction was completed in 1915 after years of delay and cost overruns. The building has become a favorite set with filmmakers as a stand-in for its bigger, more famous counterpart, but to our knowledge no one has filmed a horror movie there. Nonetheless, it might be the perfect setting for a ghost story because the building really is haunted, according to Spirit Seekers Paranormal Investigation Research and Intervention Team (SPIRIT).

The capitol was built atop the site of the state's first prison, so naturally, what we have here is failure to communicate. Rather than the usual chain rattling and screams of the damned, the phenomena reported include faint voices, barely audible except when recorded on sensitive microphones and played back through powerful amplifiers. It could be old soldier Douglas McArthur in the process of fading away, or the voices of dead politicians still doing what they did best . . . talking. Who you gonna call? Ghost filibuster busters, of course.

Using special recording equipment that can pick up the faintest sound, SPIRIT taped the voice of a ghost who, when asked his name, replied "Edward." Visual contact has been reported, too, mostly in the form of spirit orbs (glowing orbs of light), but on at least one occasion, a ghost materialized. The cheeky specter was said to have stopped and doffed his hat to a witness before continuing up the steps of the House of Representatives.

★ ★

The capitol building is located on Capitol Avenue in downtown Little Rock. It is open to the public Monday through Friday from 7:00 a.m. to 5:00 p.m. and on weekends and holidays from 10:00 a.m. to 5:00 p.m. Call (501) 682-5080 for more information.

The Name's Friday, *Arkansaurus Fridayi*
Little Rock

On a warm summer day in August 1972, J. B. Friday of Sevier County was having a "severe" problem. One of his cows was missing. He set out to look for it on his farm near Lockesburg. Instead, in an abandoned gravel pit he discovered a window into a lost world: the foot bones of a creature that roamed the coastal lowlands of our state more than one hundred million years ago.

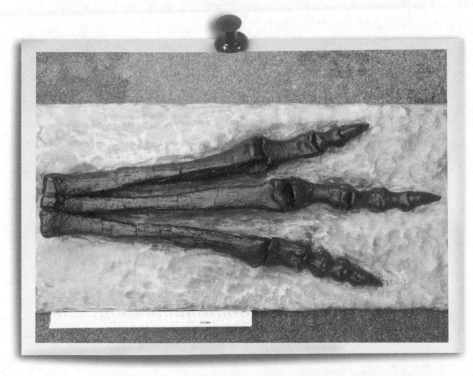

Does this look like the foot of a dinosaur or more like Big Bird's?
ARKANSAS GEOLOGICAL SURVEY

Later named *Arkansaurus fridayi,* the two-legged animal was at first believed to be an ornithomimid, an omnivorous dinosaur resembling a modern ostrich in both body shape and dietary habits. Fossils of this type had been recovered in Texas and Oklahoma, but more complete skeletal remains, showing similar bone structure, were recently found in Colorado, leading paleontologists to revise their opinions. They reclassified the animal as a possible raptor, like the velociraptors that pursued the hapless humans in the movie *Jurassic Park.*

Raptors were carnivorous predators, scavenging or hunting in packs like hyenas or African wild dogs. They preyed on the old, young, weak, and sick, perhaps following the herds of plant-eating dinosaurs, such as the much larger *Pleurocoelus* or *Astrodon.* Pleurocoelus tracks from roughly the same period were later found in a gypsum quarry that was once part of an ancient beach at nearby Nashville. (See Sauropod Promenade.)

Only a handful (or should we say footful) of bones were recovered. The rest of the skeletal remains are believed to have been scattered or used as road-fill beneath what is now AR 24. The actual bones are now being studied at Dinosaur National Monument in Utah. Fortunately, casts made of the reconstructed foot bones are on display at the Arkansas Geological Survey (3815 West Roosevelt Road in Little Rock), at the Museum of Discovery (500 President Clinton Avenue in Little Rock), and at the Mid-America Museum in Hot Springs.

All the Pretty Wooden Horses
Little Rock

Just inside the entrance to the Little Rock Zoo, you'll find a reminder of a bygone era, and it's not a replica. It's the real McCoy, the one and only. Literally. The Over-the-Jumps Arkansas Carousel is a one-of-a-kind merry-go-round that almost didn't survive into the twenty-first century.

Even when it was made in 1924, the carousel was unusual because of its undulating track, which gave riders the feeling that the

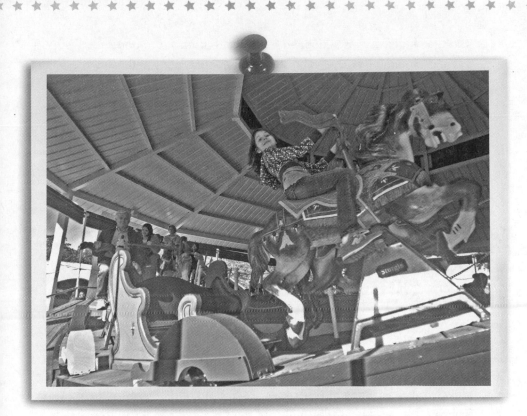

Whee!
ARKANSAS DEPARTMENT OF PARKS AND TOURISM

pretty painted horses were galloping over hills and valleys. Built by
the Herschell-Spillman Engineering Corporation in North Tonawanda,
New York, the carousel was originally a traveling amusement ride and
visited Arkansas in the 1920s and 1930s before becoming a permanent fixture at War Memorial Park in 1942. For a nickel per ride, it
was affordable entertainment for generations of children.

In 1989 the carousel was put on the National Register of Historic Places. But when the park closed two years later, it looked as
though the joyride might end. Volunteers rallied to save the beloved
antique and raised money to restore it. One of the most successful

★ ★

fund-raising ideas was "adopting" the forty horses out to donors. For a minimum of $5,000, a person could adopt a pony and name it. Adoption fees for the four lead horses ranged from $25,000 to $50,000. State funds also played a part in the financing.

The project took a long time and had its ups and downs, but six-teen years and $1 million later, the carousel was returned to its former glory. Old paint was scraped off the ponies—one had forty-three

Confederate Cache

The Hatfield community (pop. 300) in Polk County hides a secret, and Bob Brewer has spent a good portion of his life trying to uncover it, as he explains with his co-author Warren Getler in their book *Rebel Gold.* The gist of his story is this: At the end of the Civil War a faction of Freemasons composed of die-hard Southern sympathizers known as the Knights of the Golden Circle (KGC) took what was left of the Confederate treasury and hid it in remote parts of the south and southwest. One such area was the Ouachita Mountains in west-central Arkansas. The flurry of gold mining activity there in the 1880s was, they say, a cover for the KGC's true purpose of digging secret underground repositories. These caches ranged from mason jars full of coins buried just beneath the surface to large underground vaults containing weapons and bullion. Brewer claims these depositories were laid out in an elaborate circular grid system like those said to have been used by the Knights Templar, who based the grid pattern on medieval maps that showed Jerusalem as the center of the universe. Coded directional markers using Masonic symbols were carved into rocks and trees to help KGC initiates navigate layers—and fresh, vibrant colors applied. After mechanical, electrical, and structural repairs and updates were made, the Over-the-Jumps Arkansas Carousel debuted in its new home at the Little Rock Zoo in 2007. It was a merry occasion.

To get to the Little Rock Zoo, take exit 4 (Fair Park) off I-630 in Little Rock. Turn left onto Fair Park Boulevard and then right onto Zoo Drive. For hours of operation, visit www.littlerockzoo.com.

the rugged terrain. The purpose of these stockpiles was to fund a future second rebellion when the South would rise again. Originally, ex-Confederate soldiers, called sentinels, were used to guard the caches, and Brewer claims his grandfather became one such guard sometime after the turn of the century.

Brewer and Getler assert that Albert Pike was a founder and leader in the KGC and one of the masterminds behind the hidden Confederate treasure depositories. Pike was the famous polymath who moved to Arkansas in 1832 and became head of the state's Know-Nothing Party prior to the Civil War. He later rose to become the highest ranking Freemason in the world. Most mainstream historians see no evidence to back up the portrayal of Pike as a villainous leader of a super-secret organization, but true believers think this lack of proof is itself proof of how successful Pike really was. Factual or not, one thing is certain. When he wasn't busy openly or secretly plotting the overthrow of the U.S. government, Pike must have enjoyed relaxing at his lovely antebellum home that is now the Arkansas Arts Center Community Gallery at Seventh and Rock Streets in Little Rock.

★ ★

John R. Brinkley, the Goat Gland Doctor
Little Rock

Long before the advent of Botox and Viagra, promises of a new lease on life were offered to the public by physicians with credentials that were questionable, to say the least. In Arkansas, medical quackery had become so rampant by the 1880s that the state legislature felt compelled to pass the following resolution: "It is the opinion of this house that surgery and medicine are Humbugs, and that all medical colleges should be declared nuisances injurious to the health of the Commonwealth and therefore should be abated." In 1939 the *Journal of American Medical Association* named Arkansas one of the two worst states for quackery. The rival for this dubious honor was California.

Perhaps the most notorious of the medical scam artists was Dr. John R. Brinkley (1885–1942). Brinkley became known as the goat gland doctor because of the operations he performed in which he allegedly replaced men's prostate glands with billy goat testicles. These sex rejuvenations cost the patients a minimum of $750—twice that if the donor goat was especially youthful.

The procedure was so popular that Brinkley became a millionaire. He set up his lucrative practice first in his home state of Kansas, then Mexico, and finally on Marylake Drive in Little Rock, where he opened an office and hospital in 1937. By that time, however, questions about his procedures and ethics had risen along with the number of malpractice suits filed against him. Mounting legal expenses depleted his finances, and he filed for bankruptcy in 1940. He died soon thereafter. Ironically, the hospital he founded in Little Rock—a facility dedicated to the extension and enhancement of male potency—became a Carmelite monastery.

Honey, I Stole the Town!

Little Rock

There was once a custom on the frontier known as a barn raising or cabin raising, where neighbors got together, threw a party, and helped newcomers build a shelter. In Arkansas, every so often we had a "town razing," sometimes confused with hell raising.

It happened in June 1821 in Little Rock (or Arkopolis, as it was sometimes called). Citizens were whooping it up, and the whole place was afire. The town had only recently been named the territorial capital and, thanks to its new status, had overnight become a prime real estate market. Two competing groups of land speculators claimed ownership of the town site, and the court system had to rule on the dispute.

The losing faction, faced with the prospect of having their houses and buildings confiscated, staged a protest a la Boston's tea party. After first fortifying themselves with many drams of an elixir considerably stronger than tea, they painted their faces to disguise themselves as drunken Indians (or Indians masquerading as soused white men) and went to town. Using ropes and chains, they hoisted the wooden structures up on sledges or rollers, and like marauding drag queens, dragged the buildings over into the Quapaw Quarter. They were unable to move the lone remaining two-story stone building, so as a parting gesture, they blew it up and set it ablaze.

Today you can see some of the buildings that survived the birth of a capital by touring the grounds of the Historic Arkansas Museum. The structures include antebellum homes and the building that was probably the first to be moved to safety, the Hinderliter Grog Shop.

The museum, formerly known as the Arkansas Territorial Restoration, is located at 200 East Third Street in Little Rock. Tours are conducted only at certain times during the day, so call (501) 324-9345 for schedules and other information.

Visit soon, before the liquored-up reenactors arrive and drag it all away.

★ ★

The Biggest Dam Bridge in the World
Little Rock

At 4,226 feet, the Big Dam Bridge over Murray Lock and Dam in Little Rock/North Little Rock is the world's longest bridge built strictly for pedestrians and bicyclists. The Chain of Rocks Bridge in St. Louis, Missouri, is 5,350 feet long, but it was constructed as a highway bridge. Only 3,463 feet of the Big Dam Bridge are actually over water; ramps on both sides of the river add the additional length.

Pulaski County's Judge Buddy Villines was the visionary who spearheaded the campaign to build the bridge. He saw it as a bridge to good health that connects people with other people. He has called

Bridge of the dammed.
ARKANSAS DEPARTMENT OF PARKS AND TOURISM

it a "Bridge of Dreams," but Villines is also responsible for giving the structure a name that evokes laughter from young and old alike.

The bridge was eight years in the making and beset with all the problems inherent in such an ambitious undertaking. At times the people involved with the project were ready to throw in the towel. Then one day during a meeting, when emotions were about to get the best of them, Villines stood up and said, "We are going to build that dam bridge." Everybody laughed, and the Big Dam Bridge got its name.

The bridge is 14 feet wide, cost nearly $13 million to build, and rises seven stories above the Arkansas River. Capable of withstanding winds up to 100.58 miles per hour, the bridge connects 17 miles of walking trails in Little Rock and North Little Rock, with more trails being added all the time. The point of access to the Little Rock side of the bridge is 7600 Rebsamen Park Road; from the North Little Rock side, it is 4000 Cooks Landing Road.

On September 28, 2006, Rich Cosgrove and Nancy Green became the first couple to be married on the bridge, with Judge Villines officiating at the rite. All in attendance agreed it was the best dam wedding there ever was.

Take Me to the River Market
Little Rock

The biggest fad to hit the market in 2000 was the robotic singing fish-on-a-plaque, Billy Bass. It was the bane of every fisherman's existence, especially at Christmas or on Father's Day. Even lovers of the motion-activated toy eventually grew tired of it and had to admit there was truth in the old saying, "Fish and guests stink after three days." But what to do with Billy after the novelty wore off? He had become like a member of the family or, at the very least, like a car you had named. You can't just throw away something like that.

Enter Shannon Wynne, owner of a chain of restaurants called the Flying Fish. Wynne had received a lot of Billy Basses as gifts over the

A catchy gimmick.

years, and they were taking up attic space. He decided to incorporate the animatronic fish in the decor of his upscale eateries, so he established the World's First Billy Bass Adoption Center at the Flying Fish location in Little Rock's River Market District. The restaurant adopts Billy Basses brought in by customers, and several hundred adorn the walls. You'll see more fins there than you would at a 1950s auto show. Displayed under each Billy Bass is the date of adoption and the name of the parent relinquishing custody. The parent fills out adoption papers and receives a certificate along with a free basket of catfish. The gimmick is so popular, it has spawned adoption centers in other Flying Fish locales.

The sign on the wall says, "Bring us your Billy, we'll fill your belly! Plus we will take on the responsibility of feeding, loving, cleaning up after your Billy Bass as long as he shall live. You may visit on weekends or weekdays, but you must NOT bring him treats, as the other Billys get irked and this may start some Billy aching amongst the school!"

Before a Billy Bass goes up on the wall, his battery is deactivated. Otherwise, a cacophony of "Take Me to the River" and "Don't Worry, Be Happy" would serenade restaurant patrons. Children should be seen and not heard.

The Flying Fish at 511 President Clinton Avenue is open 11:00 a.m. until 10:00 p.m. daily. For more information call (501) 375-FISH (3474).

Leadership of the Highest Caliber
North Little Rock

An interpretive panel near the railroad tracks just south of the junction of US 165 and US 70 (East Broadway Street) in North Little Rock tells about an incident that occurred there on September 6, 1863. In the midst of a Civil War that pitted brother against brother and friend against friend, two fellow officers of the Confederacy met and faced off in what many historians consider the last duel fought in Arkansas.

Dueling was not all that unusual among the gentry in the Old South. A man who thought he had been wronged or insulted considered a duel to be the honorable way to restore his reputation. Imagine if we dueled today every time someone uttered a put-down or disagreed with another about politics. Nobody would be left standing. We've even managed to turn the word "disrespect" into a verb.

In the Civil War South, though, an aggrieved individual could demand satisfaction, and if the adversary accepted the challenge, the two men would meet at dawn to settle their differences.

Brig. Gen. John C. Marmaduke and Brig. Gen. L. M. Walker, both graduates of West Point, had fought together in a battle at Helena,

263

★ ★

where Union forces were headquartered. Walker was supposed to protect Marmaduke's flank but was concerned about his own men's safety and made the tactical decision not to intercede when Marmaduke came under heavy fire. After the Confederate forces were repulsed, word got back to Walker that Marmaduke had denounced his conduct on the battlefield. Walker laughed at first but then grew angry. Fearing the criticism might have a damaging effect on his military career, Walker demanded an apology from Marmaduke. When he didn't receive it, Walker challenged Marmaduke to a duel. Marmaduke accepted. With pistols at the ready, the two men aimed at each other and fired. Both missed, but Marmaduke was faster with the second shot. Walker couldn't dodge that bullet and died the next morning.

Marmaduke went on to become governor of Missouri and died in office.

Across the railroad from the interpretive panel is a bronze plaque also commemorating the duel, but it is harder to find. The site is on the itinerary of the Little Rock Civil War Campaign Tour. To request a brochure call (501) 699-1403 or (800) 844-4781 or write to Little Rock Campaign Driving Tour, Central Arkansas Civil War Heritage Trail, P.O. Box 2125, Little Rock, AR 72203.

From a Little Acorn Grew . . .
North Little Rock

Joyce Kilmer would appreciate this one.

A tree of distinction grows in North Little Rock. It is the official city tree, so designated by a proclamation from the North Little Rock Tree Board. It even owns the land on which it stands. Former Mayor Patrick Henry Hayes and then-Governor Bill Clinton signed a deed on March 19, 1990, bestowing ownership rights to the tree and its heirs and assigns.

The tree is a beautiful live oak, which is not, for all you smart alecks, an undead oak. Although oaks are deciduous trees, live oaks do not lose their leaves in wintertime. That's one reason this tree is

★ ★

so easy to recognize, but there's just something special about this particular live oak. It's the kind of tree children love to climb—plenty of good, strong limbs.

The tree is on the west side of Pike Avenue in the 1500 block. Much of that area, especially the other side of the street, is filled with small businesses and industry. The tree, we suppose, was lucky to have sprouted where it did. Otherwise it would have been cut down ages ago. As a matter of fact, not long before the tree became a landowner, the Arkansas Highway Department extended Pike Avenue, and the oak narrowly escaped a fate with the woodchopper. Thankfully the tree had friends in high places. One of those friends was former Mayor Casey Laman, who was ninety-four years old in 2008 when he spoke about his personal bond with the oak.

When Laman was a teenager, he would meet his sweetheart under the tree's broad canopy. The young couple would sit and talk and hold hands. This was about 1929, and boys and girls used to take things a bit slower then. The girl, Arlene Ellis, became Mrs. Casey Laman in 1933.

Laman's words were laden with nostalgia as he said, "That tree is still sacred to me. I still drive by there on occasion, and it comes all over me all over again."

No Run-of-the-Mill Mill

North Little Rock

In the opening sequence of the movie *Gone with the Wind,* the narrator eulogizes the passing of the Old South over a montage of quaint, picture-postcard scenes. None is more evocative of pastoral bliss than the brief shot of a nineteenth-century gristmill. What few movie fans realized then was that the Old Mill, as the building came to be called, was neither old nor a mill; and rather than being located in some sleepy, rural hamlet, it stood in a park off a busy thorough-fare in downtown North Little Rock, Arkansas.

(Continued on page 268)

Scope This Out

Quick! What's the first city you think of when you hear the words "rock and roll"? Is it Cleveland, Ohio? We didn't think so. But that's where the Rock and Roll Hall of Fame is located, so maybe the idea of a maritime museum in North Little Rock isn't as loopy as it sounds. Actually, it's the Arkansas Inland Maritime Museum, but we just got to thinking about other possible museums for Arkansas. The Arkansas French Foreign Legion Museum and the Arkansas Samurai Museum would be interesting.

Our maritime museum features the USS *Razorback,* a vintage World War II submarine with a very distinguished background. It saw action in the Pacific Theater, where it sank at least five ships and was awarded five battle stars. The *Razorback* also served in the Vietnam War before being transferred to the Turkish Navy, where it was renamed the *Muratreis.* Its actions there were classified, so if we told you what they were, we'd have to kill you.

After the sub was decommissioned in Turkey, North Little Rock bought it and rechristened it the *Razorback.* Because of the high cost of bringing the sub to Arkansas, some locals referred to it as the turkey, but this bird is truly an eagle. The oceanic hero is the centerpiece for the museum, which opened May 15, 2005. The *Razorback* is the world's longest-serving submarine and one of only two surviving subs that were present at the formal surrender of Japan on September 2, 1945.

When you call (501) 371-8320 for more information about the Arkansas Inland Maritime Museum, ask about a possible overnight stay, but be forewarned: You might be sandwiched in the sub with a ghost. Staff members have reported hearing strange noises on board the *Razorback,* and alarms sometimes go off for no apparent reason. We wouldn't worry, though, unless you start hearing "Daydream Believer." Then you'll know you're in Davy Jones's locker.

The USS *Razorback* anchors the Arkansas Inland Maritime Museum.

Rhett and Mammie's secret love nest.
ARKANSAS DEPARTMENT OF PARKS AND TOURISM

Built in the early 1930s, the two-story structure was designed by architect Frank Carmean. But it is the work done by Dionico Rodriguez that makes the site so noteworthy. With a keen eye for intricate detail, he sculpted concrete to look exactly like wood, stone, and iron.

Rodriguez called the Old Mill his masterpiece, boasting that he used the finest quality concrete, steel, and copper reinforcements. He kept his formulas and methods hidden as much as possible, even going so far as to prepare paint mixtures out of the trunk of his car. The end results are amazing. Walkways and bridges look as though they were made from trees and driftwood instead of concrete. Even the small mundane items, such as planking and an old rain barrel, are remarkably realistic. We had to touch them to be sure. Only the feel of the cool, hard surfaces is convincingly concrete.

The Old Mill is deserving of its listing on the National Register of Historic Places. To anyone who disagrees, we say, "Frankly, my dear, I don't give a damn!"

To visit the Old Mill, take McCain Boulevard East, turn south onto Fairway Avenue, and then take a left onto Lakeshore Drive.

You'll find a great place to mill around.

Haven't We Met Before?
Petit Jean Mountain

In elementary school our teacher laid flowers on Petit Jean's grave, and we cried after hearing the various tales of the girl's tragic end: mauled by bears that were annoyed at her flute playing or shot by her lover after she turned rabid. Or how about this one?

Long ago in France, when folks wore powdered wigs and bathed once a year whether it was necessary or not, a young man sought his fortune in Arkansas. He'd planned to leave his beautiful, nitpicking fiancée, Adrianne Dumont, behind, but she secretly assumed the identity of a cabin boy and joined the voyage. The crew called her Petit Jean because of her complaints about their habit of spitting in

Petit Jean's grave? Could we also interest
you in the Brooklyn Bridge?
ARKANSAS PARKS AND TOURISM DEPARTMENT

the sea and ending their sentences with prepositions. (Where was her head at?)

They finally reached Arkansas and sailed upriver, where, much to everyone's relief, Petit Jean caught a fever and died. Helpful Indians, attempting to place her spirit as far away as possible, took her up the mountain and used primitive jackhammers to bury her on the plateau that now bears her name.

Still, one wonders, what sailor wouldn't know that a beautiful young woman was living in his midst? We're to believe a change of clothing rendered her unrecognizable? And why continue so long with the masquerade? Was she love-struck or a frustrated transvestite? Perhaps Petit Jean State Park should sponsor a cross-dressing contest.

We read an article online (so it must be true) that said the Petit Jean legend is—as the French say—*merde*.

At the turn of the twentieth century, a family named Stout owned a lodge on the mountain. They concocted the Petit Jean story in an effort to gain the honeymoon market. The ruse was so popular that around 1912, they hired someone to go up to the overlook, break up some rocks, and create a grave.

When we told our old teacher the truth, she replied, "You mean for years I've been decorating a phony grave?"

We shrugged and said, "Yes, but you can still put flowers on it."

"Maybe so," she said, adding, "I think fake ones would be appropriate, don't you?"

To visit Petit Jean's grave or whatever, take AR 154 to the top of Petit Jean Mountain and follow the signs.

Rockefeller's Autotorium
Petit Jean Mountain

We once had a friend who loved his car more than he loved his wife. He ended up living in his car; his wife took everything else. Even if you're not as crazy for cars as our friend, you'll still enjoy a visit to the Museum of Automobiles on Petit Jean Mountain. They have more

★ ★

than fifty cars that are noteworthy either because of their classic engineering and design or because of their connection to a famous person. Since the autos are privately owned, the displays change—at least one-third are rotated each year. Winthrop Rockefeller, thirty-seventh governor of Arkansas, founded the museum in 1964. Two of Rockefeller's own cars are on display there: his first Cadillac, which he kept for sentimental reasons, and the Caddy he owned at the time of his death in 1973. Both Cadillacs are maroon, the Rockefeller family's signature color.

The rotating collection includes two presidential vehicles: John F. Kennedy's 1963 Lincoln Continental and Bill Clinton's blue Mustang.

Another museum showpiece belonged to the King of Rock 'n' Roll. Elvis Presley bought the black Ranchero in 1967 when he owned a ranch in Mississippi. Elvis a rancher? Who knew?

We called one display the May-Mae car. It's a pink 1937 Packard that may have belonged to Mae West, the sultry cinema siren.

Other automotive symbols of man's ingenuity and style include a 1912 Paige Beverly Touring Car, touted as the most beautiful car in America; a 1923 Climber, a very limited edition; and a 1924 Red Bug, which was powered by a twelve-volt battery.

The museum also has a 1914 Cretors Popcorn Wagon and a vintage gas pump that was used when gas was 9 cents a gallon. No, we weren't high on fumes when we read that, although fumes are about all you can buy for 9 cents these days.

Other antiques on display include a collection of license plates, a player piano, and penny arcade machines. One of the arcade amusements is a combination fortune-telling dispenser and scale that reads, "YOUR FATE AND YOUR WATE!"

Located at the eastern end of Petit Jean State Park on AR 154, the Museum of Automobiles is open year-round (except Christmas Day) from 10:00 a.m. to 5:00 p.m. Call (501) 727-5427 or visit www .museumofautos.com for admission rates; but trust us, you don't have to be a Rockefeller to get in.

Trivia

The Climber Motor Corporation was established in 1919 in Little Rock, and over the next five years the company produced between 200 and 300 cars and trucks. The vehicles were attractive and durable and handled well on Arkansas's rough roads, but financial problems and parts shortages plagued the manufacturer. The country was in a recession, and Climber cars were expensive ($2,250 versus $355 for a Model T Ford). Bankruptcy closed the doors on the Climber factory in 1924. Today only two Climber cars are known to exist, both located at the Museum of Automobiles on Petit Jean Mountain.

O Space Brother, Where Art Thou?

Petit Jean Mountain

In 1943 Ray Palmer was editor of *Amazing Stories,* a popular pulp fiction magazine devoted to science fiction. One day a rambling, 10,000-word manuscript arrived in the mail. Its author, Richard Sharpe Shaver, claimed to have esoteric knowledge of Earth's ancient history and mankind's origins.

According to Shaver, millions of years ago the world was ruled by beings from Atlantis, some of whom fled into space when Earth's atmosphere deteriorated to a point where it was no longer inhabitable. Those who stayed behind were divided into two groups: Those who lived on the earth's surface were angelic Teros; their underground counterparts were devilish Deros. Teros became the ancestors of humans.

Palmer was fascinated by the story and serialized it as fact in his magazine. The series was a hit for about three years. Many critics, however, thought that Palmer was exploiting Shaver and that Shaver's writings were the delusions of a paranoid schizophrenic. When the fad faded, the magazine's publishers fired Palmer and pulled the plug on "The Shaver Mystery."

Meanwhile, Shaver continued to write and self-publish his books and pamphlets. He moved to Summit, Arkansas, where he and his wife ran a rock shop. He spent the last decades of his life searching for physical evidence of ancient alien civilization. A spot on Petit Jean Mountain piqued his interest as possible proof.

Off Cedar Creek Trail lies a boulder of sandstone and conglomerate, a naturally occurring cementlike material. Called Carpet Rock because of the unusual design on its surface, it is a fragment, broken off from an overhanging ledge above it. Shaver thought the groove patterns were the imprints of steel reinforcement rods that had long ago rusted away. He speculated that the chunk of concrete was part of an ancient dam built by a prehistoric alien super-race. Shaver died in 1975 without knowing what his ultimate place in history might be.

Carpet Rock is located on Cedar Creek Trail. A shortcut starts behind the log structure called Pioneer Cabin, 1 mile west of the Petit Jean State Park Visitor Center on AR 154. Carpet Rock is out in the open on the right side of the trail, but you must go around to the north side of the huge boulder to see the design on the overhang's underside.

Indian Rock House Cave
Petit Jean Mountain

In ancient times, talking to God meant going up on the mountain. Greeks believed their gods lived on Mount Olympus. Peruvians built shrines in the Andes. Tibetans have long revered Mount Everest. Many Native American religions also share the belief that if one wants to commune with the gods, one must get high—literally and not just in the Rastafarian sense. The walls and ceiling of Indian Rock

House Cave, atop Petit Jean Mountain, display evidence of this old truism in the form of pictographs believed to have been painted by Native Arkansans more than 300 years ago.

Many examples of rock art are found at scenic overlooks on ridges and benches or atop mountains. These are thought to have been sites of group rituals or public events. Because of the secluded nature of Indian Rock House Cave, it was probably the site of secret rituals requiring privacy; only the special initiates were allowed to see and participate.

We'd always figured that the designs were done by hunter-gatherers living atop the mountain. However, pottery from Carden Bottoms near Russellville displays the same red pigment and many identical motifs as the images painted on the walls at Indian Rock House Cave. It is likely that the people from the towns at Carden Bottoms were the same ones who painted the designs atop the mountain. If so, it means the pictographs probably were done at the same time as the pottery—in the sixteenth century, when the Mississippian culture was on the verge of collapsing.

Modern historians believe this is the site of Tanico in the Kingdom of Cayas, the town that Hernando de Soto invaded in the fall of 1541. (See Everybody's Out of Town.) Archaeological examinations of trash dumps at Carden Bottoms show heavy use until about 1650, when the site was abandoned. Like most of the Arkansas River Valley, the area was largely uninhabited when French explorer Bernard de La Harpe visited the area in 1722. What caused this widespread depopulation still remains a mystery.

In recent years Indian Rock House Cave has been the target of vandals armed with spray paint, and air pollution is considered the cause behind the accelerated fading of Indian rock art paintings, so see them while you can. For directions contact Petit Jean State Park at (800) 264-2462.

Mountain Valley or Valley Mountain?

The handsome young model in the photograph is standing at the bottom of a slot canyon. These depressions form when swift streams flow off steep elevations and cut deep, narrow channels in the lower bedrock. This formation is similar to those found along the modern Colorado River, where a few years back, a sudden downpour high in the mountains sent a wall of water rushing down on a group of unsuspecting hikers, who were trapped and drowned.

But the man in the picture is in no danger from flash floods. He isn't at the bottom of a valley; he is 1,000 feet above the valley, standing in Bear Cave—the remains of a canyon atop Petit Jean Mountain in the Arkansas River Valley.

Petit Jean is a plateau. Rock strata on the southern end tilts upward at an angle of 5 degrees south, while south of Petit Jean, across the river valley on the next mountain, the layers of rock rise 5 degrees north. If lines were extended off these two inclines, they would intersect about 1,200 feet above Petit Jean's modern summit. A similar set of inclines exist on Petit Jean's northern edge, although the distance between the two inclines is greater, indicating a higher elevation of 2,000 to 2,500 feet. Geologists deduce that in an earlier time, Petit Jean was the valley floor between a mountain to the south that was about the height of modern Petit Jean and a taller mountain to the north that was about the height of Mount Magazine or Rich Mountain.

Several other features are worthy of note. Cedar Creek on the plateau's west end flows over a precipice to create Cedar Falls, which drops nearly 100 feet. The creek then goes 1.5 miles down Cedar Canyon to a depth of 385 feet at the point where it enters the Petit Jean River.

Seven Hollows is a group of parallel canyons atop Petit Jean. They are about 200 feet deep and 2 miles long. The easternmost hollow has a natural bridge that is the third tallest in the United States behind southern Utah's Rainbow Bridge and Virginia's Natural Bridge.

★ ★

Shop at the Gap . . . Pickles Gap

Pickles Gap

Growing up, we often heard the phrase "old as the hills," but we never stopped to think about how old that really is. Hills and mountains are older than Adam's apple and Eve's leaves. The Ouachita Mountains, for instance, are about five times older than the Alps. As ancient as the hills are, though, the gaps that slice through them are even older.

Ancestors of the modern Mississippi River wandered all over the Midwest. (If rivers don't have ancestors, where do little rivulets come from?) Initially, most rivers flowed north to south off the Laurentian Range, America's oldest mountains. As these rivers reached the continental shelf in northern Arkansas, the sea floor descended an average of 10 feet per mile for about 60 miles until it reached the continental slope. There the ocean bottom plunged like the slope of a steep mountain for more than 2 miles. Sediments built up on its edge, causing mudslides and creating steep-sided underwater canyons.

Around 300 million years ago, South America collided with North America. As the ocean floor buckled and the sea drained away, rivers kept on flowing through their old channels, maintaining their courses and cutting through the rising Ouachita Mountains. Seventy million years ago the Rocky Mountains formed, shifting drainage to the southeast, drying up the old northern rivers, and leaving the gaps through the ridges that we see today. First, game trails followed through these passes; after the first humans arrived, the gaps became roads. Many of the modern north–south highways follow these ancient river channels. In time, trading posts and stores sprang up near the gaps.

We tend to think of our pioneer ancestors as a pious, God-fearing bunch, at least when the neighbors were around. However, one can't help but notice the Freudian affinity for names like Woolly Hollow, Toad Suck, and Pickles Gap.

With its general store, knife shop, and "pickin' porch," Pickles Gap

Village is a Knott's Berry Farm version of a nineteenth-century community, with a couple of exceptions: They have modern bathroom facilities, and the owners aren't likely to rob you or decapitate you and throw your head in a ditch. Watching tourists take pictures of a wandering guinea fowl was a high point for us. And we can personally recommend the Pickle Barrel Fudge Factory. Willie Wonka, eat your heart out.

Pickles Gap Village is located on US 65 between Conway and Greenbrier. For more information visit their Web site: www.picklesgap.com.

Ah, Love Is in the Air!
Romance

Sometimes it's hard to keep romance in your life, but we know a place where you can always find it. Nestled in the gently rolling hills of central Arkansas, the little town of Romance was first settled by Kentuckians and was supposed to be called Kentucky Valley, but the U.S. Postal Service rejected that idea. According to some sources, the name Romance was suggested by local schoolteacher J. J. Walters, who thought the view was romantic. Others say the town was named for a local spring that was a popular trysting spot for the smitten. Whatever the origin, the name has given the tiny town a special place in America's heart.

Over the years, the post office at Romance has received thousands of Valentine cards and wedding invitations from people who want their mail to have a little something extra. At no charge for the service, the nice folks at the Romance Post Office will remail your cards and letters so that the cancellation will read "Romance." To have correspondence remailed with the Romance postmark, send it with proper postage in larger envelopes and address it to: Postmaster, Romance, AR 72136. The U.S. Postal Service chose the Romance Post Office as the first one in the country to sell the 1990 Love stamp.

Other small towns in the vicinity of Romance also have idyllic names: Harmony, Joy, and Rose Bud. Everything you need for a wedding. There's even a Hart. A waterfall on Little Clifty Creek is an especially lovely setting for nuptials. There is a Romance Road, and although some may say it's rocky, we tend to believe in the positive spirit of human nature. After all, no town has yet been named Divorce—at least not to our knowledge.

Romance is about 45 miles northeast of Little Rock off AR 31.

Catch a Wave and You're Sitting on Top of the World
Saline County

Sixty-five million years ago, the sea had risen northward, engulfing Arkansas's eastern and western borders. The Mississippi Delta was a bay off the Gulf of Mexico, running as far north as Cairo, Illinois. On our western border, the ocean covered the central United States, splitting North America into two distinct landmasses. The dome of the Ozarks formed a large peninsula or island. Across a strait to the south was a parallel series of long, narrow islands formed by exposed tops of the flooded Ouachita Mountains.

Large seagoing reptiles, mosasaurs and plesiosaurs, hunted offshore, oblivious to the dim star growing ever brighter in the night sky. An asteroid 6 miles across, weighing 200 thousand tons and traveling at 10 miles per second, was coming to alter their world forever. It struck the Yucatan Peninsula 600 miles south of present-day New Orleans with the force of one hundred million one-megaton H-bombs. Far away in Arkansas, the impact appeared as a flash of light on the horizon. An eerie calm followed. Then the ground began shaking from the first shock waves. The sky began to glow, turning bright red as the atmosphere grew searingly hot, burning away everything not protected belowground.

The shock waves radiated outward, creating earthquakes and sending a gigantic tsunami northward. As it reached Arkansas's shoreline, the wave's height rose to nearly a mile. When it struck, it tore away large beach rocks and pieces of the continental shelf.

Gigantic boulders, some 50 feet across, were pushed far inland. The wave reached high ground and then receded, dropping boulders atop a ridge 75 miles northeast of Little Rock.

Gary L. Patterson, an undergraduate student, first found evidence of the tsunami in Arkansas in a gravel pit about 1.5 miles north of the town of Rosie, between Newport and Batesville. Some of the glauconite boulders discovered there atop a 250-foot hill are as large as city buses.

Since then, debris has turned up in other areas. Three car-size boulders of novaculite have been found 7 miles from their original outcrop. They sit atop a hill on US 70 just off the I-30 exit between Benton and Hot Springs. Many other erratic boulders lie scattered through the woods along this stretch of US 70. They are visible in late autumn and winter, when leaves are off the trees. A reminder: Even Chicken Little is right on occasion.

Mounds—Not a Candy Bar
Scott

Cyrus Thomas wrote in 1894, "These works form, without a doubt, the most interesting group in the state, and in fact, one of the most important in the United States." The Toltec mounds are ancient earthworks located 16 miles southeast of Little Rock near Scott. They were built around 650 AD by Native Americans known as the Plum Bayou culture. Few people actually lived at Toltec, probably just a skeleton crew of caretakers. The site was a ceremonial center where large groups from outlying farmsteads gathered for seasonal celebrations, communal feasting, and religious services.

Plum Bayou's cultural influence was extensive. Evidence of it has been found as far north as the Little Red River and as far south as Macon, near the Louisiana line. Other remnants of the culture have also been noticed at Bayou Bartholomew in the southeast and west up the Arkansas River Valley to Point Remove near Russellville. One characteristic of the Plum Bayou culture was their use of quartz crystals for tools and ceremonial objects. A trench dug in Toltec's second largest mound in 1888 uncovered several fine specimens of crystal, each measuring over 5 inches.

The site was surrounded by a ditch where dirt had been used to build a mile-long, D-shaped semicircular earthen embankment. It was 10 feet high and bordered ninety acres on three sides. Its fourth side opened to an oxbow lake. A plaza dominated by two large pyramid-shaped mounds, with sixteen smaller mounds, filled out the site.

Even the Egyptian pyramids wouldn't have survived farmers trying to get an extra acre of cotton.
ARKANSAS PARKS AND TOURISM DEPARTMENT

The mounds first came to national attention following a letter-writing campaign by the landowner, Mary Eliza Knapp, who named them Toltec mounds. In 1876 she wrote to the Smithsonian Institution, calling the site "one of the greatest wonders of the lowlands this side of Mexico city." Despite her boosterism, she seemed to harbor mixed feelings toward the mounds and their contents. At the same time she was petitioning archaeologists to come and study the mounds, her husband's cotton plantation workers were busy plowing them to pieces. Some survived, however, and Toltec is today one of the best-preserved archaeological sites in Arkansas. It became Toltec Mounds Archeological State Park in 1980.

To visit the site, take I-440 to exit 7 and go south on US 165 to AR 386. Turn right onto AR 386 and go 1 mile. For more information call Toltec Mounds Archeological State Park at (501) 961-9442 or visit www.arkansasstateparks.com/toltecmounds.

The House That Dimes Built
Searcy

While doing research for this book, one site we were excited about visiting was Mady Armstrong's house in Searcy.

Mady was the town eccentric. She started saving dimes in 1926 after hearing a church sermon entitled "Little Things Grow to Big Things." Her goal was to save enough dimes to build herself a house. She took in washing and ironing and did other kinds of odd jobs that women of her station did in those days. She saved eight out of every ten dimes she earned, and in less than ten years, she had collected a grand total of 13,000 dimes—enough to build her house.

Mady became known as "the Mistress of the Dime House," and her financial feat was recorded in *Ripley's Believe It or Not!* Her accomplishment was an inspiration to others who were still reeling from the Great Depression.

Yes, we were looking forward to seeing "the House that Dimes Built," but during our visit to Searcy, no one of the current generation remembered the dwelling. We were told that the structure must have been demolished. Apparently, it wasn't worth a dime.

A Girl's Best Friend
Searcy

In 1926 ten-year-old Alice Taylor was hoeing cotton on her parents' farm near Searcy when she picked up a smoky-white rock the size of a quail egg. Alice kept the pretty stone as a treasure, tucking it away in a safe place, the way kids do. Sometimes she let her brothers play marbles with it, but she held on to the keepsake into adulthood.

Twenty years after she had found it, Alice discovered the rock could cut glass and knew she really had something. She mailed the rock to Tiffany's in New York, and they sent her a written offer to buy it. She thought the letter said $85, but the check she received was for $8,500. Her find was a 27.21-carat diamond. ". . . among the best that have been found on the North American continent."

Many people went to the Taylor farm in search of more diamonds. One was an Australian geologist, who concluded there was no way the diamond had been formed there. So where did it come from? Some say a crow picked it up at the Murfreesboro diamond fields. Some think a Native American may have dropped it.

Tiffany's put the Arkansas diamond on display so that everyone could enjoy it.

Give Me That Old-Time Religion
White County

After a sermon in 1857, two feuding factions of a small church in Mountainburg attacked one another using utensils originally intended for Sunday potluck. Because of the Mountainburg Church Massacre, services at the church were canceled for the next seventy years.

Then came the Cobbites. A Reverend Cobb and his followers arrived in White County in 1873 and formed a commune. A couple

✦ ✦

of local families, led by Preacher Dover, joined the group.

Cobb was a humble man. Every morning he'd raise his sycamore stick and command the sun to rise, and in the evening he made it set. Followers proved their faith in him by walking the crest of their rooftops with their eyes closed. To show his skill at raising the dead, Cobb buried an accomplice alive but secretly inserted a crude, hollow-reed snorkel into the grave. Sadly, it rained that night and the tube filled with water. At last sniff, the resurrection of the would-be Lazarus didn't smell too promising.

In 1876 the Cobbites held a revival in the belief that the Second Coming was imminent. While in the grip of this religious fervor, they began dragging people off the road and forcing them to pray in Preacher Dover's house. In the best spirit of Arkansas education at the time, one of the townsfolk, a bartender named Carter Humphries, paid the Cobbites a visit with the intention of "learning them crazy folks something."

When Humphries and another man, Rufus Blake, arrived at the commune, heated words were exchanged and the Cobbites grabbed the two men. As the Cobbite womenfolk stretched Humphries's neck over a mulberry tree root, Preacher Dover beheaded him with a dull ax. After using the head as a makeshift soccer ball, they impaled it on a fence post and danced around it. During the revelry, Blake escaped and ran for help. His account of the attack galvanized the townsfolk into action. A posse raced to the scene, and Preacher Dover was shot dead. The other Cobbites were put in jail, where some of them got sick and died. Eventually the rest were released and ordered out of town. Reverend Cobb was taken to Hilger's Ferry and given the choice of riding or walking across the Little Red River. He chose the ferry.

bibliography

Allsopp, Fred W. *Folklore of Romantic Arkansas*. The Grolier Society, 1931.

Arkansas Health Counts, Vol. 3, No. 5, pg. 4; December 1997.

Arkansas Times. "Best and Worst" archives.

Arkansas Tour Guide. Arkansas Department of Parks & Tourism, 2008.

Beck, Ken and Terry. *Amazing Arkansas*. Premium Press America, 1997 edition.

Brickell, Beth. "Mystery at Camden." Arkansas Gazette. 1986.

Bruner, Andrea. "'Arkansas Ghost' Case Profiled" (based on lecture by Dr. Brooks Blevins). *Batesville Daily Guard*, March 12–17, 2008.

Corliss, William. *Strange Phenomena: A Sourcebook of Unusual Natural Phenomena*. The Sourcebook Project, 1974.

DeArmond-Huskey, Rebecca. *Old Times Not Forgotten: A History of Drew County*, pgs. 22, 24, 131.

Dillard, Tom W. "Remembering Arkansas." *Arkansas Democrat-Gazette*.

Dougan, Michael B. *Arkansas Odyssey: The Saga of Arkansas from Pre-historic Times to the Present*. Rose Publishing Co., 1995.

Earngey, Bill. *Arkansas Roadsides*. Eureka Springs, Arkansas: East Mountain Press, 1987.

Faulkner County Historical Society. *Faulkner Facts and Fiddlings*.

Hanson, William D., and J. Michael Howard. "Spherical Boulders in North-Central Arkansas." *Miscellaneous Publication 22*, Arkansas Geological Commission.

Hoffman, Michael P. "A Race of Giants." *Arkansas Archaeology*, pg. 254. Fayetteville, Arkansas: University of Arkansas Press, 1999.

Jameson, W. C. *Buried Treasures of the Ozarks*. Little Rock, Arkansas: August House, 1990.

Jeter, Marvin D. *Edward Palmer's Arkansaw Mounds.* Fayetteville, Arkansas: University of Arkansas Press, 1990.

Johnson, Claude E. *A Humorous History of White County.* 1976.

McKelvy, Jerry (editor). *The Sandyland Chronicle,* Vol. 3, No. 3; March 2003.

Martin, Fred. *Clay County Courier.* Corning, Arkansas.

Paulson, Alan C. *Roadside History of Arkansas.* Missoula, Montana: Mountain Press Publishing Company, 1998.

Rafferty, Milton D. *The Ozarks: Land and Life.* Fayetteville, Arkansas: University of Arkansas Press, 2001.

Robinson, Henry W., and Allen, Robert T. *Only in Arkansas.* Fayetteville, Arkansas: University of Arkansas Press, 1995.

Rossiter, Phyllis. *A Living History of the Ozarks.* Gretna, Louisiana: Pelican Publishing Company, 1992.

Sabo, George III, and Jerry, Hilliard. *History of Rock Art Search in Arkansas.* Arkansas Archeological Survey.

Sears, Derek W. G. *Thunderstones: A Study of Meteorites Based on Falls and Finds in Arkansas*. Fayetteville, Arkansas: University of Arkansas Press, 1988.

Stewart, David. *The Earthquake that America Forgot.* Marble Hill, Missouri: Gutenberg Richter Publications, 1995.

Wood, Ramona. *The Goat Woman of Smackover.* El Dorado, Arkansas: ABC Press, 2001.

Worthen, Bill. "Artist's Old Mill in North Little Rock Grist for Book." *Arkansas Democrat-Gazette,* pg. 5H; July 27, 2008.

index

index

index

about the authors

Wyatt and Janie Jones were both born and raised in Arkansas and currently live in Conway. They wrote about the beauty of their native state in their first book, *Hiking Arkansas,* also published by Globe Pequot Press. They still enjoy an occasional hike with their dogs, and Janie dreams of training a bloodhound to help her track down material for the true crime articles she writes for *AY Magazine.*

As struggling authors, the Joneses have worked in a variety of venues, including a stint as theatre performers at the Museum of Discovery in Little Rock. There they staged the electric and robotic shows—until they were replaced by robots.